HYPNOSIS

THE INDUCTION OF CONVICTION

THIRD EDITION

JOHN C. HUGHES, D.C.

Copyright © 2009 by
The National Guild of Hypnotists, Inc.
P.O. Box 308
Merrimack, NH 03054-0308

Copyright © TXU 416 223, 1990 by John C. Hughes, D.C.
Original title *The Essence of Hypnotism*
Copyright © 2002, 2009, The National Guild of Hypnotists, Inc.
ISBN: 1-885846-15-0
ISBN 13: 978-1-885846-15-0

All rights reserved. No part of this book may be reproduced in any form or by any electronic or mechanical means including information storage and retrieval systems without permission in writing from the publisher, except by a reviewer, who may quote brief passages in a review. Published by the National Guild of Hypnotists, Inc. P.O. Box 308, Merrimack, New Hampshire 03054. Third edition. This edition is an expansion and revision of a work previously published as *The Essence of Hypnotism,* copyright © 1990 by John C. Hughes, D.C.

Dedication

This book is dedicated to my hypnosis mentor Rexford L. North, Ph.D. Dr. North founded the National Guild of Hypnotists in 1951. I was privileged to see the Guild grow from a small group of enthusiastic hypnotists (most of whom were former students of Dr. North's Hypnotism Center in Boston) to its present status as the world's largest hypnosis organization. Indeed the name National Guild of Hypnotists is now a misnomer, as the Guild has members from all over the world and is truly an international organization.

Dr. North's vision of a world-class hypnosis society has been fulfilled under the able stewardship of the Guild's hard-working President and Executive Director, Dr. Dwight F. Damon. Committed to the advancement of the science, art, and philosophy of hypnotism, the National Guild of Hypnotism is today the largest and foremost hypnosis organization in the world.

A cloud of mystery hangs over the fate of Rexford L. North. He disappeared, under still unexplained circumstances, in 1956. Whatever may have been the cause of his vanishing, it cannot detract from what he accomplished in getting hypnosis and its practical applications to the attention of the general public and of the medical profession. In a very large sense, to those who had the privilege of knowing him, the history of hypnosis could be dated B.N. and A.N. — i.e., Before North and After North.

One generation plants the trees; another sits in their shade. Here's to you, Rexford, for planting those trees.

Cheers!

Acknowledgments

The first edition of *Hypnosis: The Induction of Conviction* was published in 1990. This extended third edition has been expanded, revised and brought up to date.

Special recognition for the title of this book goes to the late William S. Kroger, M.D., an internationally renowned pioneer and longtime proponent of hypnotism. In 1963 Dr. Kroger published one of the most highly regarded treatises on hypnotism: *Clinical and Experimental Hypnosis*. (A second edition was published in 1977.) In this book Dr. Kroger defined hypnosis as a *conviction phenomenon*. It was Dr. Kroger's belief that the conviction of hypnosis leads to hypnosis.

I am deeply grateful to my esteemed colleague Dr. C. Scot Giles, who wrote the Foreword for this edition Also I wish to acknowledge the *Journal of Hypnotism*, and the hundreds of sources from which I have gathered reading memories. I am particularly indebted to my mentor Dr. Rexford L. North, the charismatic founder of the National Guild of Hypnotists.

I would like to thank Dr. Dwight Damon and Dr. Edith Fiore, who have encouraged and supported me in my literary endeavors; and special thanks to my professional friends and colleagues who generously shared their ideas and their expertise.

Last but not least, I want to acknowledge my indebtedness to Kimberly Martin who provided the layout and formatting for this book.

John C. Hughes, D.C., June 2009
Las Vegas, Nevada

Foreword

I am honored to write the *Foreword* for the *Third Edition* of this magnificent book on the hypnotic arts and sciences. This is a book I have long admired, and it is the volume I give to clients and other helping professionals when they express an interest in knowing more about hypnotism. It is a pleasure to see it updated and expanded with none of the original clarity lost.

The author, Dr. John Hughes, is a Charter Member of the National Guild of Hypnotists and the former Research Editor for the *Journal of Hypnotism*. This book is the accumulated wisdom and insight of someone who has been part of the hypnotic community for a very long time.

While John Hughes is better known in the scholarly world for his exceptional research into the history of hypnotism, he is himself a practitioner who has had a long and distinguished career. Nowhere else will the reader find such a concise summary of what it is important to know about the practice of hypnotism today.

While necessarily less complete than his authoritative historical works, Hughes charts the evolution of the hypnotic arts from the Incubation Rites at the Temple of *Asklepeia* in classical Greece to the modern revival that began in the 1920s. The biographies of the great practitioners are given with an evenhandedness and objectivity most will find refreshing.

Even more impressive is the extensive theoretical exposition Hughes gives in this book. Covering all major theories of hypnotism, Hughes elucidates current scientific thinking on why hypnotism has a remarkable utility to help people with personal and medical problems. Dr. Hughes lays out the modern thinking on Mind-Body interaction so clearly it can be easily understood, even by a beginner.

The reason why this book is titled *Hypnosis: The Induction of Conviction*, is explained in the chapter "Fundamental Principles of Success." In this chapter Dr. Hughes shares his personal view that the precondition to successful hypnotism is the establishment of rapport with the client, and that success requires the practitioner to instill in the mind of the client the conviction that the hypnotism will succeed. Hughes presents formidable scholarship in support of this "persuasive" understanding of hypnotism that merits much study.

Finally, the hypnotist reader will find this volume full of practical help and guidance from someone who is an "old hand" at this work. Hughes gives his less-experienced colleagues sophisticated advice, tips, cautions and reassurances. Collecting in one place an overview of the history and theory of hypnotism, a summary of current research and guidance for the practitioner, this substantial volume is one of the best books on hypnotism available today.

The Rev. C. Scot Giles, D.Min.
Board Certified Chaplain
Diplomate, National Guild of Hypnotists

Table of Contents

1. History Of Hypnotism 1
2. 20th Century Practitioners 43
3. What Is Hypnosis? 85
4. Myths & Misconceptions 93
5. Is Hypnosis Dangerous? 103
6. Theories Of Hypnosis 111
7. Who Can Be Hypnotized? 123
8. How Hypnosis Works 129
9. The Power Of Visualization 141
10. Principles Of Success 165
11. The Conquest Of Stress 173
12. Suggestibility Tests 183
13. Arousing From Hypnosis 205
14. How To Hypnotize Your Client 209
15. Aid To The Medical Profession 247
16. Painless Childbirth Guideline 257
17. The Art Of Self-Hypnosis 261
18. Self-Hypnosis And You 271
19. How To Use Self-Hypnosis 289
20. Understanding Psychology:
    An Overview For The Hypnotherapist 305
21. Smoking Cessation Guidelines 327
22. Pain Management 345
23. A Marketing Tool For Referrals 357

Glossary 363
Index 373

CHAPTER 1
History Of Hypnotism

Hypnotism has come of age and is now more widely known than ever before. The practical application of hypnosis is starting to be more generally understood and accepted in the medical profession, which has until now largely derided it. This in turn is generating the greatest upsurge of widespread public interest in it that has been seen since Franz Anton Mesmer attempted to investigate it scientifically in the 1780's.

Hypnotism has had a long ancestry of both doctrine and practice, going back to the remotest antiquity of primitive peoples, and continuing through the classical high civilizations and the medieval Renaissance cultures of Europe. Yet not until a little over two centuries ago was it forcefully brought to the notice of the medical, legal, and religious establishments of Western society, then at the peak of that phase of widening outlooks generally known as the Enlightenment.

The exact origins of hypnotism have been lost in the mists of time. Paralleling man's development, and nearly as old as mankind itself, the practice of some form of hypnotism has been intimately associated with the magico-religious practices of various people.

It is doubtful if any healing modality has simultaneously received such wide acclaim and mass condemnation as hypnotism. The belated acceptance of hypnosis as a therapeutic tool was due, in part, to the extravagant claims made by the early practitioners. The zealous hypnotist of yesteryear thought that in hypnosis he had found the universal remedy for all the ailments that beset suffering humanity. When these claims could not be substantiated clinically, hypnotism fell into disrepute. In renouncing hypnosis, however, the baby was thrown out with the bath water. While the therapeutic value of hypnosis is now well recognized, like any therapeutic tool it, too, has its limitations.

Ancient healers believed that the hypnotic trance, or "sleep," was of divine nature and supernatural origin. Through an elaborate ritual of magic and incantation the tribal priest or shaman used this trancelike state for the exorcism of evil spirits or in the mollification of benevolent spirits.

Ailing and afflicted pilgrims flocked to the Hellenistic Temples of Asklepeia to take part in a ritual called incubation. (Incubation means, "lying on the ground.") At least 186 sleep temples are known to have been built in Greece between about 325 B.C. and the second century A.D.; the bulk of them within the first fifty years of that span. Since many others were probably destroyed without a trace in the later barbarian invasions, the actual total may have been around three hundred. They were uniformly dedicated to Asklepios, the Greek god of healing—supposed to be a deification of an actual physician of the ninth or eighth century B.C.—and hence were called Asklepeia. Their principal feature was the *abaton* (sleep room), which the patient could enter only after ritual purification and a large donation to the temple.

After induction into sleep—we do not know the induction methods employed—Asklepios, who prescribed the proper treatment, or sometimes healed the ailment immediately, visited the patient in a dream. According to inscriptions the god cured paralysis, epilepsy, dropsy, baldness, blindness, worms, wounds, sterility, headaches, tuberculosis, dyspepsia, gout, and many other afflictions. These "sleep temples" became so popular that they spread throughout the whole of Greece and Asia Minor and were in vogue for nearly one thousand years.

Miracles by the laying on of hands and healing by the spoken word are recorded in early writings. The shaman used variations of this primitive form of healing widely and often with results sufficiently impressive that his exalted position of authority was passed on to successive generations.

The Eighteenth Century: Franz Anton Mesmer (1734–1815)

Hypnotism in various guises has a long ancestry of practice, going back to the remotest antiquity. It was first forcefully brought to the notice of the medical, and religious establishments of Western society, through the claims and actual achievements of an educated person of high social standing, the Austrian physician Franz Anton Mesmer, whose name would for decades after him be associated with the art he revived and sought to gain acceptance of as a safe and effective therapy for many ailments.

"Natural Magnetism," or "mesmerism" as it became known, was the forerunner of scientific hypnotism. While Mesmer's theories were obfuscated with astrological notions and pseudo-scientific jargon, he did unearth a grain of psychological truth, which became the fertile starting point for later scientific investigation of hypnosis and hypnotic phenomena. Although often wrongly depicted as a charlatan, many historians regard Mesmer as the "father of hypnotism."

Mesmerism, in the form its introducer believed it to function, was tragically in error. Mesmer himself, after a brief flush of fame and success, would be discredited and die in obscurity. He did not understand what hypnosis is, nor grasp the reality of the influence of suggestion on the subconscious mind. He thought that the effects he was able to produce in his patients were due to the operation of a mysterious "animal magnetic" fluid permeating everything in the universe, which he was able to tap and direct to a degree.

Yet had not Mesmer come forward when he did, and effectively promote his concept of "animal magnetism," hypnotism could not have made the substantial advances toward the understanding and acceptance of it attained during the nineteenth century. There is a direct line of connection from Mesmer, through his followers and their heirs (many of whom disagreed with his interpretations through fully crediting the originality of his findings) to the great Victorian Era pioneers of modern hypnotherapy. It is thus necessary for a full appreciation of all the progress in hypnotism since his time, to gain a full acquaintance with Mesmer's keen mind and the vast influence he exerted on Western thinking and outlooks; and to rid our own minds of the numerous misconceptions and errors that have become attached to Mesmer in all too many histories and textbooks.

Like all who have significantly affected the society and culture of their times, Mesmer was a product of them; he did not swim against their current, but rather enlarged and widened it. There was already in the Europe of the latter half of the eighteenth century, a growing interest in how the human mind worked and how it might be acted on through natural forces, or possibly supernatural ones. The cult of Naturalism introduced by Jean Jacques Rousseau, was a manifestation of this mental climate which formed Mesmer's own thinking and led him to his discovery of "animal magnetism" — or hypnotism as we now know it to be.

Mesmer was born on May 23, 1734, in the small village of Iznang on Lake Constance, in the extensive lands held by the Prince-Archbishop of Constance in the western Alpine tip of the Habsburg Empire of Austria. He was the third of nine children of Anton Mesmer, a forester in the service of the Prince-Archbishop. At eighteen, already noted as a bright and studious youth, he decided to become a Roman Catholic priest. Through his family's connections with the Prince-Archbishop, he easily obtained a scholarship to the Jesuit seminary at Dillingen in Bavaria. He went on to the University of Ingolstadt, also a Jesuit institution, to study philosophy, then seems to have decided he was not suited to the priesthood after all, and turned to the study of science and astronomy. Both these disciplines still came under the general heading of philosophy, in which he gained a doctorate degree from Ingolstadt in 1759.

He was now twenty-five and faced with the problem of making a living, and there were not many openings for philosophers in general, or scientists or astronomers in particular. Law now attracted him, and he went to Vienna to study, but the work soon palled on him. Turning to medicine, he underwent a six-year course of training by the Medical Faculty of Vienna. Among his instructors was Gerard van Swieten, the director of the Faculty, and Anton de Haen, court physician to the Empress Maria Theresa, both of whom took a personal interest in him. Mesmer appears indeed to have cultivated contacts with prominent and wealthy persons, some of whom must have contributed to the cost of his prolonged higher education. Once he had given up the idea of the priesthood, it is unlikely the Church would have subsidized him any further, and his own family was certainly not able to do it. (One of his brothers, named Johann, did become a priest, doubtless with the aid of a Church scholarship.)

Mesmer graduated from the Medical Faculty in 1766 at the age of thirty-two. His doctoral thesis was on the influence of the planets on the human body. It was largely plagiarized from a Latin work on that subject by the Englishman Richard Mead, first published in 1704. That does not seem to have handicapped Mesmer, who launched into an immediately large and profitable practice, his cultivation of contacts in the higher levels of Vienna society again paying off for him.

A year after his graduation he entered into a professionally advantageous marriage with the widow of Ferdinand von Bosch, who had been an influential adviser of the Imperial

Court. Ten years older than her new husband, and not much taken with him romantically, Maria Anna von Bosch was nevertheless very valuable to him in widening his circle of acquaintances among those who could pay well for his services. She was herself from a medical background, being the daughter of Georg Friedrich von Eulenschenk, an apothecary to the medical service of the Austrian Army, and had many other contacts that proved helpful to Mesmer.

In short, he prospered. He was able to live on a splendid Viennese estate, with a garden adorned with classical statues, and a private theater. Mesmer was a lover of music, and one of the first in Europe to play expertly on the glass harmonica that had been perfected in America by Benjamin Franklin. He attracted visitors like Leopold Mozart, who thought that the garden was incomparable, and the leading composers Christoph Willibald Gluck, and Franz Joseph Haydn. Young Wolfgang Amadeus Mozart, whose first opera *Bastien und Bastienne* had its premiere in Mesmer's private theater, later composed the Adagios in C minor and C Major (Opuses K 617 and K 617a) for Mesmer to play on the glass harmonica.

As for the nature of the medical treatments he provided his wealthy and titled clientele, they were the standard ones of the time, such as bleeding and purgative emetics (his favorite was cream of tartar, made from the acidic residue of fermented grapes, and less harsh than the more commonly used calomel and arsenical compounds) along with herbal medicines. He also experimented, as did many of the Viennese physicians of that period, with recent innovations such as magnets and electric shocks from the crude generators then existing, actually no more than toys. He was eager to discuss these and similar methods with those who did not shun novelties. Among them the one who influenced him most was Father Maximillian Hell, a Jesuit priest who also practiced medicine, then a not infrequent combination. He was also an astronomer.

The Jesuit employed magnets in the shape of the bodily parts whose ailments he treated, and claimed a high number of cures or alleviation of symptoms. Mesmer, observing these ministrations and their results, became convinced that the shape of the magnets had nothing to do with the effects. Indeed, the metal magnets themselves were unnecessary. He tried magnetizing materials ranging from liquids to a variety of solids, and was able to achieve relief or healing in his patients as well as or even better than Father Hell.

The conclusive experiment that settled the matter for Mesmer, and led to the break between him and the Jesuit healer, involved Francisca Oesterlein, a young woman of twenty-seven, and a distant relation of his wife. Fräulein Oesterlein became a resident patient at Mesmer's home at the end of 1773, seeking relief for fifteen different symptoms that appear to have been primarily psychogenic.

Over a period of several months, Mesmer tried various forms of treatment involving magnets. The one that finally brought relief consisted of having the woman drink a decoction of iron salts and then attaching magnets to her abdomen and legs, with the aim of inducing a "tide" that would sweep the afflictions right out of her body. This indeed happened; she claimed to feel powerful streams of some mysterious fluid coursing downward inside her, and in a few hours she was perfectly well. She soon thereafter married Mesmer's stepson and bore children to him without difficulty.

This historic cure took place on July 28, 1774. Mesmer realized that it confirmed the conclusions he had already arrived at—none of the physical materials employed had any healing effect of themselves. At most, they acted as channels, directing the true healing force, which was an invisible magnetic fluid he was somehow able to accumulate within his own body and then transmit into another body in which it would have a curative result.

Since this magnetic force—which he was unable to define better, or even to explain what he meant by its being magnetic—came out of a living, i.e., animated, body and was transmissible to other living bodies, he called it *animal magnetism*. It was an unfortunate term that has continued to confuse all who do not realize its derivation from "animation," and thus tend to give it a sensual connotation.

Mesmer did at times use another term, *natural magnetism*, to indicate that the force he was dealing with had a natural origin and existed independently of any magnetizing by artificial means. However, again his definitions were not altogether clear and this term also was confusing to many.

By whatever name, Mesmer's healing force was anathema to Father Hell, who denounced it as a delusion, insisting that any cures Mesmer might have effected were solely due to his having employed magnets, even if clumsily. From this time on, the growing antagonism between Mesmer and Hell increasingly divided medical opinion in Vienna, and eventually across all Europe, into opposing camps.

It continued to be a localized squabble until early in 1775, when Mesmer submitted a summary of his animal magnetism concept to a scientific journal in Altona, Germany. He attributed the benefits of his treatments to an invisible and immaterial universal fluid, similar to electricity in that it could be generated and stored through a large number of intermediary substances.

We now know that both Mesmer and Father Hell (who took great offense at Mesmer's paper when it was published, saying it was written out of sheer spite and jealousy of his own work with magnets) were unwittingly employing therapeutic suggestion to achieve their results, and that no such magnetic healing force actually existed. Neither of them understood this.

Although the Prussian Academy of Sciences in Berlin sternly rejected Mesmer's theory, and several other leading institutions and individual men of science expressed strong reservations about it, he had made himself a noted personage in the medical field through his discovery of "Natural Magnetism." His opinion came to be sought in many cases of unusual symptoms and their treatment. One notable instance was in the fall of 1775, when the Electoral Prince of Bavaria, Max Joseph, appointed him to the Commission of Inquiry that was set up to investigate the claims of Father J. J. Gassner, a Swiss priest now residing at Ratisbon (Regensburg) in Bavaria, to be healing many ailments through exorcism of the devil.

Gassner was, in other words, attributing a large percentage of sickness to diabolical possession, and asserting that through his ability to exorcise it, these sufferers were restored to health. He staged several public demonstrations that were highly convincing. Mesmer, however, was able to duplicate in volunteer subjects the symptoms of possession and their removal, without any recourse to the rituals of exorcism. The illnesses and their cures by Gassner were,

Mesmer stated, wholly the result of the patients' imaginations being acted on by Gassner, through his unwitting use of the power of Natural Magnetism.

Had Mesmer only realized it, he was very close to the truth in that assessment; Gassner was employing what is now understood as mental imagery and suggestion, in modern hypnotic usage. Mesmer's verdict was not favorably received by most who heard it, even though Gassner's religious superiors ordered him to retire to a quiet rural parish and cease his exorcist activities. To many it seemed that Mesmer was taking on himself too arrogant a mental superiority, that only he understood these matters properly, and had shown lack of respect for the Church's stand on possession and exorcism.

Criticism also started to be directed at Mesmer because he often took patients as residents in his house for as long as he was treating them. Since these patients not infrequently were young women, it was being whispered that his interest in them went beyond a strictly medical one; even though he was always careful to have them in the keeping of his wife, while they were in his house.

His enemies were looking for some solid ground of accusation on which to discredit him. It was the most celebrated cure he had yet performed that finally provided the occasion his foes sought. The patient was Maria Theresa Paradis, a girl of eighteen, the daughter of middle-class parents, blind from the age of four, and severely manic depressive. Talented musically (she had learned to play the piano as a small child) and having come to the notice of the Empress, her education was paid for and a pension of two hundred gold ducats annually was granted to her parents. Arrangements were made for her to play at concerts. Mozart heard her once and rated her performance as competent. She even created compositions of her own on the piano, which others, of course, had to score for her.

Nevertheless she was unhappy, had fits of severe depression, and went from doctor to doctor seeking a cure for her blindness. The leading oculist of Vienna, Professor Barth, who had successfully operated for cataracts many times, told her he could not help; the optic nerve had atrophied beyond hope of repair. Baron Stoerck expressed the same opinion. Desperate, she finally went to Mesmer. His examination convinced him her blindness was not caused by damage to the optic nerve. To treat it by his method would be a challenge, to which he rose. He accepted Fräulein Paradis as a resident patient. Because he wished to be completely objective in treating her and evaluating the results, he assured her that he would charge no fees.

Her sight returned gradually, by stages, as the treatment progressed. Mesmer's magnetic treatment ritual induced an altered state of consciousness. In this trancelike state Fräulein Paradis' subconscious mind assimilated Mesmer's suggestions that she would be able to see. Her father, who followed the process closely, compiled a written report of her reactions as she regained her sight and was increasingly able to distinguish objects, people, colors and landscapes. This account is consistent with many other cases in medical literature relating to the gradual attainment of sight by blind persons.

However, the medical fraternity of Vienna was outraged. Professor Barth was adamant in his assertion that the girl was faking her newfound capability of sight. He said Mesmer was influencing her to pretend that she was really seeing. Yet the long and exhaustive documentation her father compiled, day-by-day, of her recovery is clear proof to the contrary. She was not finding sight an unmixed blessing. Bright sunlight made her giddy. She stumbled over doorsteps she had traversed easily while sightless. The quality of her piano playing fell off, as she found herself laboriously watching her fingers on the keys instead of moving quickly and easily over them as she had learned to do when sightless.

It was this last difficulty that gave Mesmer's opponents the opportunity they had sought to discredit him. They went to Fräulein Paradis' parents and indicated that the Empress would soon discontinue the annual pension, because with their daughter's sight restored, the original consideration for the grant of the pension no longer existed. It was unfortunate, they added, that the girl could no longer play the piano so well; that would seriously reduce her desirability as a concert attraction, which had largely derived from her blindness anyway.

The parents were now alarmed at this prospective threat to the affluence their daughter's affliction had brought them. Even though there had been two public demonstrations, attended by a thousand persons, of her restored sight, Herr and Frau Paradis now suddenly agreed with Professor Barth that she was merely pretending to see. They went to Mesmer and demanded, literally at sword's point, the return of their daughter. When the girl—who had gone into hysterics—refused to go with them, her mother slammed her head against the wall so hard she fell senseless to the floor. Mesmer finally persuaded the parents to leave without her, pointing out that they had made her ill and she now needed his medical care.

This shocking emotional experience caused the blindness to recur. When Fräulein Paradis recovered consciousness, she found herself blind again. It took two weeks for Mesmer to restore her vision, through repeatedly infusing her with—as he believed—animal magnetism, for which he still employed ordinary magnets as conveyers of the "invisible fluid."

The Paradises now came back, profusely apologetic for their hostile behavior. They expressed deep gratitude to Mesmer for healing their daughter, and promised if he now allowed them to take her home, she would be free to return for follow-up treatment on whatever schedule he wished. He did not believe them, for he was already under confidential notice from the Imperial Court to halt his magnetic treatments, but he had no choice. Reluctantly, he assented. Fräulein Paradis went home, and eventually returned to performing as a concert pianist, billed as being blind. It appears she never fully lost her sight again, but that it soon deteriorated to the point where for all practical purposes she could be regarded as blind. Thus she retained her earning capacity. She did not, of course, ever come back for further treatment by Mesmer.

The full extent of the opposition to Mesmer, and how it made the Paradis case a pretext for driving him out of Vienna altogether, or at least silencing him, remains buried in the Habsburg archives. It is known that Cardinal Magazzi, who largely controlled the Empress's Committee to Sustain Public Morality, had prevailed on Maria Theresa to order Baron von Stoerck to issue a formal order, in the name of the Imperial Court and the Medical Faculty, for Mesmer to "cease this humbug."

This order had been privately conveyed to him during Fräulein Paradis' recovery from her parents' abusive visit. The same high quarters probably advised the parents to go back to

Mesmer in a more conciliatory mood, as a way of getting him to let the girl leave with them.

There is also evidence, though not fully authenticated, that the Jesuit Order (which still had great influence in the Austrian Empire at that time) felt it had to sustain Father Hell in his condemnation of Mesmer's animal magnetism. The Jesuits may have worked behind the scenes to orchestrate the outcry against Mesmer that resounded from all sides in the wake of the Paradis incident. By whatever means it was instigated and sustained, this campaign achieved its purpose.

Mesmer left his Landstrasse home, though his wife remained there, and retired to the countryside for a three-month stay, during which he tried to sort out his conception of the strange new means of healing he had stumbled upon. What exactly was it? How did it work? Should he continue any further with it?

He was not able to arrive at a solution that fully satisfied him. He remained uncertain about whether to regard animal magnetism as an independent, outside force he somehow could draw upon and use beneficially. Was it perhaps an additional bodily sense, a sixth one differing from the familiar five natural ones? Was it the creation of his mind, and possibly also of the mind of the person he was treating?

Mesmer wavered between these alternatives. He tended to lean toward the second one, coming close to realizing the psychological nature of animal magnetism, yet again missing it. He concluded that since animal magnetism had demonstrated its effectiveness as a healing force, he should seek a wider audience. There was the possibility of a definitive professional acceptance for it in Paris, which was regarded the intellectual capital of Europe, where new ideas of all kinds could presumably gain a ready hearing. He decided to go there, and returned to Vienna to plan his departure.

It is probably not quite correct to say Mesmer's departure from Vienna was forced upon him. Having discredited and silenced him, his enemies would probably have been just as happy to have him stay and resume conventional medical practice. He made his preparations carefully and deliberately, with no appearance of haste. He asked for, and readily obtained, a favorable letter of introduction from the Imperial Chancellor, Prince Kaunitz, to the Austrian Ambassador in Paris. Some Viennese physicians who still had confidence in him gave him another letter of introduction to Baron d'Holbach, a prominent French amateur of science with valuable contacts among the medical and scientific fraternities of Paris. He had also hoped to have the endorsement of the Prussian Academy of Sciences, to which he sent a twenty-seven-page summary of his *Animal Magnetism*, written in quite moderate terms and making no vast claims for its efficacy. He was disappointed in the Academy's reply, which concluded tersely that he was making a mistake.

Mesmer appears nevertheless to expect that he would be able to resume magnetic healing in Vienna after the French medical establishment had vindicated him. He left two female patients in the care of his wife, and they remained there for sixteen months until compelled to leave by official order.

Mesmer made his journey to Paris in February 1778, as the French monarchy was entering into its alliance with Britain's rebelling Thirteen Colonies across the Atlantic, which would enable them to gain their independence. Though he felt his initial reception was disappointing (at a dinner party that Baron d'Holbach arranged for him, his demonstrations of the effects of animal magnetism fell flat and d'Holbach wrote him off as a mere dabbler and poseur) after a while, people of all social classes began coming to him for treatment.

Mesmer's magnetic treatment was unique as well as dramatic. John Grive, an English physician, wrote about a visit to Mesmer's house and noted that there were never less than two hundred patients at one time.

> I was in his home the other day and was witness to his method of operating. In the middle of the room is placed a vessel of about a foot and a half high, which is called here a *baquet*. It is so large that twenty people can easily sit round it; near the edge of the lid which covers it, there are holes pierced corresponding to the number of persons who are to surround it; into these holes are introduced iron rods, bent at right angles outwards, and of different heights, so as to answer to the part of the body to which they are to be applied. Besides these rods, there is a rope, which communicates between the *baquet* and one of the patients, and from him is carried to another, and so on the whole round. The most sensible effects are produced on the approach of Mesmer, who is said to convey the fluid by certain motions of his hands or eyes, without touching the person. I have talked with several who have witnessed these effects, who have convulsions occasioned and removed by a movement of the hand.

Magnets with alleged healing properties were hung overhead. Exotic incense was burned and heavy draperies over the windows put the room in semi-darkness; all calculated to induce a receptiveness to animal magnetism. Melodic strains of cadent music was heard in the background and Mesmer—who had a flair for the dramatic—made his grand entrance wearing a flowing silken lilac robe and carrying an iron wand. Mesmer would stop before his more dilatory patients, giving each in turn a piercing gaze and an occasional touch with his wand. Afflictions of every description were "cured" by this unorthodox treatment.

Two aspects of Mesmer's personality both advanced and impeded him during his stay in Paris that extended to seven years. The first was his profound sense of personal honor, which was expressed in a sincerity of word and behavior so unmistakable that he easily gained the confidence of people he had never met before. This quality also made him a very effective hypnotist--though he did not know in the modern sense that he was one. He was however unable to understand or accept that not all people had the same genteel concept of honor that he did; and consequently by expecting in others a standard of conduct as high as his own, he was continually disappointed and embittered, and made enemies of many who were at first favorably inclined to him.

The second two-edged characteristic was his strong humanitarian proclivity. He saw his method of healing as a means not only of therapy for the sick, but as a source of profound social reform that would promote and enhance the well being of all. Though he accepted fees from those able to pay, he never attempted to enrich himself from the application of his animal magnetism. He was thus naturally attracted to all the myriad of radical political, social and spiritualistic movements that were rife in France during those last years of the Ancien Regime as it drifted into the catastrophe of the Revolution; and though he was never directly involved in any of the activities of these movements, his associating with them still made him suspect in the eyes of the authorities and deprived him of official support he might well otherwise have had.

These two qualities were prominent in Mesmer's attempts to gain formal recognition and sanction of his method of healing. This involved three principal institutions: the Paris Academy of Sciences, the Royal Society of Medicine, and the Paris Medical Faculty. The interest of the first was in the strictly scientific side of all new discoveries and theories; it referred all claims of such to have healing applications, to the Paris Medical Faculty, which however was extremely conservative and reluctant to approve any innovations in medical practice. As the decade of the 1770's began, it was the last hold out in Europe against inoculation for smallpox, which had become widely accepted half a century earlier.

It would thus have been the proper strategy for Mesmer to first concentrate on convincing the Academy of Sciences that animal magnetism had scientific validity, before seeking approval of it as a treatment for illness. He was handicapped though, as already pointed out, by his not having any very clear formulation in his own mind of what animal magnetism really was or how it worked. Nevertheless, when Jean-Baptiste Leroy, President of the Academy of Sciences, visited Mesmer shortly after his arrival in Paris and heard from him an exposition of his method, Leroy was favorably impressed--not least by Mesmer's openness and frankness--and said he would report to the Academy that animal magnetism merited full and impartial examination.

The hurdles beyond the Academy, even if it should bestow its approval on Mesmer's method, were truly formidable and probably not fully appropriated by Mesmer. The Paris Faculty of Medicine was in a collective fit of hurt pride and humiliation over the open rebuke to its pretensions by the new King, Louis XVI, who shortly after coming to the throne had on April 9, 1776, set up the Royal Society of Medicine and given it authority to pass on all forms of medical treatment, both old and new. The King's action stemmed from the fact that his predecessor, Louis XV, had died in 1774 of smallpox, as a result of never having been inoculated against it, due to the Faculty's opposition.

When Mesmer arrived in Paris in 1778, the Royal Society and the Academy were wrangling heatedly, each denouncing the other as unqualified, and trying to prevent its own members from joining the opposing body. It was as unpromising a situation as could be imagined, in which to seek recognition of any new medical treatment.

Nor, despite M. Leroy's open-mindedness toward the doctrine of animal magnetism, and his sponsorship of Mesmer as an innovative pioneer to a meeting of the Academy, was that group inclined to take him seriously. Many of its members openly laughed at him. A few, however, were willing to attend private demonstrations by Mesmer of the effects of animal magnetism on both volunteers and patients. One of the academicians, M. De Maillebois, discerningly observed that imagery on the part of the subjects could account for the results obtained by Mesmer—another of the many instances in which someone came close to the essence of hypnosis and its procedure, without attaining to a real understanding of them.

Mesmer, as angered by what to him seemed belittling criticism by Maillebois, and retorted that if it was all just the imagination of his patients, how could he be achieving cures of their ailments? Later in 1781, he realized the error of that position; whether or not any cures were effected, he would then write, the phenomena of animal magnetism were just as indisputably real. But now in 1778, he allowed his irritation at Maillebois' observation to make him stake everything on his method being a cure-all, leaving him wide open for refutation by both the Royal Society and the Medical Faculty.

In May, three months after coming to Paris, Mesmer set up a clinic at Créteil, a suburban village, where he commenced receiving patients on a regular basis. The clinic had been open for only twelve days when Mesmer was informed that the Royal Society was planning to investigate what he was doing He went to the Society to find out for himself and was told that a Commission of Inquiry was being set up, to determine the medical usefulness — if any — of his method.

Mesmer objected strongly. He would welcome individual members of the Society, who might want to come and resolve their personal doubts; animal magnetism, he insisted, was not something to be prescribed and administered like a drug, it was part of a larger whole, of the mental and physical interaction by which the body and mind jointly maintained their health and capability for action.

That was a straightforward position, and the Society seemed receptive to it; but then in a mistaken attempt to prove his willingness to compromise, Mesmer said he was willing to have his patients first certified by the Medical Faculty, that they were actually ill and not merely pretending sickness. This had been urged on him by some in the Academy of Sciences, but it was a fatal concession to the conservatives in the Faculty, and did not help him any in the society, which was in its own turf battle with that group.

The Faculty sent only one patient to Mesmer. The Society, offended by his concession to the old-line physicians, sent back unopened a lengthy report he submitted on the results of his treatments of the patients who came to the clinic; and did not take him up on his offer to have individual observers come to visit it. The Academy washed its hands of the matter by stating that since Mesmer's method was claimed to have therapeutic application, it was out of its jurisdiction and properly belonged to the Faculty and the Society, to pass judgment on it.

Mesmer's hopes for recognition and accreditation in Paris had reached an impasse. In all probability he would have given up at this point and gone elsewhere, had not the Chevalier d'Eslon come on the scene to encourage him to fresh attempts.

By March 1784, the vogue of animal magnetism had attained such a pitch the medical and political establishments of France had become seriously alarmed. According to a survey made by order of the Prefect of the Paris police, M. Jean-Pierre LeNoire, at least eight thousand persons in the metropolitan area had been treated in either Mesmer's or d'Eslon's clinics.

Self-appointed magnetizers were springing up in all the leading cities of France. All sorts of radical enthusiasts, such as the crank genius Jean-Louis Carra, who claimed the extreme severity of the winter was due to atmospheric changes caused by the resistance of academic science to magnetizing, were finding in Mesmer's method a cure-all for all the ills of society. This dangerous line of thinking was starting to make serious inroads into the wealthy, titled, and educated classes.

Even if there was no other reason to call a halt to the magnetizing mania, its detractors asserted, the grave peril it presented to public morality required its prompt suppression. The scandalous "crises" into which the magnetizers induced their female patients were only a form of sexual orgasm in public, which could no longer be tolerated. It had not escaped the notice of M. LeNoir's investigators there were eight women for every man seeking treatment at the *baquets*.

With arguments of this sort, King Louis XVI (who himself had no particular feeling one way or the other about Mesmer or his therapy, but disliked "all commotions and disturbances to peace and order") was persuaded to appoint on March 12, 1784, a Royal Commission of Inquiry to determine whether there was anything to the claims made for animal magnetism. The Commission consisted of nine members, some of high distinction in the medical and scientific fields. Four members, including Dr. Joseph Ignance Guillotin (who in a few years would achieve immortal notoriety for recommending the construction of a device that would kill all persons condemned to death instantly and humanely), were physicians from the Medical Faculty, which had been lobbying intensively in the royal court for a restoration of its status and prestige. Five members were from the Academy of Sciences. These included the noted chemist Antoine Lavoisier and the astronomer Jean-Sylvain Bailly (both of whom would be guillotined nine years later during the Reign of Terror), and Benjamin Franklin, the envoy of the United States to France, famed no less for his practical research into many branches of science than for his diplomatic and political genius in bringing about the independence of the former Thirteen Colonies.

The Royal Society of Medicine, which had displaced the Faculty as the premier body of the medical profession in France, immediately complained about being left off the Royal Commission of Inquiry. Indeed, the Society made such uproar over it that on April 4th the King named a second Commission, made up of five Society of Medicine members, to conduct a parallel inquiry. Included among the five was a Dr. Poissonnier, whose wife had died of cancer after unavailing treatment by Mesmer, and a botanist, Dr. Laurent de Jussieu, who had gained repute for searching out and using new medications from plants. He was the nephew of three noted botanist brothers who had been among the scientific luminaries of the reigns of Louis XIV and Louis XV.

On the face of it, the commission members appeared reasonably objective. Lavoisier, Bailly, and Franklin were regarded as open-minded, as was de Jussieu. Poissonnier would be prejudiced against Mesmer, but it seemed most of the other members would at least try to examine the evidence fairly.

It did not turn out that way. This was mainly because the royal directives to the commissioners emphasized they were to prove or disprove the existence of animal magnetism and the all-pervading fluid that was supposed to be its vehicle. Since both of these elements were founded on thoroughly unscientific premises by Mesmer and his followers, and had no real existence, it was not difficult for the commissioners to reach negative conclusions about them. The tragedy was that the phenomena they were investigating were real enough, and instead of recognizing them as such and seeking a solid explanation for them, the commissioners dismissed animal magnetism as due merely to the imaginations of the patients. Thus the actuality of hypnotism and its mode of operation were not discerned, and a whole century may have been lost in the utilization of hypnosis for therapy.

Even to this day, there is an astonishing blindness on the part of many writers on scientific and medical subjects in acknowledging Mesmer's concept of animal magnetism as the first step toward the development of scientific hypnotism. Mesmer was the pioneer, from whom an unbroken line of further development extends to the present day. Stephen Jay Gould, the Harvard biologist, geologist, and noted historian of science, famed for his "punctuated evolution" modification of Darwinism, is one of those who have failed to see this. In an article in the July 1989 issue of *Natural History* he represents Mesmer as a fraud and charlatan, and his method as of no consequence or importance.

In Gould's view, the Royal Commission (he ignores the second Commission altogether) performed an admirable work of exposure of an imposition on the public's gullibility. "Never in history had such an extraordinary and luminous group," Gould extols, "been gathered together in the service of rational inquiry." In particular he holds up Franklin and Lavoisier as shining examples of this dedication to pure disinterested search for the truth, crediting them with having devised most of the experiments that supposedly demonstrated the fraudulence of animal magnetism.

A more critical examination of the Commission's procedure and conclusions does not bear out this eulogy. In the first place, Franklin, who was seventy-eight, ill from gout and mainly waiting for Thomas Jefferson to arrive and relieve him of his post so he could finally go home to America after an eight year stay in France, was not a leading participant in the investigation, though he lent his prestige to it. Although he allowed some of the experiments to be carried out at his home in suburban Passy, in a letter to a French scientist friend, LaCondamine, who was on neither Commission, he indicated he was not greatly interested in the debate over animal magnetism, though he suggested that imagination might account for its reported effects. In this, Franklin was on the right track, but he did not pursue it, nor did anyone else. That Franklin was not hostile to the new therapies is evident from the same letter, in which he remarked that good results seemed to have been obtained from the use of electric treatments for nerve and circulation blockages.

As for Lavoisier, his attitude throughout the investigation was one of assertion of his superior intelligence. He was convinced there was nothing to animal magnetism, and anyone who had a contrary opinion was either a fraud, a dupe or a fool. Having made up his mind in advance, he was not going to let himself be confused by the facts. Since animal magnetism had indeed no existence in the mistaken conception both Mesmer and d'Eslon had of it, it was simple for Lavoisier and his colleagues to devise experiments that proved its non-existence.

Blindfolded subjects, for example, were unable to discern "magnetized" objects from those that were not.

On that sort of premise (and with Lavoisier brusquely dismissing any attempt to consider any investigation of why, if there was nothing at all to Mesmer's discovery, it was nevertheless curing or relieving a great number and variety of illness) there was total unanimity in the Royal Commission's conclusion. The report released on September 4th stated: "No evidence could be found for the existence of a magnetic fluid and therefore no therapy could be founded on it. All the alleged effects were simply due to the over-excited imaginations of the subjects." Eighty thousand copies of the report were ordered to be immediately printed and distributed to physicians throughout France, to halt the further dissemination and practice of a mode of treatment "both false and dangerous."

A separate report, not made public though filed in the Royal Library where officials could consult it, concluded that the magnetic treatment of women patients incurred grave risks to public morals and decency, and should be discouraged, or even banned. This secret report, "not adapted for general publication," is more curious than the official version.

> It has been observed that women are like musical strings stretched in perfect unison; when one is moved, all the others are instantly affected. Thus the commissioners have repeatedly observed that when the crisis occurs in one woman, it occurs almost at once in others. . . . .
>
> Women are always magnetized by men; the established relations are doubtless those of a patient to the

physician, but this physician is a man, and whatever the illness may be, it does not deprive us of our sex, it does not entirely withdraw us from the power of the other sex; illness may weaken impressions without destroying them. Moreover, most of the women who present themselves to be magnetized are not really ill; many come out of idleness, or for amusement; others, if not perfectly well, retain their freshness and their force, their senses are unimpaired and they have all the sensitiveness of youth; their charms are such as to affect the physician, and their health is such as to make them liable to be affected by him, so that the danger is reciprocal. . . . .

The magnetizer generally keeps the patient's knees enclosed within his own, and consequently the knees and all the lower parts of the body are in close contact. The hand is applied to the hypochondriac region, and sometimes to that of the ovarium, so that the touch is exerted at once on many parts, and these the most sensitive parts of the body.

The experimenter, after applying his left hand in this manner, passes his right hand behind the woman's body, and they incline towards each other so as to favor this twofold contact. This causes the closest proximity; the two faces almost touch, the breath is intermingled, all physical impressions are felt in common, and the reciprocal attraction of the sexes must consequently be excited in all its force. It is not surprising that the senses are inflamed. The action of the imagination at the same time produces a certain disorder throughout the machine; it obscures the judgment, distracts the attention; the women in question are unable to take account of their sensations, and are not aware of their condition.

The report nevertheless failed to cite a single actual case of impropriety resulting from the magnetizing of women, nor is there anything in the record of the Commission's investigations that it ever observed a woman patient being brought to a crisis by magnetizing. In other words, the Commission was deciding from impressions and hearsay, not from firsthand observation. Obviously, there was some danger that treatment of women by Mesmer's method could be abused. The Commission made up its collective mind that widespread abuse was happening or was about to happen. It sought no corroborative, factual evidence for its conclusion.

Ten days after the release of the Royal Commission's report, the Royal Society of Medicine issued its own conclusion that also denied the reality of animal magnetism. One member of the Society, the botanist, de Jussieu, dissented and refused to sign the report. Instead, he wrote a summary of his own determinations, which he released a month later. He argued that instead of simply dismissing animal magnetism as nonexistent, without any inquiry into how something that did not exist was nevertheless producing some demonstrable real effects, the Commissions should have considered whether some emanations of the human body might account for them. Perhaps, de Jussieu, suggested, the magnetizer was in some way able to transfer "animal heat" from his own body into a sick person's, which might be deficient in this "heat." In any event, he wrote, all practitioners of the new therapy should be required to carefully observe, record, and publish all aspects of their treatments.

Well thought out and rational though de Jussieu's minority report was, it brought scant comfort to Mesmer, d'Eslon and their followers, who by that time were in disarray and retreat on all fronts. Through the five months of the investigations by the Commissions, the cause of animal magnetism had been struck one damaging blow after another. Even developments that seemed at first to redound to its credit soon turned counterproductive.

After these reports were made public the French people lost interest in animal magnetism as quickly as they had ushered in this unconventional form of healing. Mesmer, now hopelessly disappointed, went into retirement in Germany. Mesmer died on March 5, 1815. He was buried at Meersburg, under a three-sided marble monument the Berlin Medical Faculty erected in his memory, bearing a carved sundial and mariner's compass symbolic of Mesmer having charted a new course for humankind.

It now looked as if the fate of mesmerism hung in the balance, and the scales quivered. Soon after Mesmer's retirement, one of his most prominent pupils, the Marquis de Puységur (1751-1825), serendipitously discovered the phenomenon of "artificial somnambulism." Charles Richet, a late 19th century French writer on the subject, did not hesitate to place Puységur on a par with Mesmer himself. Richet asserted that while Mesmer was the initiator of hypnotism, Puységur was its true founder. Without him, the method would have been short-lived, merely another in the long series of unusual medical claims that have surfaced through all of history.

A very short time after seriously applying himself to the mastery of animal magnetism, Puységur was experimenting on the hundreds of peasants who lived and worked on his vast family estate. He set up a variant of Mesmer's *baquet* around a centuries-old elm tree in the Buzancy town square. Located next to a spring with reputed curative powers, the tree itself had come to be venerated by generations of the peasantry as possessing similar virtues, especially in its bark. Consequently it was easy for Puységur to persuade the peasants that by magnetizing them under its branches he was only continuing a long-standing tradition. Seated on stone benches under the tree, Puységur's patients would take hold of the ends of ropes dangling from it, and wrap these around the afflicted areas of their bodies. He then touched them with an iron rod, evoking crises similar to those in Mesmer's treatments, at the same time suggesting they diagnose what was wrong with them and prescribe the proper treatment. This early form of self-imaging worked surprisingly well; out of three hundred patients treated in a month's time, sixty-one were cured through treatment prescribed by the patients themselves while in mesmeric trance. When awakened — which was done by having them touch the tree — they remembered nothing of what they had said.

Puységur noted their behavior while magnetized (i.e., in hypnosis) was very similar to that in sleepwalking persons. He further observed that the crises were milder than those he had witnessed in Mesmer's clinics, and in eight of the sixty-one cures the subjects had simply fallen into what looked like natural sleep, though they continued to respond to his verbal commands. He began to think the crisis was unnecessary and that magnetizing could produce all of Mesmer's effects simply by inducing in the subject a condition of artificial somnambulism, so called because it resembled sleepwalking and was descriptive of the state. (In modern hypnotism the term "somnambulism" is used to denote one of the deepest levels of hypnosis.)

This conjecture became a conviction with his treatment of Victor Race, a twenty-three year-old peasant, whom the Marquis had singled out for individual attention. Race was suffering from an infection in his chest, either pneumonia or a severe pleurisy. When the Marquis visited him at his cottage on May 4, 1784—destined to be one of the landmark dates in the history of hypnotism—he was able to put him into a calm, deep, sleeplike state, with no attending convulsions or other manifestations of the mesmeric crisis. He then suggested to Race that he was enjoying himself at a rural fair, and the young man responded by going through motions of dancing and singing. Within an hour, he broke out into a "good sweat," and Puységur woke him up. He could not remember anything of what had passed, but he was feeling much better; his fever had subsided, he was breathing easily, and the next day he was fully recovered though still a little weak. The young peasant responded to the Marquis' suggestion that he was in good health and having a good time, and gained an immediate upper hand over whatever was making him ill. He also proved to be an ideal subject for additional experiments that further confirmed Puységur's belief he had found the true basis of Mesmer's magnetizing. It was not necessary for the

Marquis to touch him, or even to speak audibly to him. Simply by directing his mind toward Race's, Puységur was able to convey telepathic commands that the peasant carried out unquestioningly while in the sleeplike state. Race could recall none of this after being awakened.

The Marquis did not fully comprehend what he had discovered. He perceived he could make contact with the mind of another person by placing that individual in a trance resembling sleep, but he attributed this to the ability of a proficient magnetizer to communicate his wishes through the magnetic fluid, the existence of which he continued to accept. Though he realized this predicated an exclusivity of communication (i.e., the magnetizer and the subject had to be in rapport with each other only) he did not understand it was suggestion that elicited the response. In Puységur's view, he was simply giving commands to a peasant who would normally be expected to obey him anyway, the only difference being that it was done through an induced sleepwalking condition instead of in the ordinary waking state. But because the commands were given directly into the mind, they produced results, such as swift physical healing, that were not normally possible. When awake, Race would not have been able to throw off his illness simply by being told to do so. However, he was an exceptionally responsive subject. It was not feasible to treat all the sick individually, and even if it were, only a few would respond as fully as Race had done. Thus for large groups of people the most practicable method of magnetizing would still be to employ conduits such as the *baquet* or variants like the elm tree of Buzancy. They would thereby obtain at least some measure of benefits.

These were the limitations Puységur and his followers placed on the advance he had made beyond Mesmer. Until the idea of the actually non-existent magnetic fluid was discarded for good, all further advances would be limited. Even so, what the Marquis had achieved was of real importance. By demonstrating that suggestion, though he did not fully understand it as such, could be exerted without necessarily using such material aids as touching with hands or magnetized objects, he laid the foundation on which modern hypnotism rests.

Puységur's findings were first made public in a book he wrote in the summer of 1784, titled *Details of the Cures Achieved at Buzancy Through Animal Magnetism*. It was published just before the release of the condemnatory findings of the two Royal Commissions of Inquiry. There is no indication that either commission paid any attention to the book. It was followed up in the winter of 1784-85 by an even larger work, in two volumes, in which the Marquis sought to establish a solid basis for magnetizing, using what he himself had discovered. He still advocated the use of touch, stroking, and other tactile stimulation in the induction process; but increasingly asserted "The act of magnetizing is an act of the will, and the awaking from somnambulism is also an act of the will."

The Nineteenth Century

The importance of suggestion to the process of hypnosis was first elaborated by a Scottish physician James Braid (1795–1860). In November 1841 Braid, along with a Dr. Wilson, witnessed a demonstration of mesmerism by a the noted stage mesmerist Charles Lafontaine, whose itinerary through Britain took him to Manchester, where Braid was one of the most prominent and respected physicians in that great industrial center.

Braid denounced the whole demonstration of mesmerism when Lafontaine announced that his female subject was "in a mesmeric coma." His denunciation was short-lived:

I at once raised her eyelids, and found the pupils contracted to two small points. I called Wilson's attention to this evidence of sound sleep, and he at once gave me a look and a low whistle, conscious that he was in a mess. (Braid then tested the girl by forcing a pin between one of her nails and the end of her finger.) She did not exhibit the slightest indication of feeling pain, and Braid soon arrived at the conclusion that it was not all humbug.

Braid noted that most trances occurred when the subject was relaxed, with eyes closed, and in a state resembling sleep. Thus, he named this state "hypnosis"[1] from *Hypnos*, the Greek god of sleep. Immediately accepted and used everywhere since then, it replaced the older names of "mesmerism" and "animal magnetism" which had been incorrect in that hypnotism was known in antiquity and among primitive peoples thousand of years before Mesmer, and it is not any kind of magnetism. (As will be pointed out later, the term "hypnotism" with its connotation of sleep, is a misnomer.)

---

[1] To set the record straight . . . Although the literature credits Braid with coining the word "hypnotism," hypnosis historian Melvin Gravitz's research brought to light that the term had been used by the French nearly 40 years prior to Braid. *First Uses of Hypnotism Nomenclature: A Historical Record. Hypnosis, 24, 42-46.*

In 1843 Braid published a book on his findings entitled *Neurypnology, or the Rationale of Nervous Sleep*. This book accentuated the importance of suggestion to the hypnotic process. With recognition of the pivotal role of suggestion in the induction of hypnosis, "animal magnetic fluid" was superseded by "suggestive commands."

John Elliotson, a prominent English physician who introduced the stethoscope into England, and who developed the techniques for examining the heart and lungs, was ruthlessly maligned and forced to resign from the faculty of the University of London and his position of President of the Royal Medical and Chirurgical Society for experimenting with mesmerism and advocating its clinical use.

In the East India Company Hospitals of Hooghly and Calcutta, India (1842) several thousand minor operations and over three hundred major surgeries (including amputations of limbs and breasts and the removal of huge scrotal tumors) were performed painlessly through "mesmeric coma" by Dr. James Esdaile, a Scottish surgeon. In the pre-anesthesia era many patients undergoing surgery died of neurogenic shock. Dupuytren, writing about this period, stated: "Pain kills like hemorrhage." To undergo surgery in those days was tantamount to signing one's death warrant. Although the mortality rate was greatly reduced, from 50% to only 5%, the English medical journals would not print a word about Esdaile's remarkable accomplishment.

The Nancy School

Auguste Ambroise Liébeault (1823–1904), from whom the Nancy School was to originate, became interested in mesmerism while still a medical student. Liébeault, a country doctor in Pont-Saint-Vincent (a rural village near Nancy) used hypnotism extensively in his general medical practice and evolved the induction techniques commonly used today. (Liébeault is credited by hypnosis historian J. M. Bramwell with the development of modern hypnotism.) After twenty years of experimentation and practice of clinical hypnosis, Liébeault wrote a book, *Du Sommeil*, and as legend has it, managed to sell but a single copy.

Fate did smile on Liebeault's endeavors, however. A patient suffering from sciatica, who had been treated unsuccessfully by the eminent neurologist Hippolyte Marie Bernheim (1840–1919) of the Nancy Medical School, came to Liébeault for hypnotic treatment and was cured. When Bernheim heard about this, he went to Liebeault's clinic fully prepared to meet a quack. When he met the sincere, unpretentious Liébeault, Bernheim was so impressed with Liébeault and his work that he decided to return and conduct research in the field of hypnotism. Working as a team, Bernheim and Liébeault used therapeutic suggestion (i.e., hypnotism) with thousands of patients. Bernheim, in addition to being the leader of the Nancy School, was a skilled hypnotist. J. M. Bramwell reported that Bernheim had a success rate of over 85% with over 10,000 patients.

In 1884 Bernheim's book, *De la Suggestion* was published; and in 1886 his definitive treatise on the nature and uses of hypnotism, *Suggestive Therapeutics*, was published. When these works appeared in print, it was an event of major importance to the development of hypnotism as an accepted science, as Professor Bernheim had enormous prestige in the medical world. At this juncture in its turbulent history, hypnotism had begun to shake off restraining fetters and gain the scientific recognition it so rightly deserved.

The Salpêtrière School

Jean-Martin Charcot (1825–1893), the famous Parisian anatomist and neurologist, conducted a series of experiments and lectures on hypnotism in Paris at the Salpêtrière Hospital, which became known as the Salpêtrière School, as opposed to the Nancy School, which of course propagated the ideas of Liébeault and Bernheim. In the hypnosis literature, one will find many references to these two diametrically opposed schools of thought.

Since Charcot's hypnotic experimentation was confined to a limited number of hysterical women, he arrived at false conclusions. Charcot incorrectly believed that hypnosis was a manifestation of hysteria, and thus an abnormal or pathologic phenomenon. Charcot's poor judgment in respect to his findings on hypnosis is an enigma, because he was a meticulous researcher and was considered to be the greatest neurologist of his time. Charcot's presumption that hypnosis is a symptom of hysteria is untenable, as normal individuals are readily hypnotizable.

The greatest blow to the psychotherapeutic application of hypnosis came when Sigmund Freud (1856–1939), developer of psychoanalysis, resolved to give up hypnotism. It was through hypnosis that Freud gained insight into the unconscious mind; and it was this germ of thought that eventually gave birth to his system of psychoanalysis. Just as alchemy was the precursor of the science of modern chemistry, and astrology the forerunner of the science of astronomy, hypnosis gave birth to psychoanalysis.

In *The Origin and Development of Psychoanalysis*, Freud stated his reason for discarding hypnosis was because ". . . I discovered that, in spite of all my efforts, I could not hypnotize by any means all of my patients." What Freud undoubtedly meant by the statement that he could not hypnotize "all of my patients" is that he could not hypnotize all of his patients to a profound degree (i.e., "deep" hypnosis). He either did not consider or failed to realize the therapeutic possibilities in the lighter stages of hypnosis.

After Freud's psychoanalysis gained momentum, hypnotism became more and more neglected in the psychiatric realm. Freud, however, eventually recognized that psychoanalysis consumed too much time to be used widely and predicted that a return to hypnotism would be necessary if psychotherapy was to become available to the general public.

The potentialities of hypnosis as a dynamic psychiatric tool were not recognized widely before World Wars I and II. During the war it became necessary to find some shortcut form of psychotherapy to handle the myriad cases of war neuroses. The hospital beds were needed for the battlefield casualties, and it was hoped that many of the patients with war neuroses could be returned to active duty. The shortcut method employed was hypnosis--having the patients relive, as it were, the traumatic event which precipitated their "shell shocked" condition. Through hypnosis, combined with other psychotherapeutic procedures, many of these patients were quickly relieved of their symptoms. The therapeutic results thus attained with the war neuroses cases were indeed most impressive.

Outstanding among the scientists in America who have influenced the scientific development of hypnotism were William James, Boris Sidis, Clark Hull, Milton Erickson, and Ernest Hilgard.

William James, who was America's premier psychologist, made a valuable contribution to the scientific advancement of hypnotism by his open-minded approach to it in his numerous writings on the structure of the human mind.

The practice of hypnotism in America was falling back into the hands of self-taught amateurs. That is not to undervalue their contributions, one of which was the eminently practical handbook of instruction in hypnotism and suggestion published in 1903 by the stage hypnotist Herbert Flint and his wife in Chicago. This made little impression, however, on members of the medical profession, who looked to the academic community for example and direction; and the academics were largely turning their backs on hypnotherapy.

Very few American hypnotists were on a level with their distinguished counterparts in Britain and Europe, for instance, Boris Sidis, a friend and student of William James, who in 1914 opened a psychotherapy institute in Portsmouth, New Hampshire, and John D. Quackenbos who practiced in Manhattan from 1894 to at least 1907. They can be credited with certain advances in the understanding of hypnosis. Sidis, pioneered in the exploration of the hypnoidal (now called hypnagogic) state between waking and sleeping, while Quackenbos sought to reclaim youths who had gone morally and criminally astray by sympathetic and reassuring hypnotic suggestions—an endeavor in which he was remarkably successful.

In America, the revival of hypnotism in medical practice stemmed from the publication in 1926 of William McDougall's *Outline of Abnormal Psychology*, with its explanation of hypnotic control as a temporary yielding by the mind's authority to suggestions in which it has acquired confidence. The work in the 1920's and early 1930's of Clark Hull at the University of Wisconsin and Yale University was equally influential. Along with these was the emergence into active hypnotherapy of Milton Erickson, who was to become the greatest hypnotist of the century.

Ernest Hilgard, a psychologist prominent in the fields of learning and hypnosis published several important scientific papers in both areas. Hilgard was engaged in hypnosis research at Stanford University's Laboratory of Hypnotic Research until his death in 2001 at the age of 97.

While the foregoing is only a brief overview of the history of hypnotism,[2] in this chapter we have touched upon the milestones in its therapeutic evolution.

---

[2] For a comprehensive history of hypnotism see *The Illustrated History of Hypnotism*, by John C. Hughes, The National Guild of Hypnotists, Inc., Merrimack, NH © 2008.

CHAPTER 2
20th Century Practitioners

The 20th century brought about a complete transformation in the fields of hypnosis and hypnotherapy. The science matured and became an accepted and respected therapeutic tool.

This transformation resulted from a number of brilliant and committed visionaries. They succeeded not only in developing the science, but also in educating medical practitioners and the public so that most of the suspicions and superstitions surrounding hypnosis were defeated.

Three lines of study were the engines driving the development of the science. The first line was led by William McDougall and Morton Prince in the 1920's. The second was led by Clark L. Hull in the 1920's and 30's, and the third by Milton H. Erickson, who elaborated on Hull's work into the latter part of the century.

In addition to these luminaries, Dr. Rexford L. North contributed to the maturation and acceptance of hypnosis by training large numbers of hypnotists and doctors. North formed a professional association and published a journal that provided structure and focus to this emerging science

In 1950 Dr. North founded The National Guild of Hypnotists. His vision transformed hypnosis, bringing together individual practitioners, entertainers and isolated scientists into a homogeneous body that is now respected by the public, establishing an organization and structure with professional standards and regulations.

Emile Coué

Emile Coué was a major influence in the 1920's. He is not ranked with the world's greatest hypnotist, but he was essential to the development of modern hypnotherapy.

Coué became famous for his autosuggestion formula, "Every day in every way, I am getting better and better." His doctrine was based on the way the human psyche and imagination actually function, and modern self-hypnosis is really a revived form of his doctrine. That would take another half century to be fully accepted in medical practice.

A pharmacist from 1882 to 1910 and then a student of hypnotism, Coué had faith in his self-suggestion mantra, claiming he could teach people self-healing and even bring about organic changes.

As with many of the fads of the Roaring Twenties, his ideas were briefly trumpeted to the skies as the newfound magic cure for every illness. His doctrine was then rejected and scorned just as quickly. Yet Coué was essential to the development of modern hypnotherapy.

Emile Coué was born February 26, 1857, in Troyes, France, about one hundred miles southwest of Nancy. Coué became interested in Liébeault's and Bernheim's successes in treating patients without drugs after seeing the curative effects of placebos he gave to customers.

Coué went to Nancy to closely observe what was being done, and later visited the Nancy School in the United States, where he learned about a forgotten treatise by Chicago hypnotist W. B. Fahnestock, who argued that most people could put themselves into a trance and did not need someone else to do it.

Coué' started his own hypnotherapy clinic in Nancy. He believed that there was no suggestion other than self-suggestion and that all hypnosis was really self-hypnosis. He claimed to have treated fifteen to forty thousand patients annually. His method diverged from the original Nancy School toward pure self-hypnosis, and became identified as the New Nancy School.

The French press publicized Coué, who set up the Psychological Society of Lorraine, with himself and his wife as founders and directors. For five francs, anyone could become a member; ten francs secured membership to the inner council. Soon, branch institutes were springing up all over France. *Suggestion and Autosuggestion,* a book that had appeared the previous year by Dr. Charles Baudouin of the University of Geneva in Switzerland, with a dedication to Coué, became an overnight best-seller. Within weeks the British and American press started to extol the virtues of this marvelous new way of finding happiness.

People wanted to find out more about Coué's treatments, and the demand was soon met. In London, Miss Richardson opened the Coué Institute for the Practice of Conscious Auto-Suggestion. In Paris, Mlle. Anne Villeneuve, who had studied under Coué, opened a similar institute. Coué himself, now in his mid-sixties, came to New York early in 1922 to coordinate plans for a National Coué Institute in New York.

An eager disciple, Archibald Stark Van Orden of Ramsey, New Jersey, founded the Coué League of America, with himself as Secretary. Two books by Coué appeared in American bookshops in rapid succession—a translation from the French, *Self-Mastery Through Conscious Auto-Suggestion*, followed by *My Method, Including American Impressions*, which he wrote in English after returning to France. Professor Baudouin had already prepared an expanded and revised edition of his earlier book to be published in the United States by Dodd Mead. It became the bible of the Coué movement here.

Coué proposed that by training a person's imagination to create a mental picture of beneficial results, their body would mobilize to repair itself and defend against intrusion and injury. This had been demonstrated many times, using hypnotic suggestion in a trance state. But the trance state was not necessary, Coué insisted. Merely reciting a proper formula, repeated consistently and correctly over time would do the job just as well - in fact better.

The key point in Coué's assertion is the "correct persistence" in reciting the autosuggestion formula. Coué pointed out that training the imagination is not an easy thing. Merely repeating a mantra or formula will not get the imagination under control, or enable it to direct the autonomic nervous system that carries out bodily functions such as digestion and breathing.

Coué devised a four-step method, which included trance induction and hypnotic suggestions, to enable his patients to begin the rigorous process of training their imaginations. He instructed patients to suggest to themselves that three times a day they would feel like eating, that they would not have any digestive distress, that they would have an easy daily evacuation of intestinal wastes, that their bodies would properly assimilate what they had eaten to facilitate and strengthen every natural function, that they would enjoy nightly refreshing sleep, and that they would be able to fulfill any demands of work or effort, within reasonable limits.

Patients were to imagine these and other autosuggestions as actually happening, not because of an act of will but simply as the result of picturing them as real. Eventually this process would become effortless and natural, and it would not be necessary to repeat the visualization technique.

A strict translation of the original French mantric formula was, "Every day, from every point of view, I am doing better and better." To make it easier for English speakers to use, Coué shortened it to, "Every day in every way I'm getting better and better." Repeated twice daily, the formula reinforced the basic suggestions. However, without first instilling a positive expectation, reciting the formula was to no avail.

Because autosuggestion was such a simple concept, the public was convinced that Coué was a charlatan. When he died on July 2, 1926, in Nancy, at the age of sixty-nine, he had been discredited by doctors, hypnotists, and the public alike.

Coué remained discredited for almost half a century and even now is not fully recognized as having anticipated the benefits of self-hypnosis. Coué understood what had been known for centuries, that mantras could dissolve the sense of physical separation from the inner self. Repeating formulas enables the conscious personality to call on the vast powers of the subconscious. Although Coué did not realize it, the wording actually doesn't matters. The great English poet Tennyson, for instance, used to put himself into an "inspirational trance" by repeating his own name.

According to Coué, the method is effective only if the repetition becomes a habit, and is repeated with confidence. This requires thorough training of the imagination. Coué said that this training should be largely intuitive and unforced. He differed on this point from Beaudouin, who called on the intellect and will to tame the imagination and make it the trusted order-bearer of the conscious mind to the subconscious. But that, Coué argued, would constantly create conflicts between what the intellect thought was best and what the subconscious instinctively knew to be best.

Coué and Baudouin's disagreement added to the demise of the public's obsession with Coue's autosuggestion. People quickly concluded that there had to be something wrong with the whole idea if Coué and his chief disciple couldn't agree on a key point.

The medical profession in general had never warmed up to Coué and was happy to see him and his teachings disappear from the headlines. However, a few doctors thought that perhaps Coué had been on the right track. So many patients seemed to have nothing organically wrong with them, yet were always complaining of various symptoms.

A. J. Cronin, a London practitioner later noted for his medical novels, decided to tell some patients that they were suffering from "asthenia," a term he abridged from Freud's "neurasthenia." The patients were delighted to discover a doctor who, unlike the others, accepted that they were actually sick. They readily submitted to his placebo injections, for which he charged high fees. He gained a reputation with his successful results, and other doctors soon began employing similar methods.

Yet neither Cronin nor those who took their cue from him saw any connection with suggestion or hypnosis in this placebo therapy. The medical profession solidly agreed with Pierre Janet's somber assessment in 1925 that "Hypnotism is dead—until its next revival." Few expected a revival in the foreseeable future.

Coué was a folk hero of the Roaring Twenties. For two or three years, newspaper readers knew Coué's name and face as well as that of Al Capone or the Prince of Wales. Everybody was repeating the simplistic mantra, "Every day in every way, I am getting better and better."

However, few people understood the mantra and how it could effectively improve their mental and physical condition. Before long disappointment and disillusioned replaced their enthusiasm.

New fads, such as Teapot Dome, radio, and Lindbergh's Paris flight, crowded Couéism off the stage. Millions of people concluded that it had been just another fad in an age of fads.

This is how Coué and his doctrine are remembered today, if they are remembered at all. Yet Coué's teaching was in the mainstream of hypnotherapy as it had been developed over almost a century and a quarter by Mesmer and his successors. Coué's important innovation was recognizing that the patient's imagination was more important than willpower in the therapeutic use of suggestion.

B.F. Skinner

Science and medicine turned to behaviorism, which began with John Broadus Watson at Columbia University in 1912 and peaked in the depression psychology that was almost universal in 1932. The age of behaviorism retarded the progress of hypnotherapy. It remained in the establishment forefront through World War II and the immediate post-war years, attaining new prominence and avid acceptance in the 1960's, with B. F. Skinner as its principal advocate.

Behaviorism, which asserted that only observed behavior had any scientific validity, made any investigation of states of consciousness unacceptability. Watson, and later Skinner, claimed that there was no way to observe mental processes accurately. Thus science could learn nothing from them, or about them.

The behavior of organisms, on the other hand, could be observed and recorded with rigorous precision, and reduced to mathematical formulas. Under this reductionism dogma, subjective processes such as sensation, perception, emotion, and creativity were declared out of bounds because they were not linked to any definitely locatable stimulus or impulse. This was an attempt to legitimize a particular set of practices. For a generation it shut the door to any further development of the effects of suggestion and imagination that had been growing steadily from Mesmer through Coué in the 1920's.

However, across the Atlantic, behaviorism found less academic acceptance. In 1923, Professor C. D. Broad at Cambridge University derided Watson's premises as so silly and preposterous that "only very learned minds could conceive and believe in them," a shining example of the British genius for understated sarcasm. In Europe, Pierre Janet continued his lonely labors on behalf of hypnotism, and Georg Groddeck, a forgotten pioneer from whom Freud borrowed his concept of the Id, said in 1917: bacteria by themselves did not cause illness, which only occurred when our inner defenses of immunity broke down, for reasons usually related to what the mind thinks or believes.

In the United States and Europe, medical fads continued to sprout and flourish, enriching the doctors and product-makers who practiced and promoted them. Removing the appendix and "septic sacs" in the intestines, radical extractions of sound teeth to uncover such sacs in the gums and jawbones, yeast diets for skin conditions, and a host of other treatments arose and were in the limelight. They actually benefited many, but it was because the power of suggestion instilled belief in the effectiveness of the treatment. As each belief ran its course, it lost its efficacy and yielded to the next one. Few people in the 1920's and 1930's saw the potency of imagination and suggestion.

A Thread of Continuity

One important thread keeping hypnotherapy going was the work done by the Harvard trained hypnotists on trauma cases in World War 1. Because of the Harvard influence, a number of young psychologists with experience in hypnotherapy were available during World War I. They were ready to use their knowledge in treating the symptoms of battle neuroses caused by the psychic trauma of war.

War victims were hypnotized and regressed to the time of the traumatic experience, where they were encouraged to relive the event and to rid themselves of the emotions relating to the experience. (J. A. Hadfield coined the term for this procedure "hypnoanalysis".)

Thousands of battle trauma cases flooded into the armed services hospitals. The shortage of mainline psychiatrists led to using hypnosis as an abbreviated psychotherapy, and the post-war medical establishment began to regard hypnosis more favorably.

The clinical use of hypnosis in World War II and the Korean War also created a new wave of enthusiasm for hypnotherapy. The cumulative evidence proved that hypnosis was superior to pain-killing drugs in alleviating the pain of burns and severe wounds, and was of definite value in restoring healthy minds and psyches to men who had been inwardly scarred by the horrors of combat.

In 1955 the British Medical Association passed a formal resolution approving hypnosis as a valid therapeutic technique for treating neuroses and for relieving pain in surgery and childbirth. In 1958 the American Medical Association and the American Dental Association also passed resolutions recognizing hypnosis as an accepted treatment and encouraged training in hypnosis for students in medicine and dentistry. Also in 1958, the American Psychological Association recognized hypnosis as a respectable psychotherapeutic tool. Certifying boards were set up for both the experimental and clinical usage of hypnosis in 1960. With this new legitimacy an increasing number of health professionals began to use hypnosis.

William McDougall and Morton Prince

Despite the retreat of hypnotherapy in mainstream medicine, some research continued. One line advancing this research grew out of the teaching and clinical work of William McDougall and Morton Prince at Harvard in the 1920's. In his seven years at Harvard, McDougall stimulated the curiosity and interest of several students who went on to do important work in hypnotism and to influence others to follow in their footsteps.

McDougall's most prominent students who did pioneer work in hypnosis research included William S. Taylor, Paul C. Young, Frank A. Pattie, and George W. Estabrooks. In 1929 another student, Henry A. Murray, became head of the Harvard Psychological Clinic that Morton Prince had founded in 1927. Paul C. Young performed the first hypnotic experiments leading to an American doctorate in psychology.

In 1931 Murray and a graduate of the clinic, Donald W. Mackinnon, co-authored a book on the status of hypnosis research at that time. One graduate, Robert W. White, Murray's successor as head of the clinic, was a teacher of Martin T. Orne, who after World War II became one of the most important figures in the field of hypnotism.

None of the men of the generation between Prince and Orne were known outside of their own professional circles, and the hostility toward hypnotism was so great in the medical establishment at the time that they had to avoid any publicity about their interest. Yet they made a considerable contribution to the later emergence of hypnosis and its acceptance into medicine. They kept alive a spark of research that led to new insights and techniques.

Clark L. Hull

A second line of development centered on the work of Clark L. Hull, the foremost figure in American hypnotherapy from the late 1920's to mid-century. He was a psychologist at the University of Wisconsin and then at Yale from 1923 to 1931, where he was appointed to the Sterling Chair of Psychology.

Hull's book, *Hypnosis and Suggestibility: An Experimental Approach*, published in 1933, set a standard of scientific control and statistical verification of hypnotic phenomena that is still a model for the profession. But by the time it appeared in print, Hull had stopped all his research in hypnosis and closed the hypnosis research laboratory he had opened at Yale two years earlier.

Hull's abandonment of the field devastated his twenty pupils in hypnosis. Eleven went on to other studies; nine found academic or clinical positions in psychology, and only two, Arthur Jenness and Griffith Williams, ever did any hypnotherapeutic work in their professional careers.

From 1933 on, Hull quantified his ideas of the primary laws of psychology. He argued that from these primary laws all individual, group and social behavior could be derived under a set of secondary laws. He devised several mathematical equations to express these laws, which he published in 1943 in his book *Principles of Behavior*. This work was a bible of psychological theory and practice for a decade beyond his death in 1952, and seemed to assure Hull a niche among the immortals of science.

Then in the 1960's, his fame and influence seemed to evaporate overnight as the untenable nature of his premise became increasingly evident. Today, the few professionals who remember Clark Hull blame him for holding back the development of modern hypnotherapy with his attempt to numerically straitjacket the human psyche.

Hull also had a great influence on Milton H. Erickson, who became the twentieth-century's foremost hypnotist. Erickson was a student working on investigative assignments in Clark L. Hull's seminars at the University of Wisconsin. Although Erickson later disassociated himself from Hull, Erickson viewed his academic mentor generously, recalling how Hull had encouraged and directed his interest in the discipline.

Erickson and a host of practitioners after him went far beyond Hull, but without the scientific credibility Hull provided, it might have been another fifty years or more before hypnotism would be used again in therapy.

Milton H. Erickson

Milton Erickson was the source of the third line of investigation, and became the 20th century's foremost hypnotist.

Erickson was born December 5, 1901 in a Nevada mining camp. His father had been a farmer, and shortly after Erickson was born he returned to Wisconsin to resume farming. Erickson's ambition was to become a farmer too--a modern, up-to-date one. At seventeen he published an article in a national magazine on why young people did not want to stay on farms and what could be done to persuade them to do so.

Then, just after finishing his third year of high school, he was stricken with polio and almost totally paralyzed. Through a combination of mental imagery and stubborn determination, Erickson recovered sufficiently to go to university and train to become a medical doctor, the career he chose when he no longer had the physical strength for farming.

Erickson realized that recovering from a state of helplessness had been largely due to his ability to self-induce a trance state (i.e., self-hypnosis) in which he imagined step-by-step the stages in regaining his mobility. This led to his interest in Hull's classes on hypnotism.

In 1923, with Clark L. Hull's encouragement, Erickson carried out a number of experiments investigating the nature of hypnosis, the processes of induction and trance development, and the roles of the hypnotist and subject. He concluded that the controlling factor in hypnosis was the subject's individuality and how it interplayed with the hypnotist's suggestions.

He summarized his findings in two papers, but did not publish them because they went against Hull's convictions. Erickson was beginning his professional career and did not want to publicly oppose or offend Hull, who was becoming an authority in hypnotism. Erickson gradually dissociated himself from Hull's research.

In addition to his near-fatal attack of polio at seventeen, Erickson faced many other obstacles connected with his health. His earlier physical deficiencies included being tone-deaf and red-green color-blind. He also had severe dyslexia which vanished in a flash of visual illumination as he tried to follow his frustrated teacher's explanation that the characters M and 3 were not the same. From that time in first or second grade, he had only one further problem with learning to read. In his second year at high school he was unable to find words in their alphabetical sequence in the dictionary, and had to keep turning the pages to find the word he was looking for. Then, just as suddenly, this disability also vanished.

Some sixty years later, Erickson concluded that these sudden illuminations were the result of his having self-induced a trance state without realizing it. By concentrating intensely on his reading limitations, he had eliminated them. Whether this was true or not, there is no question about the role of concentration, imagery and self-hypnosis in Erickson's recovery from polio. From a state of total paralysis and a partial loss of his speech faculty, within eleven months he was able to walk with crutches and speak clearly.

His recovery enabled him to graduate from high school in 1920, and work at a sit-down job in a cannery all summer to earn money for college. He entered medical school at the University of Wisconsin that fall. Erickson believed his deep concentration and clear images were the principal factors in overcoming his incapacitating paralysis.

As his body compensated for its loss of mobility, his hearing became exceptionally sharp and sensitive, and he began to identify every sound he heard in the house and outdoors. Soon he could accurately determine who was making what sound, and the activity and mood it denoted. Next, he used his eyesight, which also became more acute, to scan windows closely while he sat in bed or from his rocking chair. His intense focus on the windows induced an auto hypnotic state where he actually started to rock the chair and very gradually slide it toward the window.

He concentrated on remembering the movements of his hands, feet, fingers and toes in grasping tools and utensils, and in walking and climbing trees, and he visualized performing the actions. Before long he was able to perform those motions. From closely watching his baby sister learn to balance and walk, he visualized himself doing the same, and was soon walking.

He used crutches through his freshman year at university, and generally felt physically weak. Determined to toughen himself up, he set out in June 1921 on a two-week canoe trek down the Wisconsin River. He was actually gone ten weeks, paddling from the Wisconsin to the Mississippi, to beyond St. Louis, then back up against the current in both streams a total of twelve hundred miles. He developed powerful shoulder muscles through strenuous paddling, and returned in much stronger physical condition, again able to ride a bicycle. He was able to discard the crutches but still used a cane occasionally for balance. In addition he had met a great variety of people and learned to conduct himself in many different situations.

But he paid a physical price for these gains. Erickson's right shoulder muscles never regained the strength of those in his left shoulder. To keep the left shoulder from becoming higher and disfiguring his appearance, he twisted himself in front of a mirror for many hours until his shoulders were approximately level. However, that severely twisted his spine, which had already been damaged by polio. This led to severe problems later in his life. For the time being, however, Erickson was nearly normal in his physical appearance and ability to move.

After his investigations into hypnotism under Hull in his senior year, he went on to postgraduate medical school at Wisconsin. In 1928, at the age of twenty-six, he qualified for his medical and Master of Arts degrees. He interned in general medicine at the Colorado General Hospital, and in psychiatry at the nearby Colorado Psychopathic Hospital where he worked under Dr. Franklin Ebaugh, a noted psychiatrist in the 1920's.

After a year at these Colorado institutions, Erickson was appointed assistant physician at the Rhode Island State Hospital for Mental Diseases, where he did intensive studies in the relationship of mental deficiencies to family and environmental factors. His findings resulted in seven papers being published in professional journals. This brought him into notice and led to a better paying tenure at the State Hospital in Worcester, Massachusetts, where from 1930-34 he progressed from junior physician to Chief Research Psychiatrist.

He first started using hypnotism extensively as a therapeutic tool at Worcester. The hospital staff was opposed to this, fearing that hypnotism was potentially dangerous to sanity. Erickson overcame this hostility through carefully controlled experiments that demonstrated its safety. His resulting paper, published in 1932 in the *Journal of Abnormal and Social Psychology*, was a significant first step toward the wider professional use of hypnotism in medical practice.

Although Erickson's career was advancing, his personal life was unhappy. He got married at 23, in his first year of postgraduate medical study, and by the early 1930's was raising a family of three children. This placed a heavy burden on his relatively low earnings, and he realized that early marriage had been a serious mistake.

To overcome his paralysis, he had focused on himself, but he had not developed social and relationship skills. He was naive and immature, and was not equipped emotionally for marriage. He divorced in 1934, and obtained custody of the children. He was then determined to learn the skills he was deficient in, and to apply this painfully gained knowledge in his professional practice. He was successful, and in the 1940's and 1950's he was the first to work with families to heal shattered relationships.

Erickson was appointed Director of Psychiatric Research at the Wayne County General Hospital in Eloise, Michigan, a Detroit suburb, in 1934. Five years later this position was expanded to cover Psychiatric Training as well. He remained there for 14 years. It was at Eloise that Erickson started to attain true maturity both as a person and as a healer.

A prime factor in his growth was meeting Elizabeth Moore, who he married in 1936. She became his fellow researcher and muse, a mother to the three children he already had, and to five they had together. Her steady presence and strength helped Erickson become the dominant leader of the hypnotherapy revival in the 1960's and 1970's.

He was thirty-four and physically still vigorous when he married for the second time. However, he had never fully overcome the limp on his right side, and it was becoming more pronounced. He now used a cane all the time, but could walk surprisingly long distances, and still had powerful shoulder muscles.

His physical deterioration began in 1947, at forty-five. He was knocked off his bicycle by a dog and suffered extensive skin abrasions. He received a tetanus antitoxin injection and developed a severe reaction from which he had great difficulty recovering. In particular he could no longer tolerate the damp, chilly Michigan winters. A friend and former Detroit psychiatrist, Dr. John Larson, who was Superintendent of the Arizona State Hospital at Phoenix, invited Erickson to join his staff. Erickson moved his family to Phoenix in 1948, and the warm dry climate improved his health markedly. He helped Dr. Larson institute many progressive changes at the hospital, which had been run in an outmoded and obsolete manner.

In the spring of 1949, political opposition forced Larson's resignation, and Erickson also decided to leave the hospital and go into private practice. He was ill again twice within a few months, apparently from allergic reactions to the desert's environment. To reduce exposure to the sand and dusk, he set up an office in his home in Phoenix.

His condition seemed to stabilize until 1953, when he suffered what was diagnosed as a second attack of polio. It is now believed to have been an episode of post-polio syndrome, traceable to the original attack twenty-four years earlier. There were further episodes through his remaining twenty-seven years of life. While they were not as severe as the first, each caused further muscle impairment until he was reduced to virtually total invalidism.

Erickson became more prominent in the hypnotherapeutic field even though he was becoming more physically disabled.

At his post in Michigan he had attracted the attention of Dr. Margaret Mead, who consulted him in 1939 about the spontaneous trances of the native dancers she had filmed in Bali.

During World War II they collaborated on still classified government projects, assessing the Japanese character and the effectiveness of Nazi propaganda. He also became the associate editor of the *Journal of Diseases of the Nervous System*, and was interviewed several times by newspapers and radio stations, as well as national publications such as *Life* and *This Week*. In addition he frequently spoke to civic and youth groups, and at graduations, using the opportunities to promote public understanding of hypnotism.

The response was slow, but he was sowing seeds for an abundant harvest later on. In the 1950's Erickson became a nationally known figure. He was featured in the news media and consulted about improving performance by famous athletes, the U.S. military, and the airline industry.

The emphasis was mainly on psychology and Erickson's masterly application through his psychiatric techniques. But it was finally getting across to the public and to some portion of the medical profession that hypnotism was the most important of the techniques.

The American Society of Clinical Hypnosis, founded in 1957 largely by Erickson's initiative, was a giant step towards greater acceptance of hypnotherapy. Erickson was its first president and editor of its Journal, and remained president for two years, and editor for ten years. By the late 1950's Erickson was receiving many invitations to speak and demonstrate his inimitable techniques to professional groups across the country and abroad. He was away from home for at least one week every month.

At the Seventh Congress of the International Society of Hypnotists in 1976, Milton Erickson received the newly created Benjamin Franklin Gold Medal award for the highest level of achievement in the theory and practice of hypnotism.

He was cited as an outstanding innovator, distinguished clinician, and the leading creator of the modern view of hypnosis as a discipline and therapy. In July, 1977 a special issue of the American Journal of Clinical Hypnosis was published in honor of his seventy-fifth birthday. (Erickson had been the founder and first editor two decades earlier). It included a tribute by Margaret Mead, the first figure of national prominence in psychology to recognize Erickson's genius.

Now, halfway through the eighth decade of his life, Milton Erickson was known and looked up to everywhere in the Western world as the premier figure in the field of hypnotherapy. He had given up active practice and was totally confined to his wheelchair. But a rising generation of psychotherapists still avidly sought him out. They hoped to be his disciples and carry his legacy of creative and innovative healing through hypnosis to new heights.

Ernest Rossi and Jeffrey Zeig were among these aspirants who rose to prominence after Erickson's death. Yet there is still no general agreement among professionals as to exactly what constitutes an Ericksonian approach to therapy. Many claimed to be doing, or trying to do, what Erickson did, but no one is following his path exactly.

Indeed, that would hardly be possible. Milton Erickson was a law unto himself, a master innovator who understood early in his career that he had to go beyond textbooks and theories. He built on their foundation, using his own best insights and judgment. His years of experience taught him to approach each case on its own merits. What worked with one patient might not work with another. However, there were general principles, mainly of common sense, that usually produced results. Effective treatment involved determining the best mix and application of these principles to each case.

Erickson did not always succeed. He freely admitted that he had encountered many patients he could not help. Some were simply not hypnotizable and offered no other access to their inner complexes. Some who could be hypnotized didn't really wish to be helped.

He taught his pupils that an important part of any therapist's practice was detecting which patients could not be helped. However, his often unconventional techniques for doing that could not be easily adapted by others. He never systematized them, because he avoided systems of any sort.

To a great extent, Erickson used indirect suggestion, confusion, puzzlement, and metaphor. "I try," he would say, "to get the patient to learn about himself, in an unstructured way." Erickson's suggestions and leading questions—at which he was as expert as any trial lawyer—concentrated the patient's attention to the point where he or she would enter the hypnotic state without the customary induction ritual. He used traditional induction procedures very capably when the occasion called for them, but they were not his primary tools.

Erickson used metaphor, but that oversimplifies his vast assortment of techniques of analogy and anecdote. He was a charismatic story-teller. Whether he was addressing an audience or a patient, people became completely wrapped up in his tales, which often seemed to have no relation at all to the patient's situation. The stories had a very distinct purpose, however. They opened up the patient's mind consciously and subconsciously to what was wrong with them, and the need to take definite steps to change the anomalous behavior.

When the situation called for it, Erickson could be extremely authoritative, issuing preemptive commands instead of softly spoken suggestions. He knew when to employ shock techniques to compel patients to make choices instead of evading them. Sometimes he enabled people with bad habits to overcome them through even greater indulgence, until they grasped just how harmful and self-destructive those habits were.

Erickson was particularly effective when he used his talent to create high drama, with the patient playing the leading role. He did not write the script, but he provided the setting and the strategy. He gave suggestions, but left it up to the patient to devise the tactics to play out the drama. Some critics charged him with being manipulative, but Erickson countered that all psychotherapy was manipulative in one way or another. What mattered was the objective and the values involved.

Erickson valued traditional morality, softened by common sense and sensitivity to suffering. He was not religious in any church-going sense, though he had experienced mystical states at various times in his life. He strongly believed that there was a right way for people to behave, with consideration and respect toward themselves and others. If a religious conviction helped someone behave properly, that was fine, but he never relied on religious motivations in seeking beneficial change in a patient.

One criticism of Erickson was that when imbuing a sense of values into patients, he tended to lecture them like a moralizing Dutch uncle. While some people found this demeaning, most people appeared to accept it and it seems to have achieved its purpose. Perhaps his speech rhythm, (about 75 words per minute - half that of most people) resembled the intonation of a priest and acted as an induction mode, facilitating a trance-like absorption and acceptance of what he was saying.

The impression of Erickson's voice was so strong that it made his posthypnotic suggestions more emphatic and effective. "My voice will go with you," he would say, and it would reinforce the suggestions in the patient's subconscious. However, it was not his custom to make overt hypnotic suggestions. He usually concealed them in the anecdote or narrative he used to concentrate the patient's attention.

As a psychiatrist, Erickson was concerned with retrieving and identifying a patient's core emotions from early life, and he used hypnosis very effectively for this purpose. He realized, perhaps more clearly than most practitioners, that valid retrievals depended on the patient's eagerness to please and satisfy the therapist.

In many cases the memories patient brought up were not of real events, but what they thought the therapist wanted and expected to hear. With this in mind, Erickson worded his questions to patients to elicit truthful answers. He was careful not to prejudge the responses, but he usually formed a pretty accurate idea of what the patient might be concealing from what came out in pre-induction questioning.

Therapists who attended his seminars and workshops often despaired of ever being able to match his flexibility and eclecticism. They realized that his unique qualities were the key to his preeminence. Patients quickly realized that they were being treated by a learned person at the head of his profession, and this made them feel special.

On a philosophic level, Erickson did not agree with Freud's belief that human biological urges and civilization were incompatible. This seemed to contradict his observation that most people lived normally with those urges, within the constraints of civilization.

He felt that the goal of psychotherapy was to free people whose rigidity and timidity prevented them from functioning usefully in society. For this purpose, hypnosis was by far the most effective means. He defined hypnosis as any state of absorption in which the attention could be concentrated on a single thought or idea. It unlocked the vast hidden powers of the unconscious, a term Erickson preferred to the subconscious.

Erickson looked on the psyche (the unconscious) as a source of power and strength, a reservoir of resources to draw on by the conscious surface personality, in order to function more healthfully. This was diametrically opposite to Freud's view, which regarded the subconscious with suspicion, as a hiding-place of malignant memories and impulses. Erickson had no illusions about people's propensity to deviousness and trickery, but his more generous concept of human nature helped him take an active interest in each patient and convey the belief that relief or cures were possible.

At the same time, he didn't believe that the human unconscious held limitless powers of healing. Everything had a boundary, and the human body, capable of marvelous resilience and recovery, still had its limits. His own steadily deteriorating physical condition was a case in point. He helped and frequently healed others, but was less and less able to heal his increasingly crippled body.

Erickson was the epitome of the archetypal "wounded healer," from world mythology and folklore, including the Christian figure of the divine Jesus, who on the cross is mocked by the crowd shouting, "He saved others, himself he cannot save." Facing the reality that his physical deterioration was irreversible, Erickson nevertheless used his inner resources to continue helping others as long as possible. In spite of nearly constant pain and almost total loss of mobility, he lived into his seventy-ninth year and was active in many ways to the very end. This medical miracle owed very little to conventional medicine, though he used it when it was of value.

Erickson's physical breakdown intensified steadily from about 1967 on, even at the peak of his fame and recognition. The once powerful shoulder muscles weakened to the point that he needed both hands to lift spoons, knives, and forks when eating. Walking, even with a cane, became too exhausting by 1969, and he had to give up traveling. A year later he moved into another home in Phoenix which had been remodeled for wheelchair living. He continued to do research, write papers, do organizational work and editing, and see patients. By 1974 he gave that up because he could no longer wear dentures or enunciate clearly due to his loss of cheek and tongue muscle control. He also had to give up much of his reading, as he could no longer focus his eyes for extended periods of time.

Yet he did not become totally inactive professionally. In the mid-1970's he was in great demand for teaching sessions at his home, but he gradually decreased his teaching schedule as his health declined. There were so many requests for his sessions that when he died in late March 1980, his teaching schedule was filled through the end of the year, and applications extended through to the following year.

Through collaboration with his favorite disciples Ernest Rossi and Jeffrey Zeig, Erickson continued to contribute to the professional literature on hypnotherapy. The demand for papers by him grew enormously after the publication in 1973 of Jay Haley's *Uncommon Therapy: the Psychiatric Techniques of Milton H. Erickson, M.D.* It was this book that first made a large sector of the medical and psychiatric professions aware of his breakthrough methods. Previously they had not paid much notice to the acclaim Erickson had been gaining from his peers.

As Mesmer and the Nancy School had done in their centuries, Erickson lifted hypnotism to previously unattained levels in the 20th century, laying the foundation for still further gains.

His achievements were not immediately followed by new ones of equal stature. No corpus of hypnotherapeutic theory or practice can be identified as strictly Ericksonian, because his unique approach was simply beyond imitation. He set examples and laid down principles to be built on, amplified, and further developed, but whatever the degree or direction of these advances, they inevitably depart from both the spirit and the letter of his approach. However, therapists who adhere to his openness and diverse approach can claim to be practicing a form of Ericksonian therapy.

Five years after Erickson's death, D. Corydon Hammond of the University of Utah School of Medicine, in a symposium at the Tenth Congress of the International Society of Hypnotists in Toronto, Canada, delivered an analysis of the varying attempts at following in Erickson's footsteps. Hammond's paper is a valid statement of the Ericksonian legacy.

Hammond described some surprising misinterpretations in light of how clearly Erickson explained his techniques in a vast body of writings. For instance, Erickson's entry into self-hypnosis in the diagnostic process, which was occasionally helpful to him in grasping the nature of the patient's problem, was misunderstood as being his standard method. The harmful result has been training sessions where aspiring therapists are encouraged to go into hypnosis and trust their unconscious to come up with the esoteric metaphors and paradoxes that Erickson often employed, and to expect this superficial methodology to produce results as positive and lasting as Erickson's.

That is merely evading the hard work and careful planning that Erickson devoted to each case. He had no intention of founding any sort of cult, or of propounding dogmas of either theory or practice. He believed, because he had seen it proven over and over again, that the results you get are in direct proportion to the effort you put into solving the problem.

Some of this misinterpretation stemmed from his teaching seminars in his last years. Because of his severe physical limitations, they were not formal classes in any sense. He would reminisce informally about many cases and describe his treatment in general terms. These narrations often gave the impression that he had achieved magical results through very simple means. But he left out the arduous trial and error he used to reach the correct diagnoses and the appropriate treatment techniques for each case. He made it sound easy because he was no longer up to explaining how hard it was. His results were miraculous only to people who did not appreciate their common sense.

Many who claim to be Ericksonian in their practice actually employ only one or a few of his many approaches. It was often asserted that the true Ericksonian method is to implant hypnotic suggestion indirectly. Actually Erickson used direct suggestion about as frequently as indirect, but because indirect suggestion had rarely been used and was unknown to many practitioners, he naturally emphasized it in his case histories. Why talk at equal length about what was known already?

Ernest Rossi summed up Erickson's genius as extreme flexibility in applying whatever was appropriate to a situation—of knowing when to use what. "It is natural," Rossi said, "when we encounter a genius who does something new (such as indirect suggestion) to jump on that one facet as being the total of what makes a genius. That totally misses the eclecticism that is often a hallmark of geniuses, and certainly was emphatically so with Erickson."

Therapist Kay Thompson said, "We simply don't believe in ourselves enough . . . we don't believe we have the power to make the direct approach work for us, as he made it work for him. We chicken out and resort to the indirect approach—and don't do so well with that either—because we lack the belief and skills needed for the direct one. Erickson was successful with both methods because he had fully mastered each."

Erickson's later followers made metaphor and story-telling a prime factor in their treatment, even though therapists such as Robert Pearson, who worked with Erickson, said that metaphor accounted for only a fifth of his hypnotic work, at most.

The misconception here was that Erickson did not trust patients to obey him or follow his directions, so he conveyed suggestions through metaphorical stories that distracted the patient and diffused resistance to what he was instilling.

According to Pearson, Erickson used stories to give his patients time to integrate what they had been told. These were not idle tales, spun on the spur of the moment. Erickson invariably made a direct connection between them and the patient's problem, carefully making essential points.

Erickson said that he often spent more time reviewing the details of each session with a patient than in the sessions themselves. He wrote down everything they said, and what he planned to say at the next session. This exhaustive preparation and review made his words and actions appear effortless and spontaneous.

Kay Thompson charged that many claim to be his followers by simply entering self-hypnosis and trusting their unconscious to come up with the right words. "They've put nothing into their unconscious, so nothing useful comes out of it," Thompson said. "They don't want to do the painstaking, exhausting work Erickson did." Nor did they want to give their patients the hours of intensive training in developing the hypnotic state that Erickson always provided before undertaking the implantation of therapeutic suggestions. Even with a patient who had previously been hypnotized, he insisted on a minimum of twenty minutes in the hypnotic state before giving the patient appropriate posthypnotic suggestions.

Erickson put his patients' interests ahead of his own. He gave them sixty minutes out of every hour, rather than the fifty which became common in the psychotherapy profession, and even with early 1970's inflation his private practice fees never exceeded $40 per hour.

The third line of development, Erickson's idiosyncratic approach, merged with the first two. Erickson had already experimented with and applied many of the wartime psychologists' hypnotherapy techniques, and had formed a circle of collaboration with a few other psychiatrists who did not accept Freud's rejection of hypnosis. They found themselves in good company with the expanding post-war associations developing the scientific and therapeutic aspects of hypnosis, and setting up research facilities.

Milton V. Kline, a psychologist, and Jerome M. Schneck, a psychiatrist, both of the new generation of clinical hypnotists that emerged after World War II, founded the Society for Clinical and Experimental Hypnosis in 1949.

Three years later the Society began publishing its Journal, with Kline as the first editor. This led to the formation in 1958 of an International Society with the same title by Bernard Raginsky, a Canadian psychiatrist. It merged its Journal with Kline's for worldwide readership.

That same year Erickson founded the American Society of Clinical Hypnosis, where he edited the first ten volumes of its Journal, until April 1968. For a while there was some rivalry between Kline's and Erickson's societies, but this gradually faded out. Most clinical hypnotists became members of both, and attended joint meetings in which the international society sometimes participated. Together these societies spurred universities and funding sources such as the National Institute of Mental Health and the Office of Naval Research, as well as private sources like the Ford Foundation, to set up and endow laboratories for hypnosis research.

Erickson left his family and colleagues a legacy of strict high principles, dedicated application, and a conviction that service to others had a value above all else.

Dave Elman

Witnessing the power of hypnosis sparked a lifelong interest in Dave Elman. He would become one of the great promoters of hypnotherapy in America in the second half of the 20th century.

Dave Elman was born in North Dakota on May, 6 1900. His father, Jacob Kopelman, was an amateur hypnotist. When Elman was 8 years old, his father became ill with cancer and was completely incapacitated by pain. An acquaintance of his fathers who was also a hypnotist visited their home and hypnotized his father in an effort to manage the pain. After just a few minutes his father was transformed from a bedridden man writhing in agony to someone who could move around and participate in daily family activities. This made a lasting impression on the young Dave Elman.

Elman was a talented child. He played the saxophone and the violin, and he wrote music. When he was a teenager he put together a comedy act that featured hypnosis. He later decided to delete the hypnosis part of his routine when he realized that he was alienating the parents of the girls he wanted to date because they were afraid he would use his mysterious powers to mesmerize their daughters.

Elman left school at 14, and soon after moved to New York. He worked for a music publisher and put on performances at night. He eventually got a job at CBS radio where he wrote, directed and produced radio shows.

One night an act he booked for a charity performance, which he was responsible for organizing, cancelled at the last moment. In desperation Elman performed his hypnosis act. This show generated immediate interest from a medical clinic that invited him to teach hypnosis to 15 of their resident doctors. This began a career that would occupy him for the rest of his life.

Dave soon became busy teaching hypnosis to medical practitioners. He promoted hypnosis as a powerful adjunct to mainstream medical treatments. He formalized his lessons into a complete course on hypnosis. These lessons evolved into a book that was published first under the title *Findings in Hypnosis* and finally as *Hypnotherapy*.

Some of Dave Elman's most important contributions to hypnotherapy were in the area of induction methods. As a performer he needed to induce trances quickly, and he developed a method based on speed. But as he spent more time with the medical community he had to adapt his techniques to find ways to induce deeper trances.

Elman's methodology became the classical script we are all familiar with today: "Take a deep breath. Relax your eyes." He would lift and drop the arm of the subject. This was all part of reaching a physically relaxed state.

But according to Elman, the more important goal was to reach a point where the subject would suspend his disbelief and critical faculties. Only then could he accept suggestions that might otherwise be considered incredible, including suggestions that the subject would no longer feel excruciating pain.

To do this the patient needed to reach a deep state of mental relaxation. Elman developed techniques to help reach the deeper levels of relaxation. He realized that each time a suggestion was repeated, it worked faster and the trance induced could be brought deeper. He would instruct his subjects to open their eyes and close them again, relaxing more each time, and expand the relaxation to their minds. Finally he would instruct them to count backwards, doubling the relaxation with each number counted until the numbers disappeared.

By the time Dave Elman died in 1967, his techniques had become popular through the medical hypnosis community. He had been instrumental in having hypnosis techniques become accepted as a medical treatment as well, and the lessons he developed and recorded in his book *Findings in Hypnosis*[3] are still widely read and taught.

Dr. Rexford L. North

Dr. Rexford L. North was perhaps the most influential hypnotist in the 1940's and 1950's and he may have been the perfect model for the stereotypical Hollywood hypnotist.

Dr. North was a slim man with a Van Dyke beard, small bespectacled eyes, and an eerie voice that was caused at least in part by the fact that he was stone deaf. He started his professional career doing a hypnosis act on the vaudeville and nightclub circuit, and he became quite popular. He also performed on USO tours.

During a USO tour he was reported to have contracted spinal meningitis, which resulted in his loss of hearing. This loss had a great affect on his act, largely because he lost confidence in his ability to perform and to "amaze" his audiences.

With the help and encouragement of his friends, he started over again in the late 1940's. He began to work night clubs and other events and succeeded in getting his name back in the public eye. This helped him regain his confidence, but he was not making much of a living.

In 1949 he found himself in Boston, down to his last few dollars. He decided to try something new. He rented a hall in the Bradford Hotel in Boston's theatre district for one night a

---

[3] Copyright 1964 by Dave Elman

week, for four consecutive weeks. He printed up flyers announcing a free hypnosis demonstration and personally posted them all over the area.

Learn Genuine Hypnotism was his announcement. The demonstrations were very successful, and were used to promote a ten-week hypnosis class. Dr. North was a charismatic individual and an experienced showman. He translated his talents into a presence that attracted a steady stream of students from the lecture hall to his hypnosis classes. Many of his students reported feeling trust, respect and affection towards him.

The lectures and flyers produced an immediate response, and Dr. North was able to rent office space in a prestigious building at 30 Huntington Avenue where he could hold classes. In those early days of the school he also used this space for his personal office and sleeping quarters.

These classes were the seeds of one of the most influential organizations for professional hypnotists in America: *The Boston Hypnotism Center*. The first class graduated in 1949, with Frank Anderson, Berchman Carville and Dwight Damon among its original graduates.

Soon the school had outgrown the Huntington Avenue offices and a new location was found at 26 St. Botolph Street in the Bohemian quarter of Boston. The new premises had enough space for the offices and classrooms, as well as for a lecture hall, which was moved from The Hotel Bradford.

A strong bond developed between Dr. North and many of his students, partly fueled by their shared passion for hypnosis. The Hypnotism Center became a gathering point for professional and amateur hypnotism enthusiasts from around the world. Dr. North, his staff, and a cadre of volunteers worked tirelessly to market the courses and lectures, and published books and other materials to promote hypnotism. From these associations new institutions were forged. These institutions provided a solid foundation for the growth and acceptance of hypnotism as a respected tool in treating a wide variety of physical and psychological ailments.

In 1950 Dr. North founded The National Guild of Hypnotists. Its charter members included Dr. Dwight Damon, Dr. John Hughes (the author of this book), Maurice Kershaw, Harry Arons, Dr. Arnold Levinson who was the original treasurer, and George Rogers, the original president. Most of the original members were graduates of The Hypnotism Center. The members of the NGH would go on to promote hypnotism throughout the world by establishing and teaching courses on hypnotism, and by publicizing the achievements and accomplishments of the discipline.

In the early years, most of its members were stage hypnotists and showmen. Only a small percentage of its members were hypnotherapists and medical practitioners.

Dr. North launched another brainchild in 1951: The Journal of Hypnotism. Once again students of the Hypnotism Center were key figures in its launch. This journal was important not only to spread the word on new developments in the field, but also as a focal point that joined the practitioners and enthusiasts around the country and the world.

Then in 1956, Dr. North disappeared under mysterious circumstances. The Guild members became fractious and cliquish. The Guild and the Journal became dormant. The organization lost its focus and energy, though some of the members remained in contact and informally continued to teach and promote hypnosis using the methods taught in The Boston Hypnosis Center.

The Guild was revived by two of the founding members and Elsom Eldridge in 1986. Dwight Damon became the President/Executive Director and John Hughes the Research Editor of the New Journal of Hypnotism. Elsom Eldridge's computer and entrepreneurial expertise played a major role in the Guild's new beginning and resurrection. Today there are chapters of the NGH in more than 65 countries. With thousands of members around the world, it is the largest organization of its kind.

Dr. Rexford L. North's contribution to the field of hypnosis was enormous. He was the most recognized hypnotist of his day, and his influence extends beyond his lifetime.

As an entertainer and showman he was able to introduce hypnosis to the general population, increasing trust in hypnosis through familiarity and knowledge. He was instrumental in developing hypnotherapeutic techniques for dentistry.

And as a teacher and mentor he used his natural gifts, charisma, generosity and passion to enthrall a large number of talented and professional hypnotists. Through their advocacy they succeeded in spreading their knowledge of hypnosis. They became many of the practitioners who brought hypnotherapy into the mainstream of western medicine in the United States and around the world. Martin T. Orne, among the luminaries he trained, started a hypnosis research center at The Massachusetts Mental Health Center.

Despite the advice of naysayers, Dr. North had the vision to start a school, an organization and a journal that transformed hypnosis. It brought individual hypnotists, artists and entertainers, and isolated scientists into a homogeneous body that is now respected by the public, with an organization and structure, and established professional standards and regulations.

Martin T. Orne

Martin T. Orne, a student of Robert White at Harvard and a graduate of Dr. North's Hypnotism Center, established another influential research center. He took his Ph.D. degree in 1958, following a medical degree from Tufts College. Orne's laboratory, set up in 1960 as the Studies in Hypnosis Project at the Massachusetts Mental Health Center under Harvard's auspices, was transferred in 1964 to the University of Pennsylvania under the name of the Unit for Experimental Psychiatry. Orne was now a professor of psychiatry in full charge of the program, along with his wife, Emily Carota Orne, who had been associated with the laboratory from the beginning. In 1962, Orne also took over as editor of the International Society for Clinical and Experimental Hypnosis Journal, founded by Raginsky.

Orne's most outstanding contributions to the theory and practice of hypnotherapy was the clear distinction he drew between the essence of hypnotism--that is, the phenomenon of suggestibility by itself--and the artifacts, or the physical effects produced by hypnosis in the body. Even the most careful investigators of hypnotic phenomena had some uncertainty about the relationship between the act of suggestion and its results. After Orne, there was no longer any intermingling of cause and effect, which resulted in greater clarity in the definition and application of hypnosis.

Ernest R. Hilgard

Ernest R. Hilgard at Stanford University established another important hypnosis research laboratory in 1957. Hilgard was a student of Hull (though not in his hypnosis class) at Yale, so he was collaterally rather than directly from the Hull line of hypnotherapy development between the two great wars. Hilgard graduated with a Ph.D. in 1930, became a professor of psychology at Stanford in 1933, and continued to maintain the interest in clinical hypnosis he had acquired from Hull.

Hilgard set up his hypnosis research facility at Stanford with the active collaboration of André M. Weitzenhoffer, who a year earlier had gained his Ph.D. from the University of Michigan with a dissertation on hypnosis. Three years prior to that, he had published *Hypnotism: An Objective Study in Suggestibility*, the best review and update of the field since Hull's book two decades earlier.

While planning the research center with Hilgard, Weitzenhoffer published a second book, *General Techniques of Hypnotism*, a comprehensive text on induction methodology. Ernest Hilgar's wife Josephine R. Hilgard joined Weitzenhoffer and Hilgard on the center's senior staff. Her degrees from Yale and Stanford and experience in both child guidance and adult psychoanalysis made her a most valuable adjunct.

She and her associates conducted interviews with a wide range of hypnotizable patients, which became the basis for the Stanford Hypnotic Susceptibility Scales. They are now the accepted standard in the profession. Over an eight-year span, from 1959 to 1967, these scales were carefully adjusted and refined to produce significant rates of correlation between measured hypnotizability and the degree of pain relief attained. They provide clinical hypnotists with a tool for judging, with a high level of accuracy, how readily a patient can be hypnotized and how helpful the treatment is likely to be.

There were few aspects of hypnosis that were not advanced in one way or another by the work at Stanford in the 1960's and 1970's. Erickson was involved in some of these research projects, which also influenced Charles Tart's investigations of the physiological and subjective patterns of the alternate states of consciousness revealed by the widespread experimentation in the 1960's with mind-altering drugs.

Tart expanded his studies into the consciousness-altering practices of Eastern religions. He found unique response patterns associated with waking states, dreaming states, and other alternate states of consciousness, such as drug-induced states, and was eventually able to distinguish three distinct states of consciousness: wakefulness, ordinary sleep, and "paradoxical" sleep. This third state is the one into which hypnotic induction provides an entry that can be controlled and adjusted. There are numerous intermediate stages between these three primary states of consciousness, but in almost all cases they shift rather rapidly into one or another of the primary states.

Theodore X. Barber

Theodore X. Barber, who had completed four years of postdoctoral study at Harvard, partly under Orne, founded a third laboratory in 1959 that made significant contributions to a more thorough understanding of hypnosis.

Greatly skeptical at first about the validity and usefulness of hypnosis as a therapeutic tool, Barber went on to define and delimit the boundaries of stage hypnosis on the one hand, and professional clinical hypnosis on the other. He drew the distinction between the two more clearly and sharply than ever before. This emboldened many researchers to seek new and more far-reaching applications of hypnotism. Barber, and many who were trained by him, have been in the forefront of these pioneering studies that are opening up vast new horizons for the hypnotists of the twenty-first century.

These horizons bring an entirely new mind-body formulation, far from the static dualistic state first defined by Rene Descartes in the seventeenth century. We now have a vast corpus of research, much of it by psychologists who were not hypnotists but who provided clinical hypnotists with whole armories of innovative uses for hypnosis.

The interrelationship of the mind and the body as a single biochemical unit is now established as a scientific fact. Neither exists or acts independently. The mind influences and controls the functions of the body. The body in turn affects the state of the mind through its own conditions of health and illness. We are only beginning to understand the remarkable ramifications.

It will take a decade or two of concentrated psychobiological research and experiments in the expanding mind-body concept to grasp all the potentialities uncovered in the second half of the twentieth century. New hypnotists with healing capabilities beyond any previously known will arise to astound the world, as Mesmer and the Nancy School did earlier, and Erickson and Dr. North did in their time.

CHAPTER 3
What Is Hypnosis?

This is a difficult question to answer. Hypnosis has always been an enigma and is one of the wonders of modern psychology. No one really knows what hypnosis is. But then no one knows what electricity is either. Yet that does not limit its usefulness.

Often the understanding of a subject can be obtained through stating emphatically what it is *not*. This rule applies directly to hypnosis, so we shall begin by eliminating some of these more obvious things hypnosis is not, namely:

Hypnosis is not a manipulative, devious way of controlling the minds and actions of so call "weak-minded people," by making them do what they would otherwise never do nor be capable of doing, at the behest of some evil Svengali.

- Although stage hypnotism is a popular entertainment, that is not its basic usefulness. In fact, many feats of stage hypnotists can be performed without actual hypnosis at all.

- Hypnosis is not a means of enticing people into any religious cult or any specific belief pattern. There is no need to believe in hypnosis any more than one needs to believe in electricity. It operates on its own. One simply makes use of it, in the same way you plug in an electrical appliance when in need of its services.

- Hypnosis is not limited in its usefulness in the easing or banishing of the pain of dental work, or surgery, or even of childbirth which are applications becoming steadily more common today. Modern research has established that the allied discipline of visualization and guided imagery can be an effective force to the body's immune system to conquer disease. Its usefulness to defeat infections such as AIDS and to check the runaway multiplication of cancer cells is just beginning to be realized. However, hypnosis is not to be looked upon as any kind of panacea for mastering all pain and illness, or of accomplishing feats of healing beyond the capabilities of medical science. It should be looked upon as a complimentary adjunct to other methods of effective therapy.

- Hypnosis cannot be regarded as a means of "proving" the theory of reincarnation or that we have lived past lives or that one has been abducted on board a UFO. True or untrue as such speculation may be, today's science can only state that such experiences of alleged regressions attest to the remarkable fantasizing powers of the subconscious mind. In other words believe it or not.

- Finally, in relation to controversial ground, hypnosis is not to be regarded as a special means of "channeling" the messages of the dematerialized gurus of the New Age enthusiasm. All such beliefs belong to the

WHAT IS HYPNOSIS?

area of believe it or not. In this book we shall adhere to that which is most scientifically provable.

In its most simple application, hypnosis can be a way of changing the mind. The classic dictum "You are what you think!" is a truism. If we change the way we think, we change ourselves. Mind is a process of producing thoughts, and when one is hypnotized it is possible to change the quality of thoughts—generating productive and helpful thoughts and eliminating unproductive and harmful ones. Hypnosis provides a means to directly reach and influence the subconscious mind. It is an amazing power that also works through self-hypnosis, which is an effective tool for self-improvement. (Self-hypnosis is an important facet of hypnotism to be considered. Since we can suggest actions to our own mind, it follows that it is possible to hypnotize one's self. Self-hypnosis brings the incredible power of your subconscious mind under your control. You will be shown how to do it and what it can do for you, as you study this book.)

To plunge a bit deeper and get more technical, it can be said that the mind tends to operate, more or less, on two levels: conscious and subconscious (also referred to as the unconscious mind). The conscious mind is the seat of conscious thought, memory, language, creativity, and decision-making, and is selective and critical of the thoughts produced; while the subconscious mind is the non-reasoning, non-selective and non-critical part of our brain, and is receptive to the power of suggestion.

In relation to hypnosis, suggestion has been defined as being the subconscious realization of thoughts or ideas, often at such an ingrained level in the mind as to be beyond reaching through normal, everyday conscious control. Since hypnotic suggestion provides a pathway to the subconscious mind, it is a means to achieve this desired control.

What is interesting is that suggestion is both the means of inducing hypnosis as well as controlling the state--often a point of confusion among even expert hypnotists as to where suggestion leaves off and hypnosis begins.

Just what is suggestion? Suggestion is the sine qua non to the induction of hypnosis and the production of hypnotic phenomena. Hippolyte Bernheim, a famous pioneer of clinical hypnosis, said, "There is no hypnosis, there is only suggestion."

The term *suggestion* is a term commonly used but subject to different interpretations. The traditional definition of suggestion is: a stimulus that evokes uncritical acceptance of an idea. James Drever[4] defines suggestion as: "A mental process which results in the uncritical acceptance and realization, in act or belief, of ideas arising in the mind, as the effect of the words, attitudes, or acts of another person, or other persons, or, under certain conditions, dependent on processes in the individual's own mind." A more succinct definition of suggestion is provided by Roy Udolf,[5] "An attempt to get a subject to produce a behavior without commanding or directing him to do so."

---

[4]Drever, J.A. A Dictionary of Psychology. Baltimore, MD: Penguin Reference Books, 1986.
[5]Udolf, R. Handbook of Hypnosis for Professionals. Northvale, NJ: Jason Aronson Inc., 1987.

WHAT IS HYPNOSIS?

Kroger and Fezler[6] described four types of suggestion:

1. *Verbal*, which includes words and refers to communication by any type of sound.

2. *Nonverbal* applies to body language and gestures.

3. *Intraverbal* relates to the intonation of words; vocal inflections greatly influence suggestibility.

4. *Extraverbal*, the implications of words and gestures that facilitate acceptance of ideas.

Thus, "The choice of words, mannerisms, inflections of the voice, as well as the implied meaning of the phrases used, plays an important role in the hypnotic process. These are potent factors in influencing suggestibility."

A characteristic of the hypnotic state is an increased capacity to respond to suggestions. The hypnotized person is said to be hypersuggestible. Reduced to its barest essentials hypnosis can be regarded as a natural method of utilizing the innate receptivity of the subconscious mind to suggestion. It is thus that the hypnotherapist uses this state to redirect the mind of the client in the direction of desired thoughtful benefit.

Accordingly, it becomes obvious that the subconscious mind can be directed in a way to be beneficial to the hypnotized person, such as giving up smoking, for pain control, in the treatment of asthma, allergies, insomnia, phobias, and to

---

[6]Kroger, W.S. & Fezler, W.D. Hypnosis and Behavior Modification: Imagery Conditioning. Philadelphia: J. B. Lippincott Co., 1976.

reduce stress. The suggestions given by the hypnotist will continue to be followed even after the hypnotic state has been terminated. In such post-hypnotic operation of the continuance of suggestions lies the very crux of the value of hypnotherapy.

Weight control or weight loss, fitness exercises, good study and work habits, can all be motivated through hypnotic suggestion. Hypnosis is also effective in the control of pain, in the treatment of burn victims, migraine headaches, high blood pressure, chemotherapy side effects, warts, and psoriasis. Indeed, although hypnosis is not to be considered a "cure all," there are few medical conditions that cannot benefit considerably by hypnotherapy; and with none of the side effects of more common or traditional therapy.

Simple anesthesia, as for dental work and minor surgery, is not difficult to induce in the hypnotized person. It has been estimated that about eight out of ten persons can be readily hypnotized. As a rule individuals with an active imagination and of high intelligence can most readily enter the state. For use in major surgery it is generally felt that a deep level of hypnosis is desirable for the subconscious mind to block off intense pain sensations.

Through suggestion directed to the immune system, augmented by mental visualization, hypnosis has proved very helpful in fighting off invading viruses and bacteria as an aid in overcoming infections. For this purpose hypnosis is applied as an adjunct to conventional medical treatment, not as a replacement for it. This aspect of immunization of the body through the use of hypnosis has seldom been mentioned in the literature. Thus an entire chapter will be devoted to this important topic in this book.

Hypnosis has excellent clinical value in psychotherapy. Many case histories indicate that not only can the psyche be helped through hypnotically induced suggestion, but also physical changes in the body can be influenced to occur. Hypnosis is commonly used to help people overcome phobias such as fear of heights, of closed or open spaces, of airplane trips, of the dark, and of many other things. Fears like these can be disabling and prevent people from living normal lives.

Hypnosis is a means of directing and using the full capacity of the mind. Hypnosis today is experiencing the greatest upsurge of widespread public acclaim that has been seen in the two centuries since Franz Anton Mesmer had the aristocracy of France agog with his healing miracles, in the 1780's. The practical applications of hypnosis are daily gaining increasing respect from the medical profession, and many physicians refer their patients to hypnotherapists. Hypnotherapy is recognized as a profession of standing in the business archives of the United States. Bookstores are filled with an ever-growing proliferation of books and publications telling about hypnosis and the wonders it can accomplish. The world's largest hypnosis organization, the National Guild of Hypnotists has over 12,000 members, with over 100 local chapters in 65 countries. A growing percentage of Guild members have academic credentials in other fields, including medicine, psychology, counseling and nursing.

This book brings the student right up-to-date as to what is going on in the field. It presents hypnosis in a scientific and logical perspective, inclusive of new procedures. The very rapidity of the spread of hypnotism has put it badly in need of being placed in proper perspective. Before we embark on the study of induction procedures it is necessary that we first pin down the basic essence of hypnotism, and disentangle it from the many conflicting claims of its effectiveness.

CHAPTER 4
Myths & Misconceptions

Because of the pervasiveness of sensational misinformation in the popular media, almost everyone has misconceptions about hypnosis. The most common of these fallacies are:

MYTH #1. LOSS OF CONSCIOUSNESS:

One of the major misconceptions is that the hypnotized person will lose conscious awareness. In hypnosis the subject does not lose awareness or fall asleep. The subject is alert and aware of everything at all times and hears everything the hypnotist says. While consciousness is entirely suspended in natural sleep, it is definitely present in hypnosis--a great difference. Hypnosis then is not sleep. In hypnosis one is awake and alert. The brain waves of a hypnotized person, even in deep hypnosis, are those of one awake and not of one asleep. As far back as the 1950's Aserinsky and Kleitman initiated Electroencephalogram (EEG) studies.[7] These re-

---

[7] Aserinsky, E., & Kleitman, N. Regularly Occurring Periods of Eye Motility, and Concomitant Phenomena, During Sleep. Science 1953.

searchers sought a physiological connection, as defined by EEG criteria, between hypnosis and nocturnal sleep. No distinct brain psychophysiology has yet been demonstrated for hypnosis. Their findings established that the EEG of a hypnotized person is indistinguishable from that of a person who is relaxed, alert, with eyes closed. Moreover, a deeply sleeping individual will not hear if spoken to, unless roughly awakened by shaking; yet, a person in deep hypnosis, though seemingly oblivious to all external stimuli, will hear and instantly respond to the hypnotist's suggestions.

Hypnosis more closely approximates normal waking consciousness than it does sleep. When a person is hypnotized, a technique is often used which will induce a drowsy lethargic state by a combined method of relaxation and suggestions of sleep. This "sleeplike condition" is the effect of suggestion, not hypnosis. Hypnosis can easily be induced without any suggestions of sleep, and hypnotic phenomena can be elicited in the waking state.

Electrocardiograph and respiratory studies[8] during hypnosis were similar to those found in the normal waking state. In sleep, the senses are in a state of inaction and there is little, if any, response to reflex stimulation. Bass[9] found the patellar reflex (knee-jerk when tapped) to be

---

[8]Levitt, E.E., & Brady, J.P. Psychophysiology of Hypnosis. In J. M. Schneck (Ed.) Hypnosis in Modern Medicine (3rd Ed.) Springfield, IL: C.C. Thomas publisher, 1963.
[9]Bass, M.J. Differences of the Hypnotic Trance From Normal Sleep. Journal of Experimental Psychology, 1931.

the same in hypnosis and the waking state. (In sleep consciousness is lost, but in a state of hypnosis a person is capable of thinking and reasoning.)

MYTH #2. HYPNOTIZED PEOPLE DO ODD AND CRAZY THINGS:

If you have witnessed a hypnotism show, you can see how one might leave the performance with that impression. The perception is that the hypnotist's commands are irresistible. The hypnotist should tell the prospective subject that the stage hypnotist is an entertainer. To put on an entertaining show the performer invokes outrageous and farcical behavior. Hypnotherapy is used for serious purposes, so naturally the subject will not be made to crow like a rooster, or engage in any other absurdity, as in stage hypnosis.

MYTH #3. SURRENDER OF THE WILL, LOSS OF CONTROL:

Novels, popular magazine stories, comic strips, TV, and the movies have perpetuated this myth. Many people believe that hypnosis is a surrender of the will to the all-powerful hypnotist. Since the ability to be hypnotized is a subjective experience, nothing could be further from the truth. Most experts agree that all hypnosis is self-hypnosis. Although the hypnotist guides and develops the hypnotic state, the ability to be hypnotized rests within the hypnotized person, and the subject is always in control.

MYTH #4. WEAK-MINDEDNESS:

A common misconception is that only weak-willed or feeble-minded persons can be hypnotized. Contrary to popular belief, there is a relationship between intelligence and hypnotizability. It is difficult—and often impossible—to hypnotize morons, imbeciles, psychotics, or severely detached individuals. (As a general rule, intelligent people make the best subjects for hypnosis.) Motivation will be increased if this myth is clarified.

MYTH #5. REVELATION OF SECRETS:

Frequently the question is asked, "Will I tell any secrets while I am in hypnosis?" The answer is no. Hypnosis is wrongly presumed to a "truth serum" that renders the hypnotized person incapable of lying, and prevents the subject from keeping embarrassing secrets confidential. While in hypnosis a person will not reveal any intimate secrets they would not tell while in the waking state.

MYTH #6. FEAR OF GETTING "STUCK" IN HYPNOSIS:

Often a prospective client will ask, "What happens if you can't get me out of this? What if you have a heart attack while I'm hypnotized?" Answer: "Open your eyes, and dial 911" Seriously, there is no danger of a person being "brought out" of hypnosis. Since the hypnotized person holds the control, there is no difficulty in terminating the hypnotic state.

On rare occasions the suggestions to terminate hypnosis will be ignored. Two possible reasons for this are: 1) the client has lapsed into a natural sleep, in which case the operator will have lost communication and rapport. 2) The hypnotic state may be so pleasurable that the client does not wish to release it, and will ignore back to awareness suggestions. If there is no response to your arousal suggestions, do not become panicky. There is no cause for alarm. To paraphrase Franklin D. Roosevelt, "You have nothing to fear but fear itself." Keep your presence of mind. Remain calm and repeat the suggestions for arousal in a more forceful tone of voice. Refusal to terminate hypnosis is so rare, it is doubtful you will ever encounter it. If it should occur, however, just remember to keep your presence of mind, as there is no cause for alarm.

MYTH #7. HYPNOSIS WEAKENS THE WILL:

The will is not weakened or changed in any way. Hypnotized clients are always in control and cannot be made to do anything against their will. It should be emphasized that it is impossible to be dominated by the will of the hypnotist.

MYTH #8. HYPNOSIS IS HABIT-FORMING:

Can a person become addicted to hypnosis or can it become habit-forming as a drug can? No. Clients can resist hypnosis at any time, no matter how many times they have been hypnotized.

MYTH #9. REPEATED INDUCTIONS WEAKENS THE MIND:

Repetitive hypnotic induction does not weaken the mind. In university psychology labs thousands of students have been hypnotized hundreds of times without harm.

MYTH #10. HYPNOSIS AGAINST WILL:

A person cannot be hypnotized against their will. Hypnosis is not a clash of wills. It is a condition of trust and cooperation between the subject and the hypnotist.

MYTH #11. CRIMINAL OR ANTISOCIAL ACTS:

Can immoral or criminal acts be induced by hypnosis? Barber[10] states, "Experimental studies conducted during recent decades have provided an answer: Some persons who are said to be hypnotized can be made to commit acts which appear to be immoral or harmful—to violate

---

[10] Barber, T.X. Suggested Dangerous, Harmful, or Criminal Acts, So. Orange, NJ: Power Publishers, Inc. 1981.

sexual mores,[11] to attempt injury to themselves or to attempt to injure others.[12] For instance, Rowland and Young[13] instructed selected hypnotized subjects to pick up a dangerous snake and to throw acid at the experimenter. (Both the snake and the experimenter were behind a plate of invisible glass.) The great majority of subjects reached for the snake and threw the acid."

Orne and Evans[14] designed an experiment to replicate and to extend the earlier studies of Rowland and Young. All subjects were asked to pick up a venomous snake and to throw acid at the experimenter. (As in the Rowland and Young studies, the snake and the experimenter were behind a plate of invisible glass.)

According to Orne and Evans, all subjects indicated in post-experimental interviews that "they were quite convinced that they would not be harmed because the context was an experimental one, presumably being conducted by responsible experimenters. All subjects appeared to assume that some form of safety precautions had been taken during the experiment."

---

[11]Kline, M.V. The Dynamics of Hypnotically Induced Antisocial Behavior, J. Psychol., 1958.
[12]Rowland, L.W. Will Hypnotized Persons Try to Harm Themselves or Others? J. Abnorm. Soc. Psychol., 1939.
[13]Young, P. C. Antisocial Uses of Hypnosis. In L. M. LeCron (Ed.) Experimental Hypnosis. New York: Macmillan, 1948.
[14]Orne, M. T. Antisocial Behavior and Hypnosis. In G. H. Estabrooks (Ed.) Hypnosis: Current Problems. New York: Harper & Row, 1962.

Weitzenhoffer,[15] after analyzing all available data, stated: "As long as the subject perceives the suggested action for what it is--one that violates his moral and ethical principles or is a danger to himself--he will not carry it out; but if he perceives it otherwise, even though it is one he would not normally carry out, he will very likely do so. If suggestions are used to distort the subject's perception so that the requested act appears innocuous or justified, the subject will most likely carry it out.

"The above statement appears to be contradicted by the specifics of many of the cases that have been prosecuted. There is little evidence of perceptual distortions having been suggested in these cases. However, it should also be noted that in at least the more notorious cases, the subjects were generally individuals suffering from severe emotional problems who also had a long, well-established, even intimate relationship with the hypnotist, and had been hypnotized by him a great many times. Conceivably, the first two features alone could have enabled the hypnotists to influence their subjects as they did without having to resort to hypnosis, with the consequences that hypnosis may really not have been a crucial factor in the outcome."

Most authorities agree that the hypnotized subject cannot be induced to commit antisocial or criminal acts. The question usually asked is whether a hypnotized

---

[15]Weitzenhoffer, A.M. Antisocial Acts and Hypnotism. The Practice of Hypnotism, Vol. 1, New York: John Wiley & Sons, 1989.

person can be made to commit acts that are detrimental to the subject or others? A hypnotized person will not do anything he or she would not do in the normal waking state. This also applies to sexual acts.

In this chapter we have taken into account the most prevalent misconceptions about hypnosis. All misconceptions should be corrected before commencing with induction. This is a vital step, which should never be omitted.

CHAPTER 5
Is Hypnosis Dangerous?

Hypnosis in and of itself is not at all dangerous. The only possible danger is in the misuse of suggestion. Thousands upon thousands of persons all over the world are hypnotized daily without harm, and yet hypnosis is considered dangerous simply because the "Svengali-Trilby" myth has been perpetuated for years.

Julius Ginker long ago stated: "The so-called dangers from hypnotism are imaginary. Although I have hypnotized hundreds of times I have never seen any ill effects from its use." And then he referred to other leading pioneers: "Bernheim, Liébeault, Ford, Wetterstrand, and a host of others who have practiced suggestive methods in thousands of instances have had similar experiences."[16]

The Russian scientist Platonov,[17] an associate of Pavlov, who used hypnosis for over 50 years in over 50,000 cases, reported: "We have never observed any harmful influence on the patient which could be ascribed to the method of hypno-suggestive therapy, presumably leading to the development of an unstable personality, slavish subordination, weakening

---

[16] Quoted in Quackenbos, J.D., Hypnotic Therapeutics, Harper 1908
[17] Platonov, K., The Word As a Physiological and Therapeutic Factor. Moscow, Foreign Languages Publishing House, 1959

of the will, increase in suggestibility, pathological urge for hypnosis, etc."

One of the most respected authorities in medical therapy was the late William S. Kroger, who taught the principles of hypnotherapy to more than 100,000 physicians throughout the world. Kroger said that the dangers of hypnosis have been exaggerated and that hypnosis is the safest of all psychotherapies. "The incontrovertible fact is that it is doubtful if, when properly used, there is another modality less dangerous in medicine than hypnosis."[18]

The responsible hypnotist, through the judicious use of appropriate suggestions, will avoid any difficulty in his or her use of hypnosis.

Unqualified Therapy

The indiscriminate removal of pain through hypnotic suggestion without regard to its underlying pathology or causative factor could have fatal consequences. It is acknowledged that pain is often a symptom of something else, a warning signal of something wrong somewhere. In the early stages, pain can be a clear signal of something organically wrong. In such cases it does perform the useful function of sending the sufferer to the doctor for proper medical attention.

For example: The patient arrives at the doctor's office with a pain in her abdomen. It has moved to the right lower quadrant, she has vomited, and she feels quite ill. The doctor finds

---

[18]Kroger, W. S., Clinical and Experimental Hypnosis in Medicine. Los Angeles, J. B. Lippincott, 1977

tenderness over the area called "McBurney's point," takes a blood sample, and observes that the white cell count is way up. The diagnosis is appendicitis. The patient goes to the hospital and the surgeon removes her appendix, and after an appropriate healing interval, she is free of pain.

That hypnosis is capable of producing a state of anesthesia has been amply demonstrated. If hypnosis were used to remove the pain in a person afflicted with appendicitis, the inflamed appendix would eventually rupture, causing intense inflammation of the peritoneum (the lining of the abdominal cavity). Treatment delay and complications of peritonitis, caused by the hypnotic removal of pain, is this case could be fatal.

On the other hand, there are numerous examples of pain, which serves no useful purpose: trigeminal neuralgia, which causes excruciating pain in the side of the face; migraine; low-back pains; phantom pain (the pain that amputees feel in a limb they no longer possess). There are pains of psychogenic origin with no detectable pathology. Countless thousands of people suffer from chronic, disabling pain with no discoverable pathology to account for it. In other cases the pathology is cured, but the pain does not go away. If the origin of pain has been medically checked out, then hypnosis may be used as an effective method of pain control. Also hypnosis may prove of value through the reduction of tension and anxiety levels. In the case of advanced cancer, the sufferer may be given post-hypnotic suggestions that will help the patient face the present and future with greater courage.

The Psychologically Disturbed Subject

Professionals using hypnosis should stay within their area of expertise. No layperson should make use of hypnosis in treatment of nervous or mental disorders, emotionally disturbed states, or psychoneurotic conditions, except under the direction and supervision of a qualified specialist.

Never hypnotize an individual who is obviously emotionally unstable or pre-psychotic. If your prospective subject acts irrational, or there is a history of emotional instability, do not attempt hypnosis. With the pre-psychotic subject, symptoms of repression such as fearful screaming may be liberated spontaneously during hypnosis.

Occasionally a hypnotized individual will experience a release of intense emotions with outbursts of convulsive crying. If confronted with this situation the main thing to keep in mind is that firm, quiet, reassurance always works. Because of the rapport (the relationship of trust that develops between the client and hypnotherapist) good hypnotic subjects are especially sensitive to emotional cues from the operator. Never panic or become frightened. If the client senses that the hypnotist is anxious, it will reinforce the client's feelings of anxiety. The spontaneous purging of intense emotional distress acts as a catharsis and this release of pent-up emotions may have a beneficial effect on the client's mental and physical well-being.

Hallucinations

When demonstrating or experimenting with hypnotic phenomena, never give a hypnotized person suggestions that could produce fright. In somnambulism (deep hypnosis) the subject can easily be induced to experience hallucinations. A deeply hypnotized person will react to the suggested hallucination with reality and emotional intensity. For example, to suggest to a profoundly hypnotized person that he or she will see a ferocious animal would be fear inspiring, and—as a consequence of its "reality" to the subject—could produce a state of emotional shock.

The late George Estabrooks, while a professor of psychology at Colgate University, told a fascinating story about his experience with a self-induced hallucination:

> The technique of autohypnosis is difficult, but it can be mastered. Once the subject has obtained this mastery, he will find that not only can he produce, say, hallucinations in the trance itself, but can actually suggest posthypnotic hallucinations to himself. It does sound weird but it can be done.
>
> For example, the writer, while in a military hospital, had ample time to experiment with autosuggestion. He was able to suggest to himself that he would wake up at 2:00 A.M. and hear a symphony. Even more interesting he could suggest that he would awaken and hear spiritualistic raps. Sure enough, at 2:00 A.M. he was wide-awake listening to very distinct raps from the spirit world. . . .

Autosuggestion gives us an excellent device with which to study many strange things. The writer had a "pet" polar bear, which he was able to call up merely by counting to five. This animal would parade around the hospital ward in a most convincing fashion, over and under the beds, kiss the nurses and bite the doctors. It was very curious to note how obedient he was to "mental" commands, even jumping out of a three-story window on command.

But autosuggestion has a certain menace, which this phantom bear illustrated. He became so very familiar that he refused to go away. He would turn up in the most unexpected places and without being sent for. The writer was playing bridge one evening and almost threw his hostess into hysterics by suddenly remarking, "There's that damn bear again. I wish someone would shoot the beast." He also had a nasty habit of turning up in dark corners at night, all very well when one realized he was just made of ghost-stuff, but rather hard on one's nerves for all that. So he was banished and told never to return. It was fully a month before the writer felt quite sure that his ghostly form would not be grinning at him over the foot of his bed during a thunderstorm.[19]

---

[19]Estabrooks, G. H., Hypnotism. New York, E. P. Dutton, 1957

Sexual Fantasies

There have been occasional reports of women who have experienced fantasies of having sexual relations with the hypnotist while in a state of hypnosis. Freudian psychiatrists explain that these sexual fantasies arise from the subject's unconscious as a manifestation of libidinal wish fulfillment. Regardless of their origin, such fantasies do occur, and, to the hypnotized person, may be projected into waking consciousness as a "real" experience. With this thought in mind, the need for the presence of a third party can be readily seen. This situation is not unique, however, as physicians and dentists who use general anesthesia have a third party present as protection against alleged malpractice.

Sigmund Freud, the developer of psychoanalysis, reported his reaction to this symbolic sexual phenomenon:

> And one day I had an experience, which showed me in the crudest light what I have long suspected. One of my acquiescent patients, with whom hypnotism had enabled me to bring about the most marvelous results, and whom I was engaged in relieving of her suffering by tracing back her attacks of pain to their origins, as she woke up on one occasion, threw her arms round my neck. The unexpected entrance of a servant relieved us from the discussion. From that time onwards there was a tacit understanding between us that the hypnotic treatment would be discontinued. I was modest enough not to attribute the event to my own irresistible personal attractions, and I felt that I had now

grasped the nature of the mysterious element that was at work behind hypnotism.[20]

As we have seen, hypnosis per se in not dangerous. There is no evidence to support that hypnosis in and of itself is dangerous. The only possible danger lies in the operator's misuse of suggestion. Therefore it behooves the responsible hypnotist to use suggestion judiciously.

---

[20]Freud, S., My Views On the Part Played by Sexuality in the Etiology of the Neuroses, London, Hogarth Press, 1976

CHAPTER 6
Theories Of Hypnosis

Therapeutic suggestion in one form or another has been used as a powerful adjunct to the witch doctor or necromancer's repertoire for thousands of years; however, it is only in comparatively recent years that hypnosis has been placed under the bright light of scientific investigation. In 1841 James Braid made a significant contribution to the scientific acceptance of hypnotism and put it on a rational basis by demonstrating that hypnosis was a personal subjective experience.

The nature of hypnosis has always been an enigma and is difficult to define in the language of psychology. Seldom has there been a subject on which so many hundreds of thousands of words have been written. Indeed there are nearly as many definitions of hypnosis as there are hypnotists. A number of theories have been proposed to explain the essence of hypnotism. While no theory of hypnosis is adequate, all of them contain some basis of truth. We will examine the most accepted of these theories.

Pathologic Theory

In the latter half of the nineteenth century serious investigation into the nature of hypnosis was conducted by three French physicians. They were Hippolyte Bernheim and August Ambroise Liébeault at Nancy, and Jean Charcot at the Salpêtrière Hospital in Paris. Bernheim and Liébeault were ardent proponents of hypnotism and treated over 12,000 patients. They believed that hypnosis was a normal phenomenon and recognized the importance of suggestion to the hypnotic process. As alluded to in Chapter 1, their work became known as the Nancy School of Hypnotism. The Salpêtrière School, which espoused the ideas of Charcot, considered hypnosis to be an abnormal or pathologic state related to hysteria. Charcot arrived at this conclusion because he confined his experimentation at the Salpêtrière Hospital to a limited number of female hysterical patients. He found that these subjects entered hypnosis through three successive stages: "lethargy," "catalepsy," and "somnambulism," each stage showing very definite and characteristic symptoms. (Bernheim reported that among the thousands of patients he hypnotized, only one--a woman who had spent three years at the Salpêtrière--displayed the three stages described by Charcot.) Since Charcot was an eminent scientist who made important contributions to the field of medicine, his theory of hypnosis gained a number of supporters. The Nancy School triumphed over the views of Charcot, however, and rejection by Bernheim and Liébeault of the pathologic theory of hypnosis brought to light the fallacies of the Salpêtrière experiments.

Hypnosis As A State Of Sleep

Hypnotism and hypnosis, denoting respectively the procedure and the mental and physical states caused by it, are terms popularized by a Scottish physician, James Braid, in 1841. Initially Braid believed that hypnosis and sleep were related phenomena. Thus the nomenclature for hypnotism, as noted in Chapter 1, was coined from the Greek "hypnos" meaning sleep.

Yet this nomenclature is not fully correct either. However, the terms "hypnotism" and "hypnosis" are now so firmly established in use, no matter how much more accurate any other words might be, it would be impossible to substitute any others for them. Hypnosis is different from sleep because a person in hypnosis is quite awake and alert. The brain waves of a hypnotized person, even in deep hypnosis, are closer to those of one awake and not of one asleep. In sleep the subconscious mind (as well as the conscious mind) is inaccessible; yet, in hypnosis the subconscious becomes accessible and responsive to suggestion. A deeply sleeping individual will not hear if spoken to, unless roughly awakened by shaking; yet, a person in deep hypnosis, though seemingly oblivious to all around him or her, will hear and respond to the hypnotist's suggestions. It is true, however, that if not aroused from hypnosis, the subject may drift off into sleep and will awaken from it naturally.

Instead of a form of sleep, it is more correct to look at hypnosis as an induced receptiveness of the subconscious mind wherein the focus of attention is concentrated or narrowed.

Ernest and Josephine Hilgard, leading authorities on hypnosis said . . .

This may take various forms, and does not necessarily mean a highly concentrated attention. In fact, the mind in hypnosis may sometimes be almost blank, attending scarcely at all. At other times the attention is only on the hypnotist's voice and on what he is saying, with inattention to any distracting sounds. When the attention is directed to specific experiences, these are often so central that conflicting thoughts do not intrude. "It's like narrowing the thread of existence to a single strand, so that things that usually drop away one by one. All that is left is the hypnotist and the hypnotist's voice." Or: "Psychologically, it was an easy way to detach myself from present problems."[21]

The term "hypnosis," with its connotation of sleep, then, is a complete misnomer. Because of its resemblance to sleep, it is easy to see why the early hypnotists believed hypnosis and sleep to be related phenomena. Even Pavlov, the eminent Russian scientist who is noted for his theory of the conditioned reflex, insisted that hypnosis was a modified type of sleep. Hypnosis, however, more closely approximates normal waking consciousness than it does sleep.

With appropriate hypnotic suggestions a lethargic drowsy state leading to sleep may be induced. Notwithstanding its resemblance to sleep, these states are not the effects of hypnosis but of suggestion.

Not infrequently, the deep somnambulistic state of hypnosis is followed with a spontaneous amnesia. (Although the subject

---

[21]Hilgard, E. R. & Hilgard, J. R., Hypnosis in the Relief of Pain, New York, Brunner/Mazel, 1994.

may remember nothing that occurred while hypnotized, putting the subject back into hypnosis may restore these lost memories.) When a person is unable to remember the events of the hypnotic experience; it is easy to see how the resulting amnesia may be misinterpreted as a state of unconsciousness. This misconception is responsible for the mistaken belief that when one is hypnotized there is a sort of "black-out," and after awakening nothing will be remembered of what has taken place. Therefore, it is important that you tell the client who is being hypnotized for the first time, that he or she will not go to sleep or lose consciousness.

Electroencephalograph tracings or brain wave patterns of a person deeply hypnotized are similar to those in the normal waking state. These brain wave tracings are markedly different, however, in sleep. Also, electrocardiograph and respiratory studies during hypnosis were similar to those found in the normal waking state. In sleep the senses are in a state of inaction and there is little, if any, response to reflex stimulation. In hypnosis there is a marked heightening of sensory acuity, and the hypnotized individual will readily respond to reflex stimulation such as the patellar reflex (knee-jerk test). In sleep, consciousness is lost, but in hypnosis a person is capable of thinking and reasoning.

A more obvious difference exists between sleep and hypnosis. If a person who is in a sound sleep is spoken to, unless the sleeper is disturbed, no response will be elicited. The hypnotized person, however, will respond immediately to any reasonable suggestion, regardless of the depth of the hypnotic state.

When a person is hypnotized, a technique is often used which will induce a drowsy lethargic state by a combined method of relaxation and suggestions of sleep. Suggestions of drowsiness or sleep may be omitted, and the subject will remain awake and alert, assuming none of the sleeplike characteristics of traditional hypnosis. Hypnosis can be induced without any suggestions of sleep, and phenomena characteristic of the trance state can be elicited in the waking state.

Back in 1924 Professor W. R. Wells, Syracuse University, conducted experiments of waking hypnosis on several hundred subjects. In an article entitled *"Experiments in Waking Hypnosis for Instructional Purposes,"* (Journal of Abnormal Psychology and Social Psychology), Wells states, " . . . in what I call waking hypnosis, sleep is not mentioned in the preliminary explanation to the subject; sleep is not suggested, directly or indirectly; the subject experiences neither drowsiness nor sleepiness, if we may trust his introspective account; and there are present none of the objective indications of drowsiness or sleep." Indeed some authorities have asserted that all hypnotic phenomena, including amnesia, can be produced in the waking state. This would indicate that the traditional induction ritual of suggesting sleep to the subject is not essential to hypnosis and that it is only one of the ways of inducing it.

Divided Brain Theory

Leading universities are pursuing ongoing research into the realm of neurophysiology--the neurophysiology of the human brain. This research provides a persuasive theory of the psychological mechanism of the two modes of consciousness.

Neuroscientists have discovered that the cerebral cortex of the human brain is divided into two hemispheres, each of which has separate and distinct functions. The function of these two hemispheres underlies the two modes of consciousness, which simultaneously coexist within each one of us. The different functions of the left and right sides of the brain give us insight into the nature of hypnosis.

A network of millions of interconnecting nerve fibers called the "corpus callosum" joins the two hemispheres of the cerebral cortex. The corpus callosum mediates mental impulses from one hemisphere to the other. The left cerebral hemisphere is predominately involved with logical, analytical, intellectual thought processes and governs judgment. The left hemisphere is the seat of reason and normally dominates our consciousness. While the right side of the brain (the right cerebral hemisphere) deals more with symbols, with feeling, with emotions, and, what is especially important to the hypnotherapist, with imagination. The right hemisphere is the emotive, creative, intuitive side of the brain.

When hypnosis is induced, the left side of the brain—that dominant, analytical part of the brain—is lulled into a state of mental passivity, and then held, as it were, in a state of abeyance. Relaxation ensues, the mind switches and the right cerebral hemisphere comes to the fore; and we have hypnosis. While this does not answer all the questions about the induction of hypnosis, it is a logical explanation.

Psychological Theory

As we have seen, James Braid first elaborated the importance of suggestion to the process of hypnosis. This was an important milestone in the history of hypnotism, as it stressed the psychological nature of hypnosis.

Hippolyte Bernheim, one of the leading champions of this theory, stated that there was no hypnosis, only suggestion. Emile Coué, the father of autosuggestion, went a step further and stated that there was no suggestion only autosuggestion — which would indicate that hypnosis is really self-hypnosis and the hypnotized subject acts under the volition of his own personality.

Lewis Wolberg, Clinical Professor of Psychiatry, New York University School of Medicine in his book *Medical Hypnosis* stated:

Most authorities feel that hypnosis is a state of exaggerated suggestibility. Increased suggestibility expresses itself both as ideomotor action, in that an idea tends to induce automatic behavior, and as a response to social stimuli, particularly to a prestige relationship.

The average individual is relatively more susceptible to suggestions uttered by a person who is impressive in terms of strength, stature, mien, gestures, eloquence, age, education, experience and magnetic personality. There is considerable evidence that the powers of the hypnotist are based to a large degree upon the mantle of prestige with which the subject cloaks the hypnotist. Some investigators claim that the successful practice of suggestive hypnosis is dependent on the establishment and maintenance of an atmosphere of faith in the hypnotist. Anything that lowers the intensity of faith decreases the strength of suggestion. Where the subject doubts the skill and power of the hypnotist, there develops a powerful deterrent to hypnosis. Where he accepts on faith the strength of the hypnotist, he will respond to suggestions for which there are no logical grounds.[22]

Instead of a form of sleep, it is more correct to look at hypnosis as an induced receptiveness to the subconscious mind to suggestion. Though there is still no fully accepted explanation of why the subconscious should be so open to acting on the suggestions given to it, the theory proposed a number of years ago by Dr. Raphael Rhodes, a New York psychologist, has stood up well as a working hypothesis.

This theory states that our objective, everyday conscious mind is capable of both deductive and inductive reasoning, whereas the subjective, subconscious mind, which appears to control the memory circuits of our brains, can only reason deductively. Deductive reasoning infers results from causes — if we are told someone is sick with a disease we know of, we infer that they are having a certain set of symptoms we recognize. Inductive reasoning works oppositely — observing the symptoms, if we have medical knowledge, we relate the symptoms to what is recorded of diseases characterized by them, and so identify the ailment.

To put it another way, the subconscious mind takes everything literally. Once rapport is established the subconscious accepts the hypnotist's suggestions, and as we shall see it is usually surprisingly easy to assert that influence, it will

---

[22]Wolberg, L. R., Medical Hypnosis, New York, Grune & Stratton, 1948.

believe whatever it is told (subject to the limitation imposed by the subject's own inner moral code) and act accordingly. Told by the hypnotist that a subject (in deep hypnosis) has a bad case of flu, there will be an immediate onset of severe flu symptoms, even if the hypnotized person is completely well. The symptoms will disappear as soon as the trance is ended. Of course, if the subject really has the flu, it does not automatically follow that the symptoms can be banished by hypnotic suggestion, for that requires a deep degree of control of the body's immune system. It can be seen, however, that hypnosis offers a means of achieving greater control of our physical as well as mental well-being.

In summary the dominant, intellectual conscious mind is capable of deductive and inductive reasoning, while the subconscious mind does not reason at all but acts automatically through a process of cause and effect. In the induction phase of hypnosis, the critical factor of the dominant conscious mind is lulled into a state of abeyance. Suggestions then slip past the conscious mind and enter the subconscious where they are accepted and acted upon without criticism. Every suggestion that is accepted and acted upon greatly increases the subject's suggestibility. This, in turn, initiates a sensory spiral of belief that results in conviction. William S. Kroger[23] advanced the theory that hypnosis is a conviction phenomenon--hence, belief of hypnosis leads to hypnosis.

Hypnosis then is characterized by an ability to sustain in response to suggestion a state of attentive, receptive, intense

---

[23] Kroger, William S., Clinical and Experimental Hypnosis, 2nd Edition, J. B. Lippincott Co., 1977.

concentration with diminished awareness of distracting or irrelevant stimuli. It is a form of intense concentration, which maximizes involvement with a single dominant thought or idea. This intensification of attention minimizes involvement with external distractions.

CHAPTER 7
Who Can Be Hypnotized?

Hypnotizability is a normal trait and almost everybody can be hypnotized to some extent. Contrary to popular belief, the best candidates for hypnosis are intelligent highly motivated individuals. Imbeciles, morons, and persons of low mentality, who are incapable of concentrating, are difficult and often impossible to hypnotize.

The depth of trance can be used to measure individual susceptibility to hypnosis. Subjects who respond swiftly are the class known as the somnambulists. They belong to the 20%, plus or minus, group who are easily hypnotizable by almost any method.

There are several scales to measure trance depth, and estimates of how many persons can be placed into each of these levels. We will examine the susceptibility scoring system introduced by LeCron and Bordeaux back in 1947. Others have not markedly improved on it since then.

According to Leslie LeCron and Jean Bordeaux, psychotherapists who used hypnotherapy in their private practices, 60% of the population can attain deep trance and 85% to 90% light trance or better. They add, "While these estimates may err slightly, they are intentionally conservative." (With posthypnotic conditioning it is estimated that 60% can ultimately attain a deep level of hypnosis.)

This scale anticipates that five persons out of every hundred cannot be hypnotized--not because they are too strong-willed, but rather for lacking a willingness to cooperate, or having an unconscious resistance that the operator cannot surmount. The next level, that of hypnoidal trance, can be induced in about 15 out of every 100 people. In fact the hypnoidal state is being induced all the time, without any need of a hypnotist, in anyone who becomes so absorbed in watching TV, or reading a novel, or engrossed in thought, or playing tennis, or in any activity requiring intense concentration. If involved enough, the person may become totally oblivious of his or her surroundings and often does not hear even when shouted at. Subjects who go no deeper then the marginal hypnoidal state, often say that they were not hypnotized.

One out of every four people will experience the next level, that of light trance. At this level suggestions are more readily accepted. The subject may be drowsy but fully aware of what is going on.

The fourth level, that of medium trance, is achievable in about 35 out of every 100 persons. Drowsiness and a state resembling sleep are typical; in this level of hypnosis analgesia adequate for dentistry and minor surgery can be induced; posthypnotic suggestions are accepted and usually carried out, including suggestions for amnesia.

Deep trance, the fifth level, can be induced in one of four people. In it the subject will accept suggestions for the alleviation of pain, and to carry out involved suggestions including negative and positive hallucinations, during and after the trance. In this level, the subject usually appears to be fast asleep, but will hear and accept hypnotic suggestions. Memory retrieval (hypermnesia) and age regression (revivification) generally require this degree of trance.

LeCron and Bordeaux add a sixth level, the plenary trance, in which the subject is in a stupor, incapable of any voluntary action but still able to follow hypnotic suggestion. This level is very rarely attained and almost always unnecessary for practically any desired result of hypnosis, including alteration of bodily functions such as digestion, heartbeat, etc. which can be achieved in the fifth level and often at a lower one.

There is a long-held assumption that the depth of hypnosis is unrelated to treatment outcome. For most therapeutic uses of hypnosis a "deep" level of hypnosis is not necessary to obtain positive benefits. Even in the marginal hypnoidal state, the subconscious mind is responsive to therapeutic suggestion.

Stage hypnotists achieve fourth and fifth level trances in their subjects by an authoritative assertiveness that breaks down any resistance on the part of the volunteer subjects, who are eager to do whatever the performer wants. The methods of the stage hypnotist, however, are not the same the hypnotherapist uses in treating those who come for help.

It may be helpful at this point to comment on the susceptibility of various age levels to hypnotic responsiveness. Olness and Gardner,[24] well-known authorities in pediatric hypnosis, state that hypnotizability in children is limited below the age

---

[24]Olness, K., & Gardner, G., Hypnosis with children. (2nd ed.). New York, Grune & Stratton.

of 3, and achieves its peak at ages 7 to 14. Beyond adolescence susceptibility decreases slightly, remaining stable through age 60, and decreasing again in the older population. But it cannot be said there is any age in which people are too old to be hypnotized.

A prevalent misconception is that only weak-willed or weak-minded individuals can be hypnotized. In an attempt to explode this misapprehension, many hypnotists have overemphasized the role intelligence plays as a factor of susceptibility. If other things such as undue curiosity, fears, and mistrust are absent or removed, then 90 percent of all people are hypnotizable. Obviously this faction of the general populace is not comprised of highly intelligent people.

While no correlation has been found between the intelligence quotient and susceptibility to hypnosis, it is extremely difficult to hypnotize persons of low mentality. (Individuals with a real intellectual deficiency usually are not hypnotizable and tax the ingenuity of the hypnotist.) Pointing this out to anyone who is being hypnotized for the first time will increase motivation and enhance hypnotic responsiveness.

Long experience has shown that there is very little, if any, difference between male and female responsiveness to hypnosis, if sex is the only criterion.

In the 19th century, when sleepwalking seems to have been more common that now, it was widely believed that sleepwalkers could be readily hypnotized. Modern experience (though having fewer sleepwalking subjects) has largely confirmed this notion. It is not surprising, for subjects in deep hypnosis do manifest much of the phenomena of somnambulism; though, unlike sleepwalkers, hypnotic subjects are aware of what they are doing. The term "somnambulism" (i.e., sleep-walking) has been ascribed to the deepest level of hypnosis, because it is descriptive of the state.

Usually subjects improve in their ability to go into hypnosis on successive occasions. If greater depth is desired, successive re-induction into hypnosis (a technique called "fractionation") is helpful in facilitating a deeper level of hypnosis.

Josephine Hilgard, while clinical professor emeritus of psychiatry at Stanford University, investigated imaginative involvement as a factor of hypnotizability. (Childhood imaginative involvement seems to be a precursor of adult hypnotic susceptibility.) Dr. Hilgard states:

> What we found out was that the hypnotizable person was capable of a deep involvement in one or more imaginative feeling areas of experience--reading a novel, listening to music, having an aesthetic experience of nature, or engaging in absorbing adventures of body or mind. This involvement is one of the things the existentialist is talking about when he speaks of the breaking down of his experience; it is what those seeking expansion of consciousness mean by their all-embracing experiences; it is something like Maslow's (1959) peak experiences. There need be nothing abnormal or extreme about it, and we shall point out that our readily hypnotizable subjects are more likely to be normal than neurotic. If we were to define this involvement, to distinguish it from its nearest relatives such as enjoyment of, or interest in, an activity, we would have to stress the quality of almost total immersion in the activity, with indifference to distracting stimuli in the environment.

The often-observed narrowing of attention in the hypnotized subject implies something like this, but concentrated attention is not the whole story. The child glued to the TV screen, who fails to hear himself being called, whether by mother or by friends, is not only attending but is having a vivid experience through involvement, an experience some adults are also capable of.[25]

Does creativity have any relationship to hypnotizability? Hypnosis researcher, Patricia Bowers, found that highly creative people and good hypnotic subjects report that creative behavior or hypnotic responses occur effortlessly. Her investigation of the variables in hypnotic responsiveness, revealed a relationship between hypnotic susceptibility and both creativity and what she has termed "effortless experiencing."

---

[25]Hilgard, J. R., Personality and Hypnosis, A Study of Imaginative Involvement, Chicago, University of Chicago Press, 1979.

CHAPTER 8
How Hypnosis Works

In this chapter we will look at some of the effects that can be produced in the hypnotized subject. It may help if we precede our discussion of the effects of hypnosis with a brief account of how it is now thought the brain works in bringing it about.

The brain carries on its functions of thinking and perception by means of internal transmission of minute electrical waves than can be detected and categorized by sensitive instruments. The brain waves typical of normal everyday waking activity, in which we are fully conscious of time and space relationships, and of striving and effort, and the tensions created by them, are called *beta* waves.

When we spontaneously enter the light hypnoidal state, which can occur several times daily without our being aware of it (for example, in simple relaxation or watching television or monotonous driving over long distance) the resulting brain waves of lower frequency are called *alpha* waves. Writers, composers, artists and other creative thinkers usually do their best work when in the alpha state, though until recently few have ever consciously thought of their entering it.

The next phase of brain wave activity, in which the waves are of still lower frequency, is known as the *theta* state; it is that which we pass through briefly in falling asleep and again in waking up. In the theta state, the imaging powers of the mind are greatly enhanced; some people experience fleeting realistic full-color visions while falling asleep, and can sometimes later recall these in considerable detail. These fleeting theta-state imaginings are called hypnagogic.

The point to observe and keep in mind is that in hypnosis beyond the superficial hypnoidal level, the subject is in the theta state and can be kept there for as long as the hypnotic session lasts. In the theta state, the mind is responsive to acting on and carrying out the suggestions of the hypnotist, for it is still attentive and knows what it is doing, just as the person seeing hypnagogic images on the verge of falling asleep knows that he or she is still awake and not dreaming.

In full natural sleep; the brain waves are damped down still more, becoming what is known as *delta* waves. It is in the delta state that the brain enacts dreams and thus gives symbolic expression to our psychological difficulties, and the physical body carries out cell regeneration and renewal of its energies.

We thus begin to see the physical framework within which hypnosis works. The hypnotist first seeks to induce the alpha state to render the subject more receptive to deeper induction; then the theta state is induced to whatever degree of depth possible.

The Information Theory Of Hypnotic Suggestion

But what exactly is the part of the brain through which hypnotic suggestion operates? It is only within the past two decades that the probable answer has begun to be understood. One of the principal keys to it, Information Theory, goes back sixty years to its first presentation in Shannon and Weaver's *The Mathematical Theory of Communication*. A prime concept of Information Theory is transduction—the transmission of whatever form the information is expressed in, into another. For instance, in the telephone the sound waves of speech are transduced into electrical waves, which in the receiving telephone are transduced back into speech.

Computers are essentially nothing but transducers, of very intricate kinds. Most of us have no difficulty accepting that, any more than the telephone; but it is not quite so easy to picture it as happening within our brains. Transduction, nevertheless, more and more appears to be the mechanism through which suggestion and hypnosis work their effects in us.

In the late 1960's, scientists began to isolate certain chemicals known as neuropeptides, which appear to be produced in the hypothalamus, a part of the "old brain" that we have inherited from our dim reptilian past, long before mammals evolved along with their increasingly complex cortexes or upper brains. At first, only five neuropeptides were found; now more than 50 have been identified and additional ones are being found all the time. The neuropeptides that have come into public awareness are the endorphins, which act like natural opiates or painkillers; but many of the other ones appear to function as boosters of the immune system.

Ernest Lawrence Rossi, a noted authority on hypnosis, has made the first thorough study of the neuropeptides and the key role they play in hypnosis and information transduction within the brain and the neural network of nerves that convey the brain's commands to every part of the body. In his landmark book[26] about the psychobiology of mind-body healing, Ernest Rossi explains how the neuropeptides circulate within the brain itself, as neurotransmitters through which whole new circuits or even networks of circuits are created whenever old thinking patterns are discontinued and new ones developed. Within the blood stream, however, and in the lymphatic system and the nerve network, the neuropeptides act somewhat as hormones.

It seems that we have to regard the cortex or upper brain as a filter that screens out enough of the torrent of information with which our bodily senses are deluging us every waking moment, to enable us to think and function rationally. The trance state then is simply the enhancing of this screening function, superficially in the hypnoidal state which is induced all the time without any hypnotist being involved at all—and then more deeply by means of modern hypnotic techniques that have been developed by trial and error.

Since screening-out is the prime function of the cerebral cortex, in hypnosis the hypnotherapist is doing no more than encouraging the carrying out of this naturally implanted functional tendency to a greater degree than would occur normally. Once the cortex starts to accept the hypnotist's suggestions to this effect, the neuropeptides within it are stimulated to form a new circuit of thinking that is willing to act on what it is told to do by the hypnotist.

---

[26]Rossi, E., Mind-Body Therapy, New York, W.W. Norton & Company, 1988.

This new information is then transduced to the hypothalamus (the body's master gland), which it interprets as a command to start releasing neuropeptides into the blood, lymph, and nerve circulations, to enable them to carry out the instructions now being accepted by the cortex in the theta state. If these suggestions are for relief or blocking out of pain, the chemicals released are endorphins; if to fight infection or other disease, then they are ones that boost the immune system.

All this may sound simple in the telling, but carrying it out in practice can be a long and tedious process. Long-habituated patterns of thought and behavior in the cortex are not easy to break down and replace with new ones. The difficulty of stopping smoking and drinking, for instance, even with hypnotic suggestion, is well known to everyone. When it comes to more basic ways of thinking and behaving, especially those implanted in childhood and reinforced over the years, it can often take a series of treatments by the hypnotherapist to effect the desired change. Sometimes the first treatment results in such marked improvement that the client wrongly concludes no more work is necessary--and then has to start all over again a short while later.

Nevertheless, with what is beginning to be understood of the way in which imagining can strongly enhance the effects sought by the hypnotherapist, it is now possible to achieve therapeutic change more speedily and with more lasting results.

In this chapter I was going to talk about the effects of hypnosis, but I see I have led you into the uncharted frontier of psychobiology. It's just as well, for now that I've told you about the classes of brain waves, information transduction, and the functions of the neuropeptides, I think it will be easier to follow what I will be saying about the effects of hypnosis, and to grasp how these effects are brought about.

I again have to remind you about what I said above, that the hypnotic state is basically a concentrating of the filtering power of the cerebral cortex or upper brain. By altering its wave transmissions first into the alpha state and then into the theta, the hypnotist is persuading it to filer out as many distractions as it can--the everyday distractions that assail us in every waking moment and often make it so hard for us to get our minds to anything demanding close attention. The more the cortex succeeds in this enhanced filtering, the deeper will be the hypnotic state into which the subject is placed.

When the concentration of the filtering process approaches 100 percent of screening out everything except the instruction—whatever it may be—on which the hypnotist is focusing the brain's attention, some remarkable effects in the subject's body can be brought about. If, for instance, the cortex is being asked to focus on blocking out all sensation of pain, it is possible in this way to reach a level of anesthesia in which major surgery can be performed without pain. The cortex can also be instructed to block out all awareness of the actual process of surgery, which might otherwise frighten or alarm the patient.

However, since chemical anesthesia is highly reliable, fast, and relatively safe, such a deep state of hypnosis is rarely required for any therapeutic work. Anesthesia sufficient for most dentistry can be attained with much less than 100 percent of concentration; indeed only 51 percent concentration is sufficient to have a direct effect on the other 49 percent of the mind.

It is the filtering out by the cortex, under hypnotic suggestion, that makes it possible to achieve a condition of marked muscular rigidity--a phenomenon called catalepsy. The stage hypnotist tells the subject that the body is getting stiff and rigid, so stiff and rigid that it is becoming as unyielding as a bar of steel. The rigid body is now placed across two chairs and another person stands on the unsupported abdomen. This is possible because the cortex filters out the inhibiting restraint of our usual waking convictions. The muscles are quite capable of such a performance; when the suggestion is accepted subconsciously the muscles will respond to the hypnotist's suggestions.

Consider also astonishing feats of superhuman strength in a moment of crisis. Like the frail old lady who single-handedly lifts a car that is crushing her grandson. In this condition of full concentration, incited by intense emotion, there is nothing left to impose a restraint. Thus the muscles will react to the emergency situation to the full extent of their strength. In this instance a hypnotist is not involved, but the principle remains the same.

The human jaw muscles can exert a pressure of about 600 pounds, but we do not normally ask them to use that power, even if we know that it is there. Circus performers do know it, and train those muscles to enable them to hang by their teeth and twirl from trapeze bars, sustaining the full weight of their bodies.

Hypnotic suggestion can likewise relax the muscles into a state of complete plasticity, making it possible to mold them into abnormal positions, from which they revert instantly when commanded to do so. Or they can be made continuously active, as for instance in the stage demonstration of having the subject rotate the hands around and around, unable to stop. There is also a phenomenon of automatic writing that can be hypnotically initiated. (Automatic writing is sometimes used in hypnotherapy to release traumatic events suppressed in the mind.)

All of the physical senses are similarly subject to hypnotic suggestion. Ill-tasting and ill-smelling things can be perceived as pleasant, or the other way around, if the hypnotist suggests that. For instance, the pungent vapors of ammonia may be perceived as a fragrant perfume. The subject can be made to hear sounds that do not exist, or be deaf to the loudest noise — even a gun fired close to his or her ear. Non-existent things are seen by the subject, if that is the hypnotist's command — the image of an imaginary pet, such as a dog or cat, can be evoked to play very realistically with the subject. University students who were hypnotized for psychological experimentation have been made to believe they were blind, so effectively that brain waves typical of real blindness were transmitted.

Usually the senses under hypnosis are also capable of being exalted to powers well above their normal state. Taste, hearing, smell, sight and touch can become much keener, detecting sensory impressions beyond normal capability. There is also a highly increased sensitivity to time, posthypnotic instructions being carried out precisely to the suggested moment. Many of us utilize this subconscious ability, without thinking it anything particularly special, when we tell ourselves on going to sleep that we want to wake up at a particular hour.

The tendency of the subconscious mind to enact roles is readily enhanced in hypnosis. Subjects can give very convincing performances of either imaginary or real personages. Submerged personalities can be brought to the fore and their characteristics revealed. This usually requires deep hypnosis on repeated occasions.

Influence of the physical functions of the so-called involuntary nervous system, such as digestion, breathing heartbeat, and the menses, can be exerted through hypnotic suggestion. High blood pressure can be relieved, though by the suggestions of relaxation rather than directly as in the case of the other functions just named.

It is apparent from what has been cited (without going into further methods of deepening hypnosis, as with medically administered drugs such as trilene) that the range of possible responses to hypnosis is enormous, and provided the therapist has a commensurate range of skills, a literal host of both psychological and physical disorders and malfunctions can be treated and relieved or cured. Imagery techniques are used in the stimulation of the immune system and the combating of severe physical illnesses such as cancer. However, more traditional methods of hypnotic treatment often yield highly satisfactory results in a substantial number of cases.

A note of caution has to be sounded at this point. Hypnotherapy is not a universal cure-all. Not all clients yield to hypnotic induction. Many come to seek treatment when the problem has progressed to a state where effective relief is no longer possible. Yet it cannot be too strongly stressed that hypnotherapy is a treatment resource of which far too few are aware, and that its proven record of success, within the limitations from which no mode of treatment is free, should make it a preferred one. Indeed there are few medical conditions that hypnotherapy cannot benefit.

A popular guidebook on hypnosis has a 24-page listing of approximately 400 conditions in which hypnosis has been shown to be of practical help. In every instance, it is the hypnotically enhanced selective thinking, which brings about this relief. Attention is so totally focused--not on the condition, but on whatever treatment or countermeasure is indicated--that the necessary changes in the body begin to occur.

"Mind over matter" has long been a cliché, but it is only through hypnosis that it can actually take place. You can grit your teeth and will your mind not to feel the pain of a bad ankle sprain, for instance, but you will find that it does not work. Too many distractions, that you cannot prevent your senses from receiving, are getting in the way of concentrating on the blocking of the pain impulses. Hypnosis, however, enables this concentration to take place without all that effort on your part.

This is not to say that cooperation on the part of the client is not necessary, or that a large degree of sustained dedication to the sought-for end is not required in the more advanced forms of hypnosis, which seeks to direct the immune system. Still, it is one of the major advantages of hypnotherapy that much can be achieved by the client permitting the therapist to take charge of the whole process. This will include appropriate posthypnotic suggestions that will continue to be carried out after the treatment session has ended.

Hypnotic suggestion can also greatly enhance the effect of conventional medication, by implanting the idea that it will help and continue to do so. It is only carrying a step further the well-known "placebo effect," in which the doctor gives the patient plain water (perhaps flavored to make it taste bad, to meet the usual expectation that only such medicines work) and says that it is some impressive-sounding new remedy. Very often the patient is markedly benefited, because the cerebral cortex was thus stimulated to screen out any doubt of the efficacy of the potion.

There are an astonishing number of physical ailments for which no clear physical cause can be found, and that keep the sufferer running from one doctor to another, without ever finding effective treatment. The vast majority of these can be treated hypnotically, for the cortex is thus steered to concentrate on the mental root of the problem. Chronic muscle spasms are one of the commonest forms of these ailments; if occurring in the neck muscles, they can in time cause a literal twisting of the neck resulting in a condition called wryneck (or torticollis). Wryneck is often caused by a psychic aversion to facing up to things any more, for example, as a consequence of the death of a loved one or some similar wrenching loss. When the suggestion is accepted that the client does have the capability of facing up to things and living effectively and productively, the stressed muscles are relaxed and return to their normal position.

Anxiety and fatigue neuroses, and illogical fears and compulsions, are also highly treatable by hypnosis. They too are usually forms of evasion, of having become convinced that one does not have––or no longer has––the ability to confront the outer world with its demands and frustrations. Hypnosis can implant the counter-belief that such ability can be regained.

Alcoholism, and addiction to smoking and drugs, are also an example of turning away from a real world that seems too hostile to cope with. In these conditions, too, hypnosis is of great help, but the overcoming of these addictions, which represent major long-standing psychological problems, can be a long and difficult process, in which the cooperation and help of other therapies may have to be enlisted.

Conditions such as stammering, bed-wetting, and stage fright are still other forms of maladjustment to one's surroundings. The first two may occasionally have a related physical defect, usually minor, that can be medically corrected. Here again, however, hypnosis with its stimulation of the cortex to screen out the negative reactions that accompany and perpetuate these conditions is the principal factor in overcoming them.

Obesity from compulsive eating, insomnia, migraine, impotence—all these and many others could be added to the list of conditions that yield to hypnotic treatment. In listing all the ways in which hypnotherapy helps to overcome problems, we should however not forget that it can also help people to achieve. Improved performances in sports, in learning, in gaining self-confidence, are all attested results of hypnosis.

In fulfilling these improved performances, visualization and imagery start to play a larger role in the hypnotic process. As Maxell Maltz, the author of *Psycho-Cybernetics*, so wisely said: *The mind cannot tell the difference between an actual experience and one vividly imagined.* Sometimes the greater part of the result comes from self-hypnosis; of seeing-in-the-mind's eye one's self doing better on the playing field or in class.

CHAPTER 9
The Power Of Visualization

Over the past few years there has been an unprecedented expansion of awareness and interest in the demonstrated power of the imaging capability of the brain to direct and control many of the physical processes of the body. By forming compelling, positive images in the mind an interaction between the brain and the body occurs. This mind-body interplay is mediated through the activity of the immune system, the body's system of defense against invading organisms and its own runaway cancerous cells. (The immune system may be thought of as intricate software linking the blood and lymph circulations with the neuron circuitry in the brain.)

Even though techniques of this consciously willed direction and control were known to primitive societies for thousands of years, under the disciplines loosely systematized under the name of shamanism. Medical science is only now, grudgingly enough, coming to admit the existence of this faculty.

The precise forms of these disciplines have varied widely in the diverse cultures that primitive societies have evolved, but a general similarity is found in them all. The principle characteristic of this similarity is the figure of the dedicated person--whether called seer, shaman, witchdoctor or by some other name--who deliberately cultivates imaging ability to the extent of being able to visualize through various symbolism the means by which the body's immune system carries out its function of defending the body and maintaining its health.

Lacking the technology of modern science, the shaman did not have--and still does not have--a mechanistically correct conception of the workings of the immune system. However, he knows how to image a "healing force" in his own mind, and through ritual and repetitive suggestion to have his patients image it in their minds. They are not always relieved or cured; the affliction can be beyond the power of the immune system to vanquish the disease. Yet surprisingly often they get well, leading to the assumption that since we now have the advantage of a scientific description of the immune system, it should be possible to image it more accurately and with greater healing effect.

In *The Mind Game*, E. Fuller Torrey compares the efficacy of witchdoctors, and psychiatrists:

> We should not be surprised to find that therapists in other cultures are as effective as those in our culture. They can name the patient's disease and raise his expectations equally as well as we can. Their selection procedures for the profession are geared to attract as many individuals with therapeutic personality characteristics as ours are. And they use techniques of therapy as effectively.
>
> It is this last, the techniques of therapy, that is most difficult for us to accept. How can witchdoctors, relying

primarily on such techniques as suggestion and hypnosis, achieve as good results as Western therapists who use techniques so much more sophisticated? The answer is twofold. First, therapists elsewhere use on occasion the same "sophisticated" techniques as Western therapists do. Second and more important, we consistently underestimate the power of techniques like suggestions and hypnosis. Their low status in Western therapy blinds us to their real strengths.[27]

For decades it was known that the white blood cells attack hostile organisms attempting to gain a foothold within the body. Only recently has it become understood there are three different types, each carrying out a specific function under the command of the immune system.

The first type of white blood cell is the neutrophil. We can image the neutrophils as the scouts and patrols of a defending army. They are being continuously formed in the bone marrow, and are about two-thirds of the whole population of white blood cells. The neutrophils circulate in the blood stream, looking out for bacteria and anything else in the way of intruders. When any are encountered, the white blood cell shoots out a foot-like extension that engulfs the alien germ, or whatever it may be, and destroys it with an enzyme so strong the neutrophil itself is wiped out. Since around 100 billion are created each day in the bone marrow of the average human, the loss is meaningless.

---

[27] Torrey, E. F., The Mind Game, New York, Witchdoctors and Psychiatrists, Emerson Hall, Inc., 1972.

If the invasion is on a more serious scale, the body calls in the reserves in the form of two other types of white blood cells. These are called T and B cells. They're also called lymphocytes—so named, because they circulate in the clear lymph fluid. They are also products of the bone marrow. The T-cells (themselves divided into three types) are stored in the thymus gland in the upper chest. Where the B-cells, which create the antibodies that identify and destroy specific invaders, are held in reserve, is still a mystery.

The three T-cell types are the killers, the helpers, and the regulators. There may be sub-types not yet known. The killers attack viruses and foreign tissues, and thus have to be suppressed for organ transplants to succeed. The helpers assist the B-cells in finding their targets. The regulators (sometimes called suppressers) have the job of reining in the immune system when it goes wild and starts attacking the tissues of the body it inhabits. The regulators do not always fully succeed; diabetes and rheumatoid arthritis are two common and serious ailments that result from this malfunctioning of the immune system. Likewise, the killer T-cells do not seem particularly well adapted to attacking cancerous tissue—as if they had not yet fully evolved this ability. It may be that through imaging, under skilled hypnotherapeutic guidance, they can do this more effectively.

Paul Pearsall, the author of *Super-Immunity,* cites an unprecedented case where hypnosis activated T-cells cured what was believed to be an "incurable skin disorder."

> A serious skin disease called *congenital ichthyosiform erythro-dermia* results in a hardening and blackening of the skin. A 16-year-old boy was seen for this condition

after being shunted by his teachers and friends. His skin condition had worsened, and bacterial infection had found a welcome environment in the rigid and cracked surfaces of his body. As the skin grew harder than the boy's own fingernails, bloodstained serum oozed from the slightest bend in the skin.

All major dermatology textbooks report no known cure for this terrible disease. Hypnotist A. A. Mason saw the boy and offered mental imagery suggestions to relax him and to help him learn to see his skin as becoming normal. Hypnotism is not some magic process that somehow overrides disease. It is a guided and carefully chosen process of learning to focus, remember, think, imagine, and experience ideas and events to help achieve a healthier state. It is really a systematic way of more effective thinking and believing, of taking responsibility for the supersystem. Within 5 days, the hard, damaged skin had fallen away, replaced by reddened but more normal-appearing skin. In 10 days, the skin had returned to normal. Dr. Mason's results, published in the *British Medical Journal*, were later verified by three other medical researchers.

Following the publication of these data, other physicians attempted to work on other "incurable skin disorders." Positive results for other conditions were obtained. T-cells are special cells in our immune system that help us deal with foreign invaders or allergens. We now know that T-cell mediated skin response relates to our emotions and beliefs, that the skin reacts intensely to our feelings.[28]

The B-cells, through the antibodies they create, can confer a lasting immunity--ranging from partial to total—against a wide host of viral and bacterial invaders. This ability is enhanced by laboratory-cultured vaccines, and extended to provide protection against a number of infectious diseases without first having to undergo an attack by them.

There is mounting evidence that hypnotically-induced mental imaging of the various white blood cells going about their respective functions can markedly increase their effectiveness. Whatever medications or vaccines have been administered will then do a better job.

Before getting into a specific discussion of how hypnosis provides a method of directing the immune system to function better, it will be both interesting and helpful to examine two cases, both over three centuries ago, where stimulation of the immune system was successful by two practitioners who had only the vaguest notion of what they were doing. Additionally, there is a third instance on record, of slightly earlier date (1625) of a deliberate deception which succeeded in producing the effect sought for.

In this last-named case, the Dutch Prince of Orange relieved the sufferings from scurvy, of his troops besieged in the fortress of Breda and cut off from fresh foods. At that time nothing was known of Vitamin C or of how citrus fruits and green vegetables prevent and cure scurvy, though some ship captains did try to carry a stock of lemons and cabbages,

---

[28]Pearsall, P., Super-Immunity, New York, Ballantine Books, 1987.

through having noticed that they seemed to help. In any event, the Prince of Orange had no way to get such foods to his besieged soldiers. He did manage to pass to them, through the Spanish siege lines, a few small vials of colored and flavored water, with a note declaring that it was an extremely rare and costly medication imported from the Orient, and that two to three drops in a gallon of plain water would impart its healing virtue.

The garrison took the Prince's word on faith and drank the prescribed dose of one glassful per man. Within a few days their symptoms of scurvy had disappeared; they were restored to health and remained well until relieved by the ending of the siege. This illustrates the amazing power of suggestion. The troops thought that the Prince had expended both a lot of money and effort to deliver this "cure" to them and it resulted in an improvement in their condition.

About forty years later, Sir Kenelm Digby in England gained considerable fame through his *Powder of Sympathy*. He accomplished healing of wounds by using this prepared powder, and by adding to it any particle of metal from the weapon that caused the wound, or even a little of the blood from it. Digby cured many dangerous wounds that the surgeons of that era had given up on. So well attested are the cases that there can be no doubt his successes were real—but they were achieved through mental imagery, and not through the powder that was medically worthless. He implanted in his patients' minds the strong suggestion that their wounds would heal through his preparation of the powder (never applied directly to the patient) and their acceptance of this suggestion directed their immune systems to do the work of healing, rapidly and completely.

One case out of the many Digby treated will illustrate his procedure. James Howell, a well-known essayist and man of letters, came across two friends fighting with swords, and attempted to separate them by grasping hold of their weapons. Through his interposition, his friends came to their senses and they gave up the duel, but one of his hands was severely wounded by the sword blade he had seized, being nearly severed just below the wrist, and deeply cut on the back.

Four or five days later, in great pain and with the hand badly inflamed and suppurating, Howell appeared at Digby's residence and asked for his curative help. The healer requested something with the original wound blood still on it. Howell gave him the garter which the wound was first bound up with; Digby washed it in a basin of water in which he first dissolved some of his magical powder, and then hung it up to dry. Howell, watching attentively, soon declared the pain gone, and within a week the wounds were fully healed and closed, with only slight scarring, and the hand restored to full use.

The cure worked because Digby's reputation had already implanted the suggestion in Howell's mind that it would be effectual. Howell's watching the washing and drying of the garter probably induced a hypnoidal state, through his fixed attention on it; his immune system then proceeded to carry out the suggestion that the hand would heal, which it was able to do since it was not yet beyond the possibility of healing.

Contemporaneous with Digby was Valentine Greatrakes, son of an English family settled in southern Ireland near Cork.

Well educated for the time, he seems to have had some sort of psychological breakdown or trauma in his late youth, and thereafter to have been moody and withdrawn. Eventually, he began telling people that he believed God had bestowed on him the power to heal the King's Evil--scrofula, a term now restricted to tubercular infection of the lymph glands in the neck and manifested through external swellings and lesions, and then also covering the similar though wholly different disorder known as lupus erythmatosis, like rheumatoid arthritis a result of the immune system fighting its own body cells.

Traditionally, kings possessed the power of touching persons suffering from these complaints, and healing them instantly. Since medieval kings did have an aura of divine commission about them, people were able to believe in this attribute so strongly that—as sometimes happens now with autoimmune diseases—the immune system corrected its error and the lupus condition was healed.

As time went on and kings were seen as common mortals, belief in their healing ability diminished, and by the 17th century few had faith in this method of healing, but the propensity to it was still strong in most people, and needed only the appearance of a self-confident claimer to the healing gift such as Greatrakes to be re-stimulated and to work effectively. He first tried out the ability he believed to have been divinely bestowed on him, on a man named William Maher, with severe lupus of the eyes, cheeks and throat. Stroking him with his hands, Greatrakes implanted in him the conviction that he would be healed; and in a few days all the lesions and swelling had disappeared. Through the intense belief in the healing powers of Greatrakes, Maher's immune system overcame its hostility to his body cells and allowed them to heal themselves.

Greatrakes now began to touch and heal many other disorders among which are mentioned ague, rheumatism, epilepsy, ulcerations, and lameness. In a short time his reputation was so great that he had to devote three whole days a week to seeing sufferers who sought his help, and before long he was called over to England to exert his powers there.

The case of Greatrakes is particularly instructive in that it defines the effective limits of hypnotic healing. Where the physical cause is beyond the reach of effective treatment, suggestion can do little. There is little question, on the basis of the testimony of a vast number of witnesses, many hostile and only reluctantly convinced, that Greatrakes did actually heal, or greatly relieve hundreds or even thousands of conditions with a ritual--augmented by the patient's expectation to get well--that unleashed the healing forces of the immune system.

The French essayist St. Vermont, who was then visiting in London, has described what caused Greatrakes' eventual downfall. Many of his cures of blindness, deafness, and of cripples, proved not to be lasting. His confident demeanor created a positive expectation of such intensity the afflicted were able to see, hear, and walk. Once the influence of the charismatic healer wore off, and they were no longer affected by Greatrakes' suggestions, in many cases the "cure" was short-lived.

Much of the same phenomena can be seen in the present day in the work of many publicized "psychic healers." They succeed only within the limits of effective suggestion acting on the immune system. Many of their "miraculous cures" prove not to be lasting, as was often the case with Greatrakes. There is a great and important difference between the suggestions employed by faith healers, and the carefully directed suggestions of a modern, competent hypnotherapist.

The skilled hypnotherapist works step by step, noting the reactions and degree of cooperation of the client. The results may not always be immediate and spectacular, but they are much more likely to be thorough and lasting. And if the client has been able to acquire the capabilities of imagery and of self-hypnosis, he or she can continue to strengthen their immune systems on their own, remembering that the object is not to replace ordinary health care, but to supplement it and render it both less often necessary and more effective when required.

The earliest widespread use of hypnosis, as a form of regular therapy in medical practice is believed to have been the Autogenic Training program of the psychotherapist Johannes Schultz in Germany, in 1932. (The method originally developed from Schultz's interests in hypnotic phenomena and is, essentially, a form of structured self-hypnosis.) The clients repeat verbal statements of the therapist, in six groupings, while consciously directing their minds to passively concentrate on their bodies' response to the commands in these formulas--limbs getting heavy or warm, heartbeat leveling to a regular rhythm, breathing and perspiration controlled, etc. While this regimen has proved very effective, when properly carried out, in treating and preventing stress disorders, its drawback is that it takes four to ten months of practice to be fully effective.

More immediately effective and illustrative of the direct action of hypnotic suggestion on the immune system has been the use of hypnosis for a variety of skin disorders from warts to Type 1 herpes infections. In both folklore and medical practice warts have long been known for being particularly receptive to "wish cures." A virus that invades a clump of skin cells that then persists as a small but painful and unsightly excrescence causes them. It is probably this very unsightliness, which makes the sufferer concentrate with unusual exclusiveness on the wish to get rid of it, a wish that the immune system is thus empowered to act on and fulfill.

Folk formulas for wishing warts away are common in every culture, two of the most familiar being those in Mark Twain's *Huckleberry Finn*. In the 1920's, a Swiss doctor, Bruno Bloch, capitalized on this susceptibility of warts to wish curing. He reaped a fortune by advertising and using an impressive electrical gadget that had all kinds of whistles and blinking lights on it, and was guaranteed to get rid of your warts. It did too, almost every time--but only because Block's patients were so strongly influenced, through reading his advertising, to believe that the impressive machine would work. (A form of spontaneous self-hypnosis.) This example exemplifies William S. Korger's premise that conviction of cure results in cure.

Type 1 Herpes is a virus that remains latent in the bloodstream of many people for years and sometimes the greater part of a lifetime before breaking out as cold sores and fever blisters. It has long been known to be frequently activated by emotional disturbances. Ted Groosbart, a psychologist at Harvard Medical Center, has been working with hypnotic suggestion to relieve these disturbances, and thereby either lessen or wholly prevent the herpes outbreaks. One of his successful treatments involved an airline pilot who always broke out with herpes blisters on his forehead when flying over a certain canyon. In hypnosis he revealed that another pilot who had substituted for him when he was ill had crashed into that canyon. The posthypnotic suggestion was implanted that he had no reason to feel guilty over that accident, and he had no further herpes problem.

In Grossbart's opinion, the human skin is one of the prime vehicles through which emotional malaise wreak their havoc on the body. Eczema, hives and rashes are fueled by resentments, lack of love, and disappointed love. His treatment is twofold: imagery, aided by hypnotic suggestion of pleasing situations and scenes for immediate relief of physical discomfort, and hypnotic therapy to find the cause of the emotional problem and dispose of it once and for all. The client's attention has to be directed elsewhere to break the obsessive grip of the problem so it can be examined calmly.

Burns and scalds are among the most terrifying injuries that can happen to the skin, accompanied as they are by agonizing pain and the equally agonizing treatment in which the dead burned skin has to be scraped off. Hypnotic suggestions for alleviating the pain and calming and fortifying the victim's mind to endure the trauma of treatment are being used with varying degrees of success in a number of burn centers. Obviously, a patient in excruciating pain from multiple burns, or shrinking from the agony of scraping is not the most likely person to respond to hypnotic suggestion. Nevertheless, relief from pain, greater fortitude to face treatment, and healing with fewer infections and lessened scarring, has been achieved with burn victims and encourage further efforts.

It was found that the more quickly hypnotic suggestion was implanted after the burn occurred, the greater its acceptance and the more pronounced its healing effects. In seeking to implant hypnotically the expectation that the treatment would be less painful than what the patient was dreading, the best results came when hypnotically induced relaxation was first carried out, followed by directed imagery of the actual treatment with emphasis on the healing process, and the smallness of the pain in comparison.

It is imagery, then, which we are now coming to see as truly the essence of hypnotherapy. Theodore X. Barber, a leading hypnosis researcher, has flatly stated that all hypnotic states require the mind of the subject to be imaging some activity or behavior that has been suggested by the hypnotist; and if the command is not thus visually imaged in the mind, it is ineffective. Hypnotic therapy and diagnosis have thus to utilize imagery on the part of the client if the latter is to be benefited--and a crucial distinction has to be made at this point between receptive and programmed imagery.

Directed imagery has been almost wholly the rule in the practice of hypnotism as it has evolved in the two centuries since Mesmer. As a result, in the past clients tended to have a preconceived expectation of the hypnotist as an omnipotent, authoritarian figure, who had to be substantially if not implicitly obeyed. Only recently has there been acceptance of the alternative way of allowing free receptivity on the client's part, to whatever mental images may manifest after the induction of hypnosis.

Michael Samuels, a hypnotherapist who has worked with a wide range of peoples and cultural levels, concludes that receptive imagery is most valuable in diagnosing the client's problem, while directed imagery continues to be the most effective in stimulating the immune system. A few persons seem capable of summoning up mental images of sufficient power and intensity on their own, to initiate and continue healing. While they are able to visualize, for instance, the disease organisms or cancer cells being attacked and destroyed by the white blood cells. The majority needs the direction and suggestions of a competent therapist to undertake this sort of sustained mental activity.

Biofeedback therapy, which entered the spectrum of orthodox medical practice in 1975, employs primarily the technique of directed imagery, but through the mediation of elaborate measuring instruments and narrowly specific suggestions. Its success rate however does not seem to get above the 60 percent range; it is expensive, time consuming and cumbrous in its reliance on instruments. Hypnotherapy, which address the client's problem more directly and broadly, appears to have a much larger probability of becoming the prime method of treatment by suggestion and imagery over the next decade or two.

About twenty years ago, Dr. Howard Hall, a Penn State University psychologist, carried out a pioneering study of imagery acting on the immune system. Twenty volunteers were inducted into a relaxation state and then instructed to visualize their white blood cells as sharks attacking and destroying weak and confused germs that had invaded the body. A substantial increase in white blood cell count was found an hour after the visualization, but only among the highly hypnotizable members of the test group. Those who tended to resist induction had no increase in white blood cells.

Dr. Hall concluded, on the basis of the study, that primitive and early-civilized cultures had been able to resist both infectious and degenerative diseases through ritual practices using hypnotic techniques that energized the immune system. "We could fight disease ourselves, with our bodies," he says, "but now we've got lazy and expect pills to do it for us."

Imaging and suggestion will not, of course, be enough to defeat a massive assault on the body's defenses. An overwhelming flood of smallpox virus invading the body tissues, for instance, could cause serious damage or death before visualization techniques could mobilize enough white blood cells to resist it. It has been proposed by scholars that the inability of the native populations of the Americas to effectively combat the advancing whites from Europe, was that the new disease organisms the latter brought with them broke down the natives' immune systems before they could rally against them. As a result Native Americans lost faith in their shamans--whose stock in trade was a primitive form of hypnotism--and in their own cultures in general.

Shaman therapy nevertheless remains very much alive and functioning in many primitive cultures around the globe, both in those areas where modern civilization has not yet deeply penetrated and in those where it has survived in the shadow of alien introduced religions. A growing number of experimenters with its techniques have resulted in the publication of several books, notably those of Michael Harner, describing these and what they seek to achieve.

Basically, they are elaborate hypnotic trances and imagery, in which disease and the inner defenses against it are visualized in terms of animals, both benign and hostile. They can be fascinating to study but it is questionable whether the methods of the shaman can be adapted for use in modern society.

What is of importance to know and appreciate is that shamans have for millennia employed the same means that the modern hypnotherapist uses to access the mind and through it control the body processes. Since the dawn of history, native shamans have utilized powerful images to reach deep inside the cellular structures of the body to change the course of diseases. They have clothed these means in various mythical and ritualistic trappings, but in essence they are the same. A Navajo medicine man, Thomas Largewhiskers, who is said to be a centenarian, freely admitted this when he attended a hypnotic demonstration staged by R. L. Bergman, a scholar studying the Navajo shamanistic practices. Largewhiskers confessed he was astonished to find that the white man was capable of doing something as worthwhile as that; the same thing as he and his fellow shamans had been doing all along. All along, in fact, from the remotest origins of the human race, for the similarity of shamanism wherever it is found, among peoples thousands of miles apart, who have never been in contact, argues strongly that hypnotic trance is a basic trait, as much as language itself, and has been everywhere utilized for the same purposes of healing mind and body.

We may however be placing too heavy a stress on the concept of healing as it is understood in our own culture today.

Earlier, more naturalistic cultures have accepted such landmarks as birth, pregnancy, menopause and aging as taken-for-granted occurrences; while we have come to look on them as pathologies requiring hospitalization and special treatment. The shaman, if he was called in to treat anyone involved in these conditions, did not--and does not—see that he is expected to do any "healing" for them; at most he might employ trance to help effect an easier adjustment to their conditions.

Adjustment and coping are in fact coming increasingly to be seen as the keys to not mere survival in a world growing more complex by the day, but to healthy and fulfilling functioning in it. Our understanding of the enormous role of stress in the working of our minds and bodies goes back over forty years to the pioneering studies of Hans Selye who first isolated stress as a factor in mental and bodily health. Since that time numerous contributions have been made by others. Our knowledge of how to cope with and adjust to stress, and to make us its masters and not the other way around, begins largely from the work of Milton Erickson, in the same time frame with Selye and associated with him in part of his efforts. Erickson, whom many regard as the father of modern hypnotherapy, showed the way in the clinical use of hypnosis and imagery to control and overcome stress. All subsequent advances, and they are numerous, stem from the roots planted by Erickson.

So effective have been the therapeutic methods of stress treatment in recent years, that research is now beginning to concentrate more on the formulation of generally acceptable theory to account for how these effects are brought about and in exactly what way they counteract stress. Donald Meichenbaum has perhaps, made the most significant progress in this direction. Using the hypnotherapeutic techniques of imagery, he has developed specific clinical methodologies, which he identifies as "Coping Imagery" and "Stress Inoculation." To account for how they are generated and function, he has formulated a model of imaging factors as mediators of change in the behavior of the physical processes of the body. He divides this mediatory pattern into three phases.

In the first phase, the client is led, through suggestion, imagery and discussion, to develop a self-awareness of the bodily reactions to thoughts, emotions and stress, which as Selye first showed can result in the adrenal glands being placed in a state of perpetual mobilization for conflicts that are never resolved or fought out, with destructive long-term effects on the immune system and the autonomic nervous system.

In the second phase, new and more adaptive images are suggested to stimulate a less self-destructive reaction to stress.

In the third phase, the client learns through suggestion and visualization, to generalize these improved adaptations and thus to apply them to the constantly recurring stresses of everyday life.[29]

Meichenbaum asserts that through repeated rehearsal of the imaged adaptations and the resulting changed inner dialogue of one's self, a sense of control and mastery is attained which replaces the previous feelings of fear and helplessness in the

---

[29]Meichenbaum, D., Cognitive-Behavioral Modification: An Integrative Approach, New York, Plenum Publishers, 1975.

face of stress. In other words, the behavioral pattern of the client's mind is lastingly altered for the better.

Isolating and identifying the specific stresses that are troubling the client appear to be vital in this process of behavioral pattern alteration. E. Fuller Torrey, calls it the Rumpelstilskin Principle, from the fairy tale in which magic happens when the right word is spoken. The mere fact of naming the particular stress, of making it an identifiable and not a faceless foe, seems to trigger a helpful chain of imagery, in which ways and means of coping with and even overcoming it, are brought up in the mind almost of themselves as it were. It is thus obvious that the therapist must be judicious in the choice of suggested images, so that they lead to the correct identifying and naming of the client's causes of stress.

Yet this theoretic pattern, which Meichenbaum proposes, and similar ones that others have put forward, lack specific links between the actual physical results in the body and these mentally rehearsed images. We are thus led back to what we discussed regarding the transduction of the brain's commands through the hypothalamus and the fifty-odd neuropeptide chemicals it secretes into the blood and lymph circulations, the autonomic nervous system, and the white blood cells that are the physical means through which the immune system operates.

New information is being constantly provided by dedicated researchers, that step-by-step is helping to complete a picture of the exact steps through which suggestion, imaging, and mental control are transduced into particular physical effects in the body. The most recent findings in this line are those reported by J. Edwin Blalock of the University of Alabama, and various coworkers mainly now or formerly at the National Institute of Mental Health in Bethesda, Maryland. In sum, they add up to a refutation of the long-standing orthodox medical view that the secretions of the endocrine system, the autonomic nervous system, and the lymphatic systems are three separate and independent functions of the body, which do not directly react on each other.

Hypnotic therapy over the past half-century has already gone a long way toward overthrowing this traditional concept, but Blalock and his associates are now showing us the physical links between the systems. Beginning in 1981 with Blalock's discovery that a hormone which was supposed to be manufactured exclusively in the brain's pituitary gland and hence was solely part of the endocrine system, could also be found as a product of the immune system's white blood cells, there have been a series of findings that can no longer be ignored by the medical establishment, though as late as 1985 they were insisting in an article in the prestigious *New England Journal of Medicine* that there was no proven connection between mental states and bodily health or the lack of it.

This attitude is a holdover from Rene Descartes classic dictum in 1619, that the mind and body were totally separate. For over three centuries that axiom served a purpose in enabling science to develop a thorough understandings of how each functions. Now the time has come to bring them together again.

Candace Pert, one of these 1980's pioneers of what is becoming the new medical discipline of *psychoneuroimmunology*, along with Michael Ruff, has shown that white blood cells are not only similar in some ways to brain cells but have tiny molecular antennas tuned to receive messages from the brain. This is the same mechanism by which hypnotic suggestion is used to stimulate the immune system; by causing a message to be sent from the brain to activate it.

The hypothalamus and thymus glands secrete neuropeptides. Blalock calls them "informational substances." He thinks they may number a hundred or more separate and distinct forms, and that they are the carriers of the messages to the immune system. It is not a one-way transfer, either, in his opinion; the immune system talks back through the informational substances to the brain, and can affect mood and emotional behavior.

Karen Bolloch, another coworker, has established the presence of connecting nerve threads from the main nerves of the autonomic system to the endocrine organs that manufacture the white blood cells, thus furnishing the anatomical link between all three systems. Other physical links, found by Pert and others including Solomon Snyder and Joanna Hill, are the receptor keyholes on cells, especially those of the brain, into which the neuropeptides fit like keys. Jesse Roth of the National Institute of Mental Health has discovered that brain cells manufacture insulin, in addition to those in the pancreas, and that insulin performs different functions in the brain from those in the metabolic process.

The neuropeptides also provide message links between other cells. Indeed, it seems the whole human body is made up of constantly intercommunicating cells, checking on what is being done to keep it functioning. The macrophages or giant white blood cells that act like scavengers and take up permanent residence in the skin, lungs and brain, have receptors that can accept every neuropeptide so far known; they may thus be the general information clearing houses of the whole complex.

Research now in progress gives promise of artificially developed neuropeptides that can be used to cap cell receptors and thus prevent access of predator viruses like AIDS. This would be a totally new departure in control of infections, away from current reliance on vaccines and antibiotics. And it opens the equally fantastic-seeming possibility that through suggestion and imaging, we may some day stimulate the creation in the body of such "capper" neuropeptides, simply through ordering them to be made. First, we have to get a clear idea of the process by which it happens, so that we can effectively image it.

CHAPTER 10
Principles Of Success

Theodore X. Barber is a leading authority on hypnotism who has conducted extensive research on hypnosis. In an interview for an article in *Science Digest* Barber said:

We found that hypnotic subjects are able to do surprising things only when convinced that the hypnotist's words are true statements. When the hypnotist has guided the subject to the point where he is convinced that the hypnotist's words are true statements, the subject then behaves differently because he thinks and believes differently.

Hypnosis initiates the evolution of a relaxed and trusting therapeutic relationship called rapport. Hypnotic rapport is a harmonious bond that develops between the client and the therapist. The empathic hypnotherapist is readily recognized, and rapport is enhanced when the client perceives the operator as a competent and caring person. With the establishment of rapport the client expects positive results and is motivated to please the hypnotherapist. This positive mindset facilitates the acceptance of therapeutic suggestions.

In William S. Kroger's landmark book *Clinical and Experimental Hypnosis,*[30] Kroger wrote about the importance of a favorable mental set or attitude:

> One of the important ingredients for hypnotic suggestibility is the expectation of help from one who is in a prestigious position. If convinced of the truth of this person's words, the subject behaves differently because he thinks and believes differently. From time immemorial, all healing by suggestion or hypnosis has been based on this mechanism. If the idea is accepted that increased suggestibility is produced by a favorable mindset or attitude, catalyzed by the imagination, then hypnotic responses fall into the realm of conviction phenomena. As such, they are subjective mechanisms that are inherently present, to a degree, in all individuals. They result from the subject's imagination compounding the sensory spiral of belief until conviction occurs. Hence, it is indeed a wise hypnotist who knows who is hypnotizing whom.

Accentuate the Positive

Communication with clients should always be positive. For example, avoid negative statements such as, "I'll try to hypnotize you." Say instead, "I will hypnotize you." If you say, "I'll try to hypnotize you," you have suggested that you might not succeed. Saying "I'll try" implies doubt--the expectation of

---

[30] Kroger, W. S., *Clinical & Experimental Hypnosis,* J. B. Lippincott, 2nd Ed., 1977

failure. Create positive expectancy by assuming a confident attitude and accentuate all of your hypnotic suggestions with overtones of positive conviction. In the words of a song that was popular a number of years ago, "You've got to accentuate the positive and eliminate the negative."

Hypnosis: A Conviction Phenomenon

It is important for the hypnotherapist to grasp the idea that hypnosis is a conviction phenomenon. Kroger's insightful pronouncement, "Belief of hypnosis leads to hypnosis," is indeed true. The power of hypnosis is the power of belief.

Some hypnotherapists do not use suggestibility tests and are not concerned about the induction procedure. This is a serious mistake. In the *Handbook of Hypnosis for Professionals*,[31] Roy Udolf asserts:

> The more important use of these prehypnosis tests is to give subjects a warm-up period and practice in the kind of concentration and uncritical thinking that they must engage in to bring about the hypnotic state. These tests provide an opportunity for the rapport between the subject and the operator to develop and for the subject to develop a 'set' for following the hypnotist's instructions.

The author agrees with Roy Udolf. The preliminary tests and initial induction initiate the foundation for successful therapy. If the client feels that the suggestions are effective,

---

[31] Udolf, R., *Handbook of Hypnosis for Professionals*, 2nd Ed, Jason Aronson Inc., 1992

there is a greater change the desired changes will occur. When specific changes do occur, the sensory spiral of belief is compounded into conviction. This positive expectation automatically produces a favorable mindset and conditioned response.

The First Interview

In that crucial first meeting with your client, you set the tone by appearing confident and friendly. The moment the client sees you; judgments are made on the basis of your verbal and nonverbal signals. He or she will react to your voice and respond to your facial expressions, gestures, and energy.

Having a good voice is an asset to the hypnotherapist. Your voice is the vehicle that drives your suggestions. Learn to drive it like a Lamborghini.

The impression you make on the client is not done with your words, but how you speak them. Dr. Albert Mehrabian, a UCLA communications researcher, assesses the three elements of spoken communications.[32] Verbal-what you say—accounts for seven percent of what is believed; vocal inflection—the way you say it accounts for thirty-eight percent; and visual messages–what the client sees—accounts for fifty-five percent of what the client believes. Communication expert Dorothy Leeds[33] stated, "No words can convey confidence, or lack of it, as quickly as body language does, and it takes many brilliant words to change poor impressions made by your nonverbal signals."

---

[32] Mehraian, A., *Silent Messages*, Wadsworths Publishing, 1981
[33] Leeds, D., *PowerSpeak*. NY: Berkley Books, 1991.

Whether you are aware of it or not, your body and voice reflect your feelings. Use them to convey confidence and sincerity. It will put the client at ease.

Before proceeding with your tests of suggestibility and hypnotic induction, always conduct a preliminary interview to establish the client's beliefs and expectations. This prehypnotic interview should be adopted as your standard operating procedure.

Ask the client to tell you everything he or she knows about hypnosis. Ask if the client has ever been hypnotized or seen anyone hypnotized. Have the client tell you exactly what he or she expects to happen when hypnotized and after being aroused from hypnosis.

Almost everyone has misconceptions about hypnosis. Frequently the client's perception of hypnosis is based upon myths derived from movies, newspaper or magazine stories, television, and stage hypnotism. Most clients believe (when hypnotized) they will experience a dazed unconscious state in which they will be oblivious to everything. In addition, they expect to be unable to recall anything that happened while they were hypnotized. Removing these fears and misconceptions makes for a better client.

If there are misconceptions, explain that being hypnotized is nothing like what the client believes. That hypnosis is a safe, pleasant, experience, and that every suggestion will be for their benefit. Point out the difference between hypnosis and ordinary sleep. If the client equates hypnosis with sleep, upon termination of the hypnotic state he or she will often say, "I was not hypnotized, I heard everything you said." Therefore, it is important that clients understand they will hear every word you say, and will remember their trance experience when aroused from hypnosis.

After misconceptions are removed--and before proceeding with the first induction--with your preinduction talk motivate the client. This will produce an expectation of positive results.

Testing During Hypnosis

It is vitally important to convince clients that they have been hypnotized. Hypnosis is often an elusive and subtle state, and people who have not previously been hypnotized may not recognize the state when they are in it. If this doubt is not removed it may hinder therapeutic results. The solution is simple: use tests to verify the trance state. This is done through the production of basic hypnotic phenomena before terminating the first induction.

These tests (eye and arm catalepsy) bring to the client's conscious mind an awareness of the presence of hypnosis.

Fear of Not Being Hypnotized

Before the first induction clients often express concern that they will not succeed in being hypnotized because they cannot control their thoughts. To counteract this false impression tell the client that being hypnotized involves no control of any kind, and not to try too hard, but to be relaxed. (Trying too hard to be hypnotized will block the trance state as much as strong resistance.)

The transition from waking to hypnosis should be gradual and pleasant. The client should be made comfortable, usually seated in a recliner (or chair) with a head support. Do not allow the hands to touch or the legs to be crossed. (If the legs are crossed the prolonged immobility, combined with deep relaxation of the muscles may cause a limb to go to sleep.)

There should be no direct light in the client's eyes. Extremes of temperature should be avoided, as well as a draft from open windows, fans, or air conditioners.

If at all possible, an induction should occur in a quiet room where there will be no intrusions, loud noises, or other distractions. While quiet during the induction process is helpful, when noises and sounds that cannot be eliminated are present, utilize any extraneous noise by suggesting, "The noise (identify the specific sound) in the background will allow you to let go and it will lull you into an increasingly deeper and deeper state of relaxation."

If you are willing to put in the time and energy, you can achieve a superior level of skill and excellence. The secret is a commitment to practice. The more you do anything, the better you get at it. If you want to excel, you can never rest on your laurels. To be a successful hypnotherapist you must have practical knowledge of the fundamental principles of hypnosis and a solid foundation in hypnotherapy. Your knowledge of hypnotherapy should be complete. Study, practice, and thoroughly learn hypnotic techniques. Master the principles of suggestion and the art of hypnotherapy. Develop a positive attitude and cogitate a self-image of success. You should have the utmost confidence in your ability to hypnotize. Because of the intensified interpersonal relationship produced by the hypnotic state, both hypnotist and subject enter into rapport. In this state of rapport the subject is exquisitely sensitive to the operator's innermost feelings. Therefore having confidence in your ability to hypnotize will maximize your effectiveness.

One of the most important hindrances to hypnotic induction is the therapist who is lacking self-confidence. Successful induction of hypnosis, as stated before, depends on the rapport or strength of the interpersonal relationship between the client and the therapist. If the client senses that the operator is not self-confident, this will be a hindrance to success.

Always be serious when discussing hypnosis. Prestige and dignity are stepping-stones to success in hypnotherapy.

The degree of success you attain as a hypnotherapist will be in direct ratio to the favorable impression created on your clients. Not only does this apply to your self-confidence and skill as an operator, but also equally important is your general appearance. Dress in good taste, and, above all, be well groomed.

The soul of effective hypnotherapy is style. A warm style invites friendliness; a competent style engraves your name on the client's memory. With a memorable personal style you become a living business card, one that cannot be filed out of sight.

CHAPTER 11
The Conquest Of Stress

Stress is neither good nor bad. The effect of stress is determined on how we view and handle that stress. When handled properly, stress drives athletes to greater heights and artists to greater achievement. Stress can be a stimulant, a spice, and a challenge.

When handled improperly, stress becomes distress. It can cause a host of psychosomatic illnesses such as heart trouble, high blood pressure and peptic ulcers.

All disease has both psychic and physiologic components. Many doctors believe that fully 80% of their patients have emotionally induced disorders.[34] Distress then is exacting a steadily increasing toll of human health and well-being.

The causes of stress fall into three broad categories:

1. Physical: Physical causes of stress are environmental. They include bacteria, viruses, polluted air and water, radiation, noise, extremes of temperature, physical injuries such as cuts, bruises, broken bones, etc. In most cases, your client has the option to avoid many of these if he or she wants to take charge of their life and are willing to expend the energy to do so.

---

[34] Cannon, W.B. The wisdom of the body. NY: W.W. Norton, 1932.

2. Social: Social causes of stress come from everyday living. Some of them are unavoidable and are part of being human, such as the death of a loved one, the loss of a job or a divorce. For a social cause of stress to be harmful, it does not have to be valued as negative. Happy stressful events, such as a marriage, a promotion, winning the lottery, a vacation, or even the birth of a baby can cause psychological and physiological responses that are indistinguishable from responses caused by negative events. The body does not distinguish between negatively loaded events and positively loaded events in its response.

3. Psychological: Emotions are the psychological causes of stress. They include such feelings as worry, anger, hate, love, fear, inferiority, anxiety and frustration.

The Cardinal Signs of Stress

Most stress is self-induced. Whether the perceived danger is real or imaginary, the body reacts basically the same way to all stressful events. The precipitating factor that leads to emotionally induced stress is expectation; the belief—real or imaginary—that something terrible is about to happen. This response to stress is called the "fight or flight" response. It can cause all or some of the following symptoms: an increased heart rate, massive changes in breathing rate, sweaty palms and perspiration, shivering, trembling, surging feelings, tense muscles, changes in how things are perceived (for example, things may be perceived as happening more slowly than they really are), inability to concentrate, stomach feels queasy, the mouth and throat becomes dry and parched.

All of these reactions to stress are there as protective defense mechanisms for survival. They evolved over millions of years, preparing our body to run away from danger or to stay and fight. When we are faced with situations that require adjustment of our behavior, an involuntary response increases our blood pressure, heart rate, rate of breathing, blood flow to the muscles, and metabolism, preparing us for conflict or to flee. The problem with these reactions comes when they occur all the time. The body can recover from acute stress only so many times before it leads to ravaging diseases such as high blood pressure and peptic ulcers. Chronic stress can make a person a prime candidate for heart attack, hypertension, peptic ulcers, bronchial asthma, ulcerative colitis, some cases of arthritis, migraine, some skin disorders, or even backache. Such disorders are generally referred to as psychosomatic. People under stress are also prone to accidents on the highway.

In time, the effects of these frustrated physical actions accumulate and join forces to damage the lungs, heart, digestive tract, circulatory system, and joints, as well as to hasten the process of aging. We don't catch migraine or coronary disease or perhaps even cancer; these sicknesses often happen to us because we are vulnerable to our lifestyles.

The stresses of our modern lifestyles are many, ranging from highly competitive jobs to a lack of roots to a decline of the knowledge that we fit securely into the social organization and that there is a contribution for each to make. Stress is certainly not new to humanity, prehistoric man faced stress much as an animal does: with immediate reaction. He either fought his enemy or ran; one way or another, the threat was soon over.

The most stable factor in modern times is change, and change is a great stress on the body. Changing jobs, getting a divorce, moving to a new place, going to jail, the death of a spouse—even getting a speeding ticket—all involve stress. Vandalism and tense neighborhood situations also cause deep stress, understandably. Add to this the fear of growing old and "useless," and one can see that stress lives with modern mortals from the cradle to the grave.

So how do we handle stress so that we can live reasonably comfortable lives? Some turn to the wrong answers—alcohol and drugs that alter the mind's view of the world. Others turn to body-fitness routines that involve diet, jogging, exercise routines, muscle-building, and so on. Undoubtedly, the latter do enable the body to perform better under stress, and exercise is an excellent way to calm the nerves.

One fad of recent years has been the encounter group in which participants learn to unleash their bottled-up emotions. But there are limits to what the encounter group can accomplish for the individual, and there are even some dangers. Psychotic breakdowns under group pressure occasionally occur. And the "grouper" can carry back into the everyday world a misconception of reality; he may have changed, but the world has not.

The encounter group movement seems to have peaked and to be headed for a decline, although some new groups, ordered on the example of Alcoholics Anonymous, have proven value; these are the groups who meet anonymously to work out their problems and improve their lives, such as spouse and child abusers. Some experts feel that the only true value of an encounter group is that participants share the same problem and are understanding of each other's stress.

Meditation: The Relaxation Response

Another widespread practice used to counter stress is meditation, a very ancient practice in the East, but relatively new to the West. Back in the 1960's and 1970's meditation was sold with remarkable success to middle-class Americans. Most of the Oriental cultural and religious trappings were shorn from the meditation movement in this country, making it more appealing to the pragmatic Westerner.

Meditation offers a degree of detachment from the turmoil of daily urban life, and there is often surrender to a group. Often diet is involved with an emphasis on vegetarianism and the Oriental staple, brown rice.

The erasure of ego is designed to produce a monkish calm and to ease many of the stresses of living. A sort of benign godliness is supposed to diffuse into the participant's life and serve as a sort of buffering aura protecting him or her from harmful thoughts. This, of course, is another example of the power of autosuggestion.

The most widespread technique of meditation in this country is called Transcendental Meditation. TM first hit the American scene back in 1967 when the Beatles and Mia Farrow went to the Himalayas to learn the technique from Maharishi Mahesh Yogi, a most colorful monk with a determination to convert followers to a secular method for achieving inner tranquility.

The Maharishi settled on the United States as the most fertile ground for his ideas, and he soon multiplied the number of transcendental meditators into the hundreds and thousands.

The early followers of TM were usually associated with rock groups, but today lectures are delivered before civic clubs and the like. The teachers dress conservatively, and they begin the course with group lectures.

After two or more lectures, the TM initiate receives an hour of individual instruction, in which he learns to sit down and close his eyes for two twenty-minute periods each day. In this autohypnotic state, meditators will themselves into a "restful alertness" by concentrating or repeating silently a word called a "mantra." The mantra is a meaningless but soothing sound that the instructor has secretly told them in an initiation ceremony.

The repetition of the mantra quite easily puts initiates into a state of quietude, and as in self-hypnosis, their hands and feet feel heavy and relaxed, their minds are at ease, and their thoughts float. Done twice a day for twenty minutes at a time, the TM prescription is quite soothing.

Following the initiation, there were follow-up question-and-answer sessions where reactions to TM were discussed, such as an increase in the number of dreams during sleep. There also was group meditation, and after several weeks the instructor gave each participant a personal checkup to monitor the lowering of his stress disorders.

There are other Eastern movements that have gained footholds in the United States: Hare Krishna, which demands surrender of all liberty and worldly goods; Sufism, which combines meditation, oral literature, and whirling-dervish dancing; and Arica, which combines meditation with a strenuous physical exercise routine.

All of these mystical and non-mystical approaches put an emphasis on developing self-awareness of the whole self, as opposed to the rational, ego-centered fragment of self so familiar in our western culture. These movements recognize that the human personality is not just a biological machine for efficient living, but that people have feelings and thoughts outside the rational intellect that need to be expressed and exercised.

We need to dream at night, for instance, and it has been demonstrated that people who do not dream enough become tense and anxious. Daydreams, night dreams, fantasy, and hypnotic trances are all forms of consciousness expansion, which enrich the functions of the human mind and relieve the stresses of our conscious moments.

Mental Control

Biofeedback is a form of self-hypnosis employing the placebo principle, and it is probably one of the most recent methods being developed in the stress field. Much of the research has been underwritten by the Pentagon, which is out to learn anything that can help servicemen withstand the specialized stress of combat or imprisonment.

Biofeedback techniques go back to the 1920's, when Hans Berger of the University of Jena in Germany established the premise that the brain puts out different electrical signals during different activities. The brain gives off its highest frequency signal, *beta,* when it is under pressure to complete tasks. Down the scale is *alpha,* which indicates a contemplative and relaxed mood. *Theta* is next, and is associated with creative thinking. Lowest is *delta,* which comes with sleep.

People have been trained in laboratory sessions through feedback to shift their brains from beta to alpha and even theta. In a quiet room the trainee is fitted with electrodes to the scalp; a ground wire is attached to an ear. An electrical indicator at the feet registers the total alpha wave score achieved during one or two-minute intervals of drilling. Success or lack of it is indicated by a tone that increases when the brain switches to alpha.

Through progressive sessions, the subject learns to find his or her way into alpha, mostly by summoning up recollections of peaceful moments from the past. We are back to the effects of self-hypnosis again; and as the subject practices, the alpha state becomes easier and easier to attain. The advantages to a person under stress are obvious, for the mind can be trained to enter a more relaxed state and thus avoid the complications of stress.

Behind biofeedback is the rather revolutionary medical theory that man can control his autonomic nervous system, the unseen regulator of pulse rate, glandular secretions, oxygen consumption, and the like—all the complex mechanisms that trigger the stress diseases.

The most dramatic demonstration of biofeedback involves the heart. With two or three days of training, subjects can be taught to slow their heartbeats, and even subtle errors in the rhythm can be adjusted. Some hypertense people have been trained to lower their systolic readings also.

One of the most famous examples in medical circles is work done at the Menninger Foundation by Dr. Elmer E. Green and Dr. Joseph Sargent with confirmed migraine sufferers. Again, the power of suggestion is used to control body reactions.

These migraine sufferers are trained to anticipate and avoid the terrible headaches that are caused by dilation of the arteries in the head and scalp. A few weeks of practice teach them to raise their hand temperatures as much as 25° by dilating the hand arteries. This causes the arteries in the head to contract and thus head off the migraine. The subjects are taught to will the hands warmer simply by recall—thinking of an open wood fire, lying in the sun, or even putting the hands under a hot-air dryer in a restroom.

Whether alpha waves are produced by biofeedback or by meditation, there is little argument that there is some self-hypnosis involved. Many experts also believe that acupuncture, like biofeedback, is merely another form of suggestion employing the placebo principle.

Even the newest techniques for battling stress may not be really "new." *Centering down,* a prominent term of awareness groups, is an old Quaker expression that meant the inward contemplation of the whole group at once. Even Navajo medicine men's rituals, chants, and dances bring the inward peace that can effect healing. The chants and rituals of all religions around the world bring the same qualities of the mind and the body to the fore to successfully battle their old enemy stress.

CHAPTER 12
Suggestibility Tests

How can you tell in advance who can be hypnotized? Why is it that some subjects can be readily hypnotized by one hypnotist and are completely unresponsive with another? Is it possible to predict hypnotizability?

Prediction of susceptibility to hypnosis through personality factors or on the basis of physical appearance is not possible. (However, a positive correlation between rapport and susceptibility to hypnosis has been established; the better the subject-hypnotist rapport, the higher the hypnotizability.) The only way to determine individual hypnotic susceptibility, with any degree of certainty, is to actually try to induce hypnosis. Preliminary waking hypnosis tests, however, have been found to furnish a satisfactory way to evaluate individual suggestibility.

These preliminary tests are also of important psychological value in preparing the client for hypnosis. A skillful hypnotist can enhance suggestibility through the strategy of psychological conditioning. By experiencing the effects of suggestibility tests — and most people are responsive to these tests — the subject believes the responses are produced by the hypnotist. In reality, it is the subject's expectant attitude that initiates the response. When one suggested act after another is carried out, suggestibility is further enhanced by a favorable mental attitude. Thus the tests compound conviction by initiating a mindset of positive expectancy.

In addition to their importance as a psychological conditioning tool, the tests also provide the hypnotherapist with a means of gauging the client's suggestibility.

Relaxation Test

This simple experiment is an excellent test to use as a prelude to a first induction. It was introduced at the turn of the twentieth century by one of the pioneers of hypnotism, Dr. X. La Motte Sage, formerly President of the New York Institute of Science.

In an introductory manual, published in 1899, Professor Sage offered the aspiring hypnotist tips and advice for the study of hypnotism. That advice is just as relevant today as it was over a century ago. Before we look at the Relaxation Test, I would like to share with you selected examples of Dr. Sage's advice for the successful practice of hypnotism:

- Be sure that you thoroughly understand just what to do before attempting to hypnotize anyone.

- If you stop and hesitate and wonder what to do next, you will never influence anybody. Go about your work in a business-like way and show people by your actions that you thoroughly understand what you are doing.

- You must not expect to hypnotize everybody you try. Remember all successful operators and noted hypnotists came to be such only by long practical experience.

- If you do not succeed with the first five or ten that you try, do not give up, but continue trying. Try twenty or thirty different persons, or more if necessary, and just as sure as the sunshines you will find someone whom you can hypnotize. You cannot fail if you persevere. After you hypnotize one or two, it will be easy, and soon you can affect the majority of those whom you try; and with still more practice will be able readily to hypnotize 70 to 90 percent.

- Determine to succeed and you will succeed. If you undertake this study in a half-hearted way, if you go about it in a perfunctory sort of manner, it were better a thousand times over that you never undertook it. The greater your deficiencies in personal magnetism the more difficult will it be for you to master these sciences, and the more evident your need of further knowledge of this mysterious power. Bear in mind that perseverance is the price of success; knowledge does not come unsought.

- You must be sure to give all your suggestions in a very positive tone. A feeble, whining way of speaking never accomplishes anything. Be a person of some force of character. Speak positively and directly to your client, and influence is certain. Do not give up until you have tried at least fifty persons between the ages of 15 and 30. We ask you to do this because we know positively that after you hypnotize one, the work will be very easy and you can influence a large percentage. There is a certain knack required, and while nearly all persons get this knack very readily from proper instruction and can soon hypnotize, still there is occasionally a person who has to try over and over before he acquires just the proper method of procedure. Many, however, who find the work a little difficult at first, make the finest hypnotists.

- To be successful in influencing people one must have confidence and perseverance. A weak, vacillating disposition never accomplishes anything. People will influence you or you will influence them; it is for you to decide whether you will direct or be directed, whether you will be a master or a servant. Self-esteem, stubbornness, and an arrogant, haughty disposition are not the necessary elements with which to influence people.

The Relaxation Test

Try this simple test on a friend. Get in conversation regarding the difficulty of experiencing physical relaxation, of relaxing the muscles. Remark that the majority of people keep their muscles and nerves in a state of tension all the time, and they never experience absolute rest. The person who is able to sit down in a chair and relax completely, will have more rest in ten minutes than someone who cannot will have in half an hour or an hour. In normal sleep the muscles are completely relaxed, and it is apparent that one who can most nearly approach this condition in the waking state will secure the most rest. Many people are tired all the time, simply because they keep their muscles in a state of tension. Impress these points upon your friend, and after talking for a few minutes, remark that it is more difficult to relax one's muscles than people ordinarily suppose. To demonstrate this, propose the relaxation test of letting the hand rest upon the finger. If you place a book on your hand and hold it out at arm's length and then remove your hand quickly the book will fall to the floor, hence, it is obvious that if a person places their left hand upon one of the fingers of the right hand, using the finger as a means of support, that the left hand will fall whenever the support is removed. This admits of no argument. If the hand does not fall it is because the full weight of the left hand did not rest upon the extended right finger.

The Relaxation Test

This procedure can be used as an individual test or a group experiment.

Say to the subject, "Few people know how to relax sufficiently. When a doctor examines your throat he frequently has to take an instrument to push your tongue down. This is because you do not relax the muscles of your tongue. Most people do not obtain the rest that they should when they sit down, for the reason that they are unable to relax their muscles. They keep them in a state of tension and are consequently tired all the time. A person, who can sit down and completely relax the muscles, can obtain more absolute rest in a short period of time than a person who cannot relax their muscles. Anyone can learn to relax."

Tell the subject to raise the left arm up at a right angle out in front of the chest, then extend the index finger of the right hand and place it directly under the palm of the left hand. Explain that the full weight of the hand is to rest upon the finger, using the finger as a means of support only. After you have given these preliminary instructions, ask the client if the full weight of the hand is resting upon the finger. If the client says yes, then say, "When I count three I wish you to remove your finger very quickly. Ready . . . one . . . two . . . three." As you say "three," if the subject is truly relaxed, the left hand will fall into the lap as the finger is removed. If the hand should not fall the subject has not complied with your instructions, that is, have not relaxed the muscles. In a group experiment you would probably find that a number of the hands remain up.

If the hand does not fall when you count three, but remains up, you should explain to the client that relaxation was not achieved and repeat the test. Upon a second trail the client will invariably comply with your directions. The left hand must not be pushed or forced downward into the lap, but all the muscles in the left arm and hand should be completely relaxed and the hand and arm should fall as a dead, inert body--the same as a book would fall.

Making A Point

If you wish to make a strong point about how most people do not know how to relax there is a "psychological trick" that you can employ while giving your instructions for the relaxation test. To illustrate to the individual subject (or to the group) exactly what you want them to do, hold your left index finger erect and place the right hand on top of it. When you count to three and remove the left finger *do not let the right hand drop.* Hold it in place for a few seconds and then as you continue talking bring it down and into usage as you speak. This devious little maneuver will make an impression on a large percentage of the group and when you actually do the test with them they will keep the right hand up after removing the left hand and erect finger . . . just as they saw you demonstrate.

Eye-Locking Test

This unprecedented conditioning test is based upon a little known physical principle. As a consequence of this physical principle, suggestion plays a secondary role and the experiment cannot be used to assess hypnotic susceptibility. Its true significance is psychological. A successful result will instill conviction in your client and create a mindset of positive expectancy. The eye-locking test may be used on an individual subject or as a group experiment. In either case the suggestions would be the same.

In this experiment the client should be seated, with feet placed flat on the floor and hands resting on the thighs. Speaking clearly, and in a confident manner, say:

It is important that you follow my instructions completely. Listen carefully and concentrate on my voice. Please close your eyes. Take a good long deep breath. Now, with your eyelids closed, roll your eyeballs upwardly. Now fix your gaze, just as if you were looking at an imaginary spot in your brain. Now continue looking upward, as you listen to my voice. With your eyeballs rolled upward, you now notice that your eyelids are beginning to stick tightly together. (Use vocal inflection and convey a sensation of tightness with your voice.) *Your eyes are stuck shut. They are stuck tight . . . glued shut. Keep your eyeballs rolled upward, and, at the same time, you may try to open your eyes; but you will find them locking tighter and tighter together. Try to open your eyes, but you will find them locking tighter and tighter together. Indeed, the harder you try, the tighter they stick. TRY AS YOU WILL, BUT YOU WILL FIND THEM LOCKING TIGHTER AND TIGHTER TOGETHER!* (Allow a few moments for the client to make an effort to open his or her eyes.) Continue: *All right . . . stop trying. Relax. Relax your eyelids and your eyes completely. Now you can open your eyes.*

If your suggestions were followed precisely, the client would have found it impossible to open his or her eyes at your challenge. When the eyeballs are rolled upward with the lids closed the levator palpebrae superioris (the tiny muscles that raise the eyelids) interrupt the reflex arc with their nerve supply (the oculomotor nerve) and, as long as the eyes remain rolled upwardly, it becomes physically impossible to open the eyes.

Never inform the client of this physical phenomenon. Instead, let the client believe that it was the power of suggestion that did the trick. Always keep in mind that hypnosis is a conviction phenomenon. A successful response to this test will create positive expectancy and begin the sensory spiral of belief leading to conviction.

The effects of the following suggestibility tests are the result of a subtle mind-body phenomenon called ideomotor action. The theory of ideomotor action was an early attempt to explain voluntary action. Ideomotor responses are evoked unconsciously by ideas or images in the mind that generate impulses in the nervous system. William James[35] stated the principle thus: "Every representation [i.e., idea] of a movement awakens in some degree the actual movement which is its object; and awakens it in a maximum degree whenever it is not kept from doing so by an antagonistic representation present simultaneously to the mind."

Ideomotor activity is the involuntary and instantaneous response of muscles to thought, feelings, and ideas. The client does not realize that the responses elicited by the suggestibility tests are ideomotor activity, and thus the result of his or her own thoughts. Ideomotor responses are evoked unconsciously by ideas or images in the mind that generate impulses in the nervous system.

To cite some everyday examples of ideomotor action: You are a passenger in a car, when suddenly the car in front of you swerves and makes a sudden stop. You instantly move your foot to apply the "brakes." At a sports event you make involuntary movements in response to the athletes' motions. For example leaning in the direction of the ball at a tennis match . . . or while watching a boxing match you wince when you hear the thud of the boxer's glove on the jaw. You become so

---

[35] James, W. Principles of Psychology. NY: Henry Holt & Co., 1890.

identified with the sporting event that you vividly imagine you are doing what the athlete is doing, and your absorption turns your mental image into muscular reality.

Because ideomotor activity is such an important aspect of hypnosis, I want to deal with it in a more specific manner. To gain insight into how it works, we will consider two alleged psychic phenomena: The Ouija Board and contact "mind reading."

A number of years ago the Ouija Board was a popular fad. The Ouija Board is a board bearing the alphabet and various other symbols, consisting of a planchette (a small three-cornered device) having as one of its supports a pencil that is supposed to write out a message or point to letters or words, as it moves with the fingers resting lightly on it. This device was used in spiritualistic séances, supposedly to convey and record messages from spirits. The force behind the Ouija Board was not a manifestation of supernatural power; the mysterious messages were created subconsciously through ideomotor activity.

The pseudo-psychic Kreskin includes a demonstration of "mind reading" in his theatrical presentation of alleged psychic powers. In an article entitled *The Power Behind Suggestion* (Journal of Hypnotism, December, 1987) Ormond McGill wrote:

> The experiment of "contact mind reading" is another excellent example of ideomotor action. In such feats, the performer is led from the room, and in his absence a spectator volunteers to hide an object. On being recalled, the mind reader grasps the volunteer by the hand, and at once leads him or her unerringly to the hidden object.

Wonderful? Yes, indeed, but it is not mind reading! Rather, all such demonstrations are based on this incipient obedience of muscular contraction to ideas, even when the deliberate intention is that no contraction shall occur.

William James suggested that voluntary behavior is a function of thinking about the behavior, with the thought being "father to the act."

Bugelski and Graziano[36] made these cogent remarks in relation to James' theory.

> If one thinks of doing something, he will do it unless he thinks of doing the opposite or of doing something else. Thus, if you think of raising your hand, your arm will begin to move upwards. James did not explain how or why this might come about, but later psychologists suggested that as we grow up and develop, we are always moving our musculature about and that the actions involved generate stimuli in the muscles, tendons, and joints (feedback stimuli). These feedback stimuli always accompany movement, and when a movement is initiated by some external stimulus, the feedback stimuli will soon follow and will tend to occur earlier and earlier in any movement sequence. Eventually, the feedback stimuli will occur before the movement itself, to some degree, and will become conditioned to the movement. Thus, if the feedback stimuli can be associated (conditioned) to any

---

[36]Bugelski, B., & Graziano, A. The Handbook of Practical Psychology, NJ: Prentice-Hall, Inc., 1980

other stimuli — for example, suggestions — they can be aroused and can excite the movement itself.

A beautiful description of ideomotor activities is found in the book *Hypnosis and Behavior Modification: Imagery Conditioning*[37] by Kroger and Fezler:

> Ideomotor activity also facilitates suggestibility. It refers to the involuntary capacity of muscles to respond to external stimuli. The induction technique, in part, depends on the patient's being unaware that he has made such physical responses to suggestion. Little does he realize they are a function of his own thoughts in response to external stimulation. However, he thinks he is making the responses. This further heightens his belief and expectations of the success of future suggestions
>
> Hence, the hypersuggestibility leading to the production of a great many hypnotic phenomena is brought about by the resultant of two forces, ideosensory and ideomotor activities. When ideosensory and ideomotor activities are paired, they bypass criticalness and are interpreted as reality. The resultant synergistic effect in part leads to hypnosis.

Ideomotor action is exemplified in our next suggestibility test.

---

[37] Kroger, W. & Fezler, W. Hypnosis & Behavior Modification: Imagery Conditioning. PA: J. B. Lippincott Co., 1976.

Chevreul Pendulum

As a further aid in getting the client into the proper frame of mind and to increase expectancy, ideomotor action may be demonstrated by means of Chevreul pendulum (named after a long-lived French chemist, 1786-1889). The pendulum is easily constructed by tying a thread about 10 inches long to some light object such as a finger ring, earring, iron washer, or anything light. On a sheet of paper draw a 10-inch circle, now inside the circle draw a cross making four radii at right angles to each other. Mark the top of the vertical line "A" and the bottom "B", the left of the horizontal line "C" and the right "D".

> Seat the person to be tested at a table with the diagram in front of the client. The thread is held between the client's thumb and index finger. The elbow rests on the table, so the pendulum dangles at the center of the circle about one-half inch or so above the surface. The client is now told to imagine the pendulum swinging up and down the full length of the line A-B. Tell the client not to swing the pendulum voluntarily, but just to hold it motionless. With the great majority of subjects the pendulum will swing in the imagined direction. Continue: *Look at the pendulum and imagine that the pendulum is moving — backward, forward, backward, forward, A-B, A-B, A-B. Persistently and continuously repeat the words to yourself and imagine the direction of the movement of the pendulum.* If the client is suggestible the pendulum will sway up and down the line A-B, although a conscious effort is made to hold the pendulum motion-less.

After the pendulum is moving vigorously, tell the client to change thoughts and to focus now on line C-D. To think of the pendulum moving back and forth, from left to right, back and forth, the full length of the line C-D. Tell the client that the pendulum will soon begin to swing back and forth, from left to right. Point to line C-D, moving your finger in rhythm with the client's eye movement, as you suggest its movement back and forth, from left to right.

Next tell the client to let their eyes travel completely around the circle in either a clockwise or counter-clockwise circle. *Soon the pendulum will be moving around and around in a circle, as your eyes travel around the circle the pendulum moves faster and faster, faster and faster, and now the arc of the circle is growing wider and wider as it swings around and around, around and around.*

Nearly everybody responds positively, and the pendulum will instantly begin to swing in direct response to the suggested movement. Leslie LeCron,[38] a leading authority on hypnotherapy, said: "In my experience and that of many other psychotherapists and physicians who have learned how to use this ideomotor technique, only with perhaps three or four people out of one hundred will the pendulum fail to move." Chevreul's pendulum demonstrates that all thoughts tend to express themselves in action.

---

[38]LeCron, L. The complete Guide to Hypnosis. NY: Barnes & Nobel Books, 1973.

Arms Rising And Falling Test

The Arms Rising and Falling Test is an effective indicator of hypnotic susceptibility. This impressive preliminary test of suggestibility can be used individually or with groups.

> Request your subject to stand erect, with feet placed closely together. If you are conducting a group experiment, be sure the subjects have sufficient space so they do not touch each other. Tell the subject:

> *Extend your arms straight to the front, at shoulder level, with the palms facing inwardly. Now, turn your left arm so that the palm is facing the ceiling and extend your right thumb so that it points at the ceiling.*

> Imagery and imagination are important ingredients in this test. To enhance the effect be graphic and descriptive. Through vocal inflection *paint a verbal picture*, and play upon the subject's imagination. When you say the left arm is growing heavy, project a feeling of *heaviness* in your voice. Conversely, when you say the right arm is growing light, project a feeling of *lightness* in your voice. Voice includes not only the pitch of your voice but also volume, inflection, and pace. Vary the volume level, place emphasis on certain words and phrases, and speak at a varying pace.

> Continue: *Close your eyes and keep them closed until I tell you to open them. Now activate your imagination and imagine as clearly as you can everything I tell you. Now fix your attention on your left arm . . . concentrate on your left arm. With your eyes closed, you can see your left arm clearly*

in your mind's eye. As you focus your attention on your left arm, you notice that it is beginning to grow heavy, h-e-a-v-y, v-e-r-y h-e-a-v-y. Your left arm is growing h-e-a-v-i-e-r and h-e-a-v-i-e-r. Visualize a large book on your upturned left palm -- let us say a red dictionary, pulling it d-o-w-n, d-o-w-n. Picture your left arm and the book as being so heavy that you cannot hold it up. In your mind's eye see your left arm falling, lower and lower, going down, down, down. Your left arm is so heavy, that it is going down, down, down. As your left arm continues going d-o-w-n I now want you to shift your attention to your right arm.

Your right arm is beginning to grow light, so very light that it feels as if it were devoid of weight. You can see your right arm in your mind's eye. As it grows lighter and l-i-g-h-t-e-r, it will commence to rise. It is so very light that it feels as if a balloon filled with helium were fastened to your right thumb, pulling your arm u-p, u-p. It is growing lighter and lighter, and as it grows lighter and lighter the balloon floats up, rising higher and higher. Your right arm is growing lighter and lighter and rising higher and higher. Your right arm is rising, h-i-g-h-e-r, h-i-g-h-e-r, going u-p, u-p, higher and higher. Now open your eyes and examine the position of your arms.

When working with a group, make a careful comparison of the various responses. This will enable you to select the best subject for your next experiment.

Postural Sway Test

The Postural Sway Test (sometimes called the Backward and Forward Falling Test) provides a more substantive exploration of individual hypnotic susceptibility. Unlike the previous procedures, this is an individual test.

> Tell the subject: *Please stand erect with your feet closely together, hold your head up and let your hands relax at your side. Now close your eyes and relax.* (If the subject is wearing high heels, have her remove her shoes.) To find out if the subject is relaxed, put your hands on the shoulders and pull back slightly. If the body comes back easily, the subject is complying with your directions. If, however, the limbs are stiff and there is resistance, the subject is not following your instructions.
>
> **IMPORTANT: Stand behind the subject and assume a stance that will provide you with a balanced and solid foundation.**
>
> Make it clear that the influence is not to be resisted, and that the subject is to "let go" when the inclination comes to fall backward. Emphasize that you will be there to catch the subject.
>
> Begin your suggestions:
>
> Please keep your eyes closed so that you can more easily concentrate on everything I say. Now activate your imagination and imagine, while standing in this posture . . . with your feet closely together and your arms hanging limply at your sides . . . that you are beginning to lose your sense of balance. Your balance is growing

very precarious and you are beginning to sway to and fro, to and fro.

Continue in that vein until the subject actually begins swaying. Then place your hands lightly on the subject's upper arms (deltoid muscles) and move your hands in a small circular pattern. While maintaining light contact, glide your cupped hands from the shoulder to the wrist. By discerning the weight of the body on the heel of your hands you will be able to detect the subject's response to your suggestions. (This knowledge will aid you in your pacing of the procedure.) Your movements should be smooth and in tempo with your suggestions. Continue:

In a moment . . . when I release you . . . you will experience an uncontrollable impulse to fall back into my arms. I will catch you. The impulse is growing stronger and stronger . . . you are beginning to fall. I'm right here to catch you. Just let yourself go. You are coming back . . . back . . . falling . . . falling.

At this point break physical contact and be prepared to catch the subject. Now speak up and suggest in a more authoritarian tone of voice: Just let yourself go . . . all the way back!

If there was no response—which is highly unlikely—place your hands firmly on the subject's shoulders and rock back and forth. You will more often than not find that the body is tense and that there is resistance. Point this out, explain the necessity for complete cooperation and repeat the test.

When the subject falls back, you may wish to proceed with the second phase of the test.

Turn the subject around to face you. Position your hands on either side of the head, being careful not to touch the subject. Adjust your stance so that the subject will be looking down into your eyes. If shorter than you, this is accomplished by placing your right leg at his or her side and moving your left leg back until your stance has been adjusted so that your eye level is just beneath the subject's eye level. Your proximity is close. Being careful not to touch the subject's face, extend your fingers fully; place your fingertips near the temples, and the tips of your thumbs near your eye level. This bridge with the hands will create the illusion of being drawn forward. In this position, you are now ready to proceed. Say:

Do not close your eyes. Keep your eyes open and look directly into my eyes. Do not blink. Concentrate on my suggestions. Now use your imagination and imagine that my eyes are drawing you toward me.

That's it . . . activate your imagination. Imagine that my eyes are two powerful magnets pulling you toward me. At this point, bend your knees and slowly pull your body back, then continue: *As you gaze deeply into my eyes, you feel yourself being drawn toward me. You are beginning to topple forward . . . forward . . . forward. Just let yourself go. I will catch you. That's it. You're falling . . . falling . . . falling. Let yourself go. All the way forward. I will catch you.*

Continue along these lines until your subject topples forward. When the fall forward reaches a point of momentum, quickly bring your hands down to the subject's shoulders and check the fall.

Be sure to have a good solid stance and be prepared to catch your subject.

NOTE: In the forward falling test, the subject is told to gaze into your eyes, but you do not return the gaze. Instead of looking directly into the subject's eyes, focus your gaze on the bridge of the nose. This will give the impression of a direct gaze without actually doing it. The reason you avoid direct eye contact is because the physical strain is lessened, and you will be able to maintain a steady gaze longer without blinking.

Hand Clasp Test

This excellent conditioning test can be used as a group experiment, but is more effective as an individual test. Do not attempt the Hand Clasp Test until you have been successful with the preceding tests.

> For best results use an authoritative approach. Taking care, however, not to be too forceful or overbearing, speak in a tone of voice that commands compliance and attention. Study this technique carefully, so you can execute it convincingly.

> Emphasize that this test requires the subject's undivided attention. Ask the subject to stand erect with feet close together. Tell the subject to hold their upper arms

firmly to the side, and raise the arms at the elbow and interlace the fingers in front of the stomach.

The following verbalization is used:

Fix your gaze on mine and look deeply into my eyes . . . do not blink. Concentrate intently on my voice and on my suggestions. Activate your imagination . . . and imagine that your hands are now being placed between the jaws of a massive steel vise. The vice is beginning to tighten and draw your hands together . . . tighter . . . tighter . . . and it is now squeezing your hands together tightly. (Use appropriate intonation to convey a feeling of tightness.)

At this point, grasp the subject's hands within yours and firmly, but gently, squeeze the hands to accentuate your suggestions. Continue:

I now want you to squeeze your hands together more tightly . . . tighter . . . tighter still. (With the inflection of your voice convey a feeling of tightness.)

Maintain a steady gaze. While there will be a natural inclination to look down at the hands, refrain from doing so as it would interfere with the subject's concentration. Continue:

Your hands are now being squeezed together so tightly that they are becoming fused together. They are beginning to stick together. They are squeezed together so tightly that you cannot differentiate your left fingers from your right. Your hands are locking together inseparably. Your hands are now glued tightly together. Tighter! . . . Tighter still!

While maintaining a steady gaze, slowly step back. This will increase your range of vision, enabling you to see the subject's hands without breaking eye contact. Continue:

Your hands are locked together so tightly that you cannot take your hands apart. You may try . . . but the harder you try . . . the faster they stick. Try as you will . . . you cannot take your hands apart!

Permit the subject to make an effort to release the hands. When you are satisfied that the subject could not pull the hands apart, remove the suggestion. Continue:

All right, stop trying. Stop trying to pull your hands apart. Relax your hands. When I count to three, you will be able to pull your hands apart. Ready . . . one . . . two . . . THREE! Now you may pull your hands apart.

When you first make the challenge, if the hands do come apart do not act surprised or disappointed. When the hands are intertwined in this way there will be some difficulty in separating the hands. (When the fingers are thus interlocked, the articulations of the knuckle act as a locking device, making it difficult to release the hands while clasped together.) So, if your subject's hands do come apart after your challenge, do not indicate that the test was not a complete success. Simply comment: *See how difficult it was for you to take your hands apart.* Unless the subject is familiar with this procedure (which is highly unlikely) he or she will accept the test as being a success. This ruse will allow you to save face, and it also has a good psychological affect on the subject.

CHAPTER 13
Arousing From Hypnosis

Textbooks on hypnosis, which purport to teach one "how to hypnotize," place a great deal of emphasis on induction procedures but devote very little space to the technique of arousing the subject from hypnosis. This lack of emphasis is unfortunate, as the procedure for terminating the hypnotic state is of vital importance and will enhance the effectiveness of the hypnotherapeutic session if properly administered.

Re-alerting the subject is a straightforward process. Subjects are brought out of hypnosis in the same manner they were hypnotized—through verbal suggestion. A gradual re-alerting procedure is best. If a deeply hypnotized person is brought out of hypnosis too suddenly, the subject may react with a headache or other side effects brought about through the abrupt psychic change. To avoid adverse reactions intersperse your suggestions for arousal with positive suggestions of well-being. If future sessions are scheduled, implant posthypnotic suggestions to facilitate a deeper level of hypnosis when the subject is hypnotized again. The following verbalization includes posthypnotic suggestions for rehypnotization.

In a few moments, but not just yet, you'll open your eyes. You have had a good rest and will come up feeling refreshed and completely relaxed. You enjoyed being hypnotized and found this hypnotic experience to be pleasant and refreshing. You look forward to being hypnotized again in the future. (This posthypnotic suggestion will help to ensure that your clients will keep their next appointment.) Indeed . . . each and every time you are hypnotized, you will achieve a deeper level of hypnosis . . . even deeper than now. . . . That's right. . . . Each and every time you are hypnotized, you will go deeper and deeper . . . more quickly and more easily. All right, ready now . . . at the count of five you will open your eyes, feeling rejuvenated, refreshed, and completely relaxed. ONE. . . . You can feel the energy flowing back into your body. . . . TWO. . . . Your mind and your body feels so wonderfully relaxed, refreshed and alert. . . . THREE. . . . You feel yourself coming up more and more. . . . FOUR. . . . Your mind is perfectly clear and alert . . . and FIVE . . . SLOWLY OPEN YOUR EYES FEELING WONDERFULLY REFRESHED . . . ALERT . . . AND . . . RELAXED!

As was pointed out in Chapter 4, misconceptions about hypnosis flourish. Some people mistakenly believe that if they allow themselves to be hypnotized, the hypnotist may not be able to bring them out of hypnosis. Another fear some people have is if something should happen to the hypnotist while they are hypnotized, they would remain in hypnosis indefinitely. People who harbor these fears regard hypnosis as a comatose state. To allay this fear, in the pre-induction talk explain that there is absolutely no danger of this ever happening. In reality there is no authentic case of a person failing to come out of hypnosis. Indeed, if something were to happen—for example, if the hypnotist had a heart attack—after the passage of a short period of time, the hypnotic state would terminate or drift into a natural sleep from which the subject would awaken of his or her own accord. This would be true regardless of how deeply hypnotized the subject may be.

While extremely uncommon, suggestions to terminate the hypnotic state may go unheeded. Occasionally a subject will lapse into a natural sleep, in which case the hypnotist will have lost rapport and communication with the subject. While it is rare, another possibility is that the subject enjoys the pleasantness of the experience so much that he or she wants it to continue and purposely ignores the hypnotist's suggestions to come out of hypnosis. If your subject does not respond to your suggestions of arousal, do not become panicky. There is no cause for alarm. In the memorable words of Franklin D. Roosevelt, "You have nothing to fear but fear itself." Remain calm and in an authoritative tone of voice repeat the instructions for arousal. Difficulty in terminating hypnosis is so rare, it is doubtful that you will ever encounter it. In the unlikely event that it should occur, just remember to stay calm and keep your presence of mind.

CHAPTER 14
How To Hypnotize Your Client

This chapter will introduce practical techniques for hypnotizing and testing your client. The old adage "nothing is new under the sun," is a truism. The induction techniques presented in this book emerged from over half a century of experience as a student of hypnotism and as a professional hypnotist. Therefore, the induction procedures in this chapter are not untried theories. You can put them into use as soon as they are understood.

Before methods of induction are examined, we will take note of important preliminary steps that facilitate the induction process.

First, go back to Chapter 6 and have another look at the difference between hypnosis and sleep.

A hypnotized person never loses touch with their surroundings and—even in the deepest levels of hypnosis—may be aware of extraneous noises and sounds. Clients, who believe that hypnosis is a state similar to sleep, will assume they were not hypnotized since they were able to hear everything that was said. This uncertainty or self-doubt can nullify the beneficial effects of your suggestions. *If the client believes that your suggestions are effective, there is greater probability that the desired changes will occur.* Therefore it is crucial that the client understand that hypnosis and normal sleep are totally different, and that in hypnosis he or she will be awake and alert and not unconscious or asleep.

Before we begin our study of hypnotic induction, we will first take a look at:

- The approach or style of induction.
- Types of suggestion.
- Qualities of the voice.
- The objective signs of hypnosis.

Permissive Versus Authoritarian Approach

While there are many methods for inducing hypnosis, the hypnotist's approach to induction generally falls into one of two categories; namely, a *paternal* (authoritarian) or *maternal* (permissive) approach.

As the name implies the *paternal approach* is characteristic of a father and is strongly authoritarian. Suggestions are given emphatically as commands and the hypnotist assumes an authoritarian and omnipotent role. Conversely, the *maternal approach* is more permissive and symbolic of a mother. With the permissive approach to induction, suggestions are given in a smooth, tranquil flow without a note of authority or command.

The stage hypnotist, to whom speed is of the essence, frequently uses the domineering paternal approach. While the hypnotherapist, who must win the trust and respect of the client, will most often use the permissive maternal approach.

Your approach will depend on the particular induction technique that you choose to use. Nearly all clients react negatively to a method that attempts to browbeat them, as it were, into the hypnotic state. Therefore, it is generally advisable to use permissive induction procedures.

Types Of Suggestions

The two general categories of hypnotic suggestion are:

1. *Heterosuggestion,* a suggestion given by the hypnotist to the subject.

2. *Autosuggestion,* a suggestion given to oneself.

From a practical point of view we need only consider the four types of suggestion as described by Kroger and Fezler[39]:

1. *Verbal suggestion,* which includes words and refers to communication by any type of sound.

2. *Nonverbal suggestion* applies to body language, facial expressions, posture, eye contact, and gestures.

3. *Intraverbal suggestion* relates to the intonation of words; vocal inflections greatly influence suggestibility.

4. *Extraverbal suggestion,* the implications of words and gestures that facilitate acceptance of ideas.

Thus, the choice of words, mannerisms, inflections of the voice, as well as the implied meaning of the phrases used, all

---

[39]Kroger, W.S. & Fezler, W.D. Hypnosis and Behavior Modification: Imagery Conditioning. Philadelphia: J. B. Lippincott Co., 1976.

play an important role in the hypnotic process. These are potent factors in influencing suggestibility.

It should be noted that the terms "autosuggestion" and "autohypnosis" are often incorrectly used as synonyms. If referring to a self-induced trance or its phenomena, the term "autohypnosis" or "self-hypnosis" is correct. When referring to self-suggestion, the term "autosuggestion" would be the proper usage.

Qualities Of The Hypnotic Voice

The spoken word is the primary conveyance of hypnotic communication. Your effectiveness as a hypnotist will be greatly enhanced through the cultivation of good language skills. A quiet, audible, sincere tone of voice will gain the trust of the client. Speak clearly and use proper grammar. Develop a pleasing voice. The lower tones are more melodious and resonant. Because of its tiresome sameness, the monotone is ideal for induction. After the induction phase—when the client has achieved hypnosis—modulate your voice so that it conveys positive conviction and assurance.

The heart of effective induction is style. A competent style commands agreement and rapport. A polished personal style will imbue your suggestions with the power of conviction.

The beginner often makes the mistake of speaking too rapidly. Use a slow, d-r-e-a-r-y, t-i-r-e-s-o-m-e voice. To assure assimilation of your suggestions be repetitive, repeating your suggestions over and over again. There is a definite knack in giving suggestion to the subject. After you have gained experience and self-confidence, you will acquire this important skill.

A Note On Using The Induction Scripts

The effective hypnotist has an expressive well-modulated voice. Ideally the hypnotist's voice should be distinct, intelligible, and easy to understand. Investing a little time to develop a powerful controlled, and resonant voice will pay you large dividends for the rest of your career. Before using any of the procedures outlined in this book, the author urges you to practice by reading the induction scripts aloud. If you are reluctant to take the time to practice, consider this story[40]: A young musician approached an old master who had just completed the most beautiful rendition of a complex collection of great compositions he had ever head.

> "Sir," the young man said admiringly, "It must be great to have all the practicing behind you and be able to simply sit down and play like that."
>
> "Oh!" the old master replied, "I still practice eight hours every day."
>
> "But, why? I mean . . . you are so good!" exclaimed the young musician.
>
> "I wish to become superb!" answered the old master.

---

[40]Qubein, N.R. Story adapted from Communicate like a pro. NJ: Prentice-Hall, Inc., 1983.

We have found that many hypnotherapists are quite satisfied to become "good." Few, very few, are willing to invest the countless hours of practicing that are required to become "superb."

Mastery of any skill comes only after hours of refinement through practice, practice, and more practice.

Read the scripts in a soothing, confident tone of voice, using a kind of lullaby pattern. Speak slowly and distinctly, elongating the vowel sounds slightly. In the scripts the cue, ". . ." means to pause; make these pauses natural not mechanical.

Rapport And Self-Confidence

In order to successfully and effectively hypnotize a client, the hypnotherapist must show confidence. A lack of confidence is instantly recognized by the client, and is a hindrance to the successful performance of hypnotic experiments. Self-confidence must not only be apparent to the client, but must be actually experienced by the hypnotherapist.

As we saw in Chapter 10, hypnosis initiates the evolution of a relaxed and trusting relationship called *rapport*. (You will recall that rapport is a harmonious bond that develops between the subject and the hypnotist.) The empathic hypnotherapist is readily recognized, and rapport is enhanced when the client perceives the operator as a competent and caring person. When rapport is established the client *expects* positive results and is motivated to please the hypnotherapist. This positive mindset facilitates the acceptance of suggestions, which are then acted upon without criticism.

To enhance rapport speak assuredly and let every word, action, and expression, denote absolute confidence. If you are confident you will create confidence.

Signs Of Hypnosis

A proficient hypnotherapist carefully observes the client, taking note of any physical cues. Be sensitive to the feedback from the client; watch for signs of physical relaxation, changes in the breathing rate, arm and leg position, etc.

The term *trance*, denoting an altered state of consciousness, is often used as a synonym for hypnosis. The hypnotic trance state is unique as it is influenced by the suggestions made, and the client's expectations of what a hypnotic state is like.

While there is a great deal of variability in response to induction suggestions, certain experiences subjects have are regarded as *signs of hypnosis*.

The signs of hypnosis are divided into two categories: *objective signs*, i.e., subtle indicators the hypnotherapist can observe directly; and *subjective signs* that the client must be asked to describe.

The presence of one or more of the signs is presumptive evidence that the client is hypnotized. The skillful hypnotherapist carefully observes the client and looks for physical cues or signs of hypnosis.

The most common objective signs are:

1. Eyelid fluttering. Eye closure if the induction requires fixation on a target object. Tearing.

2. Physical relaxation. Limpness of the limbs. Blank sober facial expression.

3. Respiration is altered and the client breathes more slowly and deeply.

4. Protracted immobility. Client will remain in an awkward position for great lengths of time.

5. Lack of spontaneity. The client will not initiate any action unless told to do so by the hypnotherapist.

6. Lack of a sense of humor. In general a hypnotized person will neither smile nor laugh even when everyone else present is laughing.

7. Dilation of the pupil.

8. Trance stare. On opening the eyes the client seems to be staring at some point in space. The eyes are glazed and expressionless.

9. Uncontrolled movements of eyeballs. Eyeballs roll back into head; if the eyelids are opened only the sclera or whites of the eye will be seen.

10. Literalness. Hypnotized individuals respond with a literalness or pinpoint specificity to the suggestions of the operator. For example, if told to raise the hand, the hand alone may be raised without moving the arm.

11. Trance logic. The hypnotized person has a tolerance for incongruities, and will rationalize any occurrence they experience no matter how improbable or absurd it may be.

12. Lip pallor. This is a sign of somnambulism (deep hypnosis) and has been observed in several thousand subjects. Crasilneck and Hall report, "This is a circumoral area of pallor about the lips for a space of approximately 1 centimeter just beyond the mucocutaneous margin. If present, this seems to appear when the somnambulistic stage is reached and persists about a minute after the subject is brought out of trance. Other clinicians have independently observed this sign."[41]

The following are subjective experiences that may accompany hypnotic induction:

1. Complete physical relaxation with a disinclination to think, act, speak, or move.

2. Sensation of heaviness, especially the limbs. Feeling physically light, as if floating.

3. Feeling warm or cold. A drop in the skin temperature of the hands often accompanies the feeling of being cold.[42]

4. Time distortion. The subject has a distorted sense of the passage of time. For example, a common subjective experience is that very little time passed between entering hypnosis and coming out of it.

---

[41]Crasilneck, H.B. & Hall, J.A. Depth of Trance. Clinical Hypnosis Principles and Applications, 2nd Ed., 1985.
[42]Weitzenhoffer, A.M. Clinical signs of hypnosis. The Practice of Hypnotism, Vol. 1, NY: John Wiley & Sons, 1989.

5. Dissociation. A hazy feeling of physical detachment. Hypnotized persons may report feeling distant, or, of leaving the physical body and watching themselves perform without participation.

6. Fading and increase in cycles of the sound of operator's voice (like a radio station fading in and out).

7. Color sensations experienced.

The above signs may or may not be present in your client. Every individual is unique. (Even identical twins possessing the same genetic constitution and coming from the same ovum are different persons.) Thus, everyone experiences hypnosis in a different way.

Factors Influencing Hypnotic Induction

Do not accept the challenge of anyone who says: "I'll bet you can't hypnotize me." It is a waste of time and energy to trifle with persons who intend to resist your efforts.

Before the first induction clients often express apprehension that they will not succeed in being hypnotized because they cannot control their thoughts. To counteract this misapprehension tell the client that being hypnotized involves no control of any kind, and not to try too hard, but to be relaxed. (In actual fact, trying too hard to be hypnotized will block the trance state as much as strong resistance.)

The transition from waking to hypnosis should be gradual and pleasant. The client should be made comfortable, seated in a recliner (or chair) with a head support. Do not allow the hands to touch or the legs to be crossed. (If the legs are crossed the prolonged immobility, coupled with the deep relaxation of the muscles, may cause a limb to go to sleep.) There should be no direct light in the client's eyes. Extremes of temperature should be avoided, as well as drafts from open windows, fans, or air conditioners.

If at all possible, an induction should occur in a quiet room where there will be no intrusions, loud noises, or other distractions. While quiet during the induction process is helpful, when noises and sounds that cannot be eliminated are present, utilize any extraneous noise by suggesting: *The noise* (identify the specific sound) *in the background will allow you to let go and it will lull you into an increasingly deeper and deeper state of relaxation.*

Words are the primary conveyance of hypnotic communication. Your effectiveness as a hypnotist will be enhanced through the cultivation of good language skills. Do not speak too fast. Suggestions should be phrased so they are clear and easily understood. Develop a pleasant voice; the lower tones are more melodious and soothing. A quiet, audible, sincere tone of voice will gain the trust of the client, and give your suggestions authority and conviction.

Standard Induction Technique

The induction procedure is the vehicle that originates, or produces, the hypnotic state. The method that follows is a permissive technique. The client is directed to focus on breathing, and the relaxation of specific areas of the body. When you have mastered this standard induction technique, with slight modifications, you will find it can be adapted to other induction procedures. It will serve as a model for diversified technique.

Before you begin with the induction have the client remove chewing gum, take out contact lenses if worn, and, if so desired by the client, remove shoes and loosen any tight-fitting garments. If available use a recliner or soft chair that supports the client's neck, head and back. To assure immediate relaxation, allow a few moments for the client to get settled comfortably.

Counting Method

In the induction scripts that follow the cue, ". . ." means to pause.

> Look up, do not move your head, just your eyes, let them roll way back . . . the farther the better . . . as high as you can get them. Try to see the top of your head.
>
> Keep your eyes rolled upwardly, and, as you keep looking, you will notice that your lids will get heavier and heavier. Soon you will wish to close your eyes.
>
> Your eyelids are getting very . . . very heavy. Imagine . . . think . . . and feel your eyelids getting heavy . . . very heavy. Now slowly close your eyes and, at the same time, take a deep breath. Breathe in . . . in . . . in . . . filling your lungs all the way up to capacity . . . and hold it for as long as you can . . . and then breathe out slowly. That's fine. And as you exhale allow your eyes to relax. Now keep your eyes closed and breathe slowly and naturally. With every breath you take, you are getting more and more relaxed. More and more

relaxed with each and every breath. It is so easy to do, as you listen to my voice.

And now your body is beginning to relax. Take another deep breath and hold it for as long as you can and then breathe out slowly . . . that's it, and as you exhale . . . let your body go limp and loose and relaxed. Just think about relaxing every muscle in your body from the top of your head to the tips of your toes.

Notice how very comfortable your body is beginning to feel. Enjoy this pleasant relaxation . . . as you relax more and more you will experience a sense of inner calmness and peace . . . a feeling of letting go. Just let go now . . . and relax . . . mind and body deeply relaxed.

Now, I am going to count from ten down to one . . . with every number you hear . . . you will go down deeper and deeper . . . deeper and deeper . . . into a pleasant state of deep relaxation.

TEN . . . take a deep breath in . . . breathing in deeply . . . and hold it for a moment of time . . . now exhale all the air from your lungs. You feel yourself letting go and relaxing . . . just let go . . . go deeper and deeper into pleasant relaxation. With each and every gentle breath you become peacefully relaxed . . . drifting and drifting . . . more and more. The tiny muscles of your scalp and face are beginning to relax . . . as the facial muscles relax, you feel the lines of care and worry being erased from your forehead. Your jaw muscles are relaxing . . . just allow your jaw muscles to relax completely. Your temples . . . your eyes . . . your eyelids are letting go and relaxing completely.

NINE ... *feel the tension leaving the back of your neck and in your shoulders. The muscles of your neck and shoulders are deeply relaxed, just relax ... relax ... and feel the tension washing away ... just letting go. Notice the tension leaving between your shoulder blades ... your shoulder and back muscles are relaxed ... relaxing and letting go. Feel this soothing relaxation calming your brain and relaxing your mind and body. Feel the tensions drain away from your body. Just letting go. Let go now ... and relax completely. Drifting ... down ... deeper and deeper relaxed.*

EIGHT ... *Your body is now deeply relaxed ... and a pleasant heavy numbness is spreading up through your body; and with each and every gentle breath you feel a little more and more relaxed ... drowsier ... dreamier ... your mind and body are now so deeply relaxed that you feel yourself going down, down, down into a pleasant restful state of complete relaxation. So drowsy and so relaxed. Relax deeply ... drifting down into deep pleasant relaxation.*

SEVEN ... *the tension is leaving from the root of your neck ... on out your shoulders ... and down your arms. You can feel the tension leaving your shoulders ... your arms ... your hands ... and now radiating on out your fingertips. Both shoulders ... both arms ... and both hands are deeply relaxed. You feel so happy as you internalize this deep relaxation and drift with my words. You grow dreamier with every breath you breathe out. Just let go now ... and go deeper into pleasant, deep relaxation.*

SIX ... *you notice that you are breathing more slowly ... more deeply ... more rhythmically. The muscles of your chest are beginning to relax as you breathe more slowly ...*

and more rhythmically. Take another deep breath . . . slowly breathing in, in, in, up, up, and hold it as long as you can . . . now as you exhale you notice the gentle rising and falling of your chest with each breath. More and more relaxed . . . more and more comfortable with each breath . . . take another deep breath in now and draw that relaxation up into the center of your chest and hold it . . . and as you exhale there will be a feeling of letting go, like a balloon letting all the air out and becoming completely flat and relaxed. Relax . . . relax . . . relax . . . your mind and body are deeply relaxed.

FIVE . . . your body is now so deeply relaxed; you feel the pleasant heavy numbness that is relaxing your abdomen. Your stomach muscles are growing soft and relaxed. Your head . . . your neck . . . and your body are completely relaxed. So drowsy and so relaxed. Relax . . . deeper . . . and deeper.

FOUR . . . you find this deep relaxation very enjoyable. Just let yourself go . . . and go deeper and deeper . . . drifting and drifting . . . more and more . . . go deeper and deeper into pleasant deep relaxation.

THREE . . . this relaxation is progressive in its nature . . . now focus your attention on the muscles of your hips and thighs. Your buttocks and pelvic muscles are relaxing as this relaxation moves downwards into the great muscles of your thighs . . . and you are now deeply relaxed from your waist to your knees. Both thighs . . . both knees . . . relaxed . . . relaxed. The relaxation continues to move downward . . . and now you feel the tension leaving your calves, your lower legs, and your ankles. The tension is leaving your feet and

> *radiating now on out your toes. Both feet . . . both legs . . . completely and deeply relaxed.*
>
> *TWO . . . you are now completely relaxed from the top of your head to the tip of your toes. Enjoy this wonderful feeling of inner calm and well-being. Nothing will disturb your deep, pleasant relaxation.*
>
> *ONE . . . DEEP . . . DEEP RELAXATION! Nothing will disturb your pleasant restful state of mind. You are now so deeply, so wonderfully relaxed that nothing will disturb you. Just let go now and go down . . . down . . . deeper . . . and deeper . . . into this pleasant, restful state of mind.*

Automatic Motion Test

This excellent technique to induce automatic motion was developed by Charles Edward Cooke,[43] a noted teacher of hypnotism. If your client responded favorably to the induction and achieved a deep level of hypnosis, before arousing the client, say:

> *Now we can demonstrate how the subconscious mind can keep you doing something even against your strongest effort to stop. Would you like to see how this works? If you would, just nod your head. Nod your head.* **Wait for the acknowledgment.**
>
> *That's fine. Please raise the hand with which you write. Put it up in front of you. Now imagine that you are back in*

---

[43] Cooke, C. E., & Van Vogt, A. E., The Hypnotism Handbook, LA, Griffin Publishing Co.

school standing at the blackboard with chalk in your hand. You are about to practice making ovals. You remember the ovals? Please start making ovals. Round and round. Round and round. That's right. Remember how you used to make them? Round and round, round and round. Keep on making the ovals, round and round. So far you are doing this because I asked you to and because you want to, but we are going to turn this motion over to your subconscious mind.

As you continue to make the ovals round and round, the action is becoming just as automatic as the beating of your heart. As you know, the action of your heart is not subject to your control. Your heart speeds up and slows down in response to the needs of your body in a completely unconscious way. Thinking about it will not change its action. It is automatic, beyond your control. You cannot stop your heart from beating by thinking about it.

In the same way the motion of your hand is now completely automatic. The motion of your hand is just as automatic as the beating of your heart. It is now impossible for you to stop making ovals. Your subconscious mind is forcing your hand to go round and round. Round and round, in spite of any effort you may make to stop it. Try to stop it. It will not stop. Try hard to stop it. Your hand keeps going round and round, round and round.

Pause for the test. As soon as the client has made an obvious effort to stop the motion, continue. If the motion slows down, but does not stop, continue saying, "*Round and round, round and round*" until the client stops fighting it. If the client simply relaxes the arm and stops the motion, the test has failed. Admit it as a failure on the part of the client and continue.

Now the motion is slowing down, slowing down. Now your conscious control has returned. Now your arm is relaxed and you may do with it as you wish. Relax completely and go deeper and deeper. Deeper and deeper. Far deeper than you have been before.

Testing During Hypnosis

It is important to utilize the hypnotic state to convince clients that they have been hypnotized. Hypnosis is often an elusive and subtle state, and people who have not previously been hypnotized may not recognize the state when they are in it. If this doubt is not removed it may hinder your results. The solution to this problem is simple: use tests to verify the trance state. This is done through the production of basic hypnotic phenomena before terminating the first induction. These tests (eye and arm catalepsy) bring to the client's conscious mind an awareness of the presence of hypnosis.

Eye Catalepsy Test

Use the eye and heavy arm catalepsy tests following the client's first induction into hypnosis.

You are now so deeply relaxed that the muscles around your eyes are beginning to fuse your eyelids together. Your eyelids are beginning to stick tightly together. They are stuck together. Glued shut. Your eyelids are so completely relaxed that they are fused together . . . fused together so tightly that they will not open.

As I count from five down to one, they lock tighter with every number. Five . . . locking tighter and tighter. Four . . . glued tightly shut. Three . . . Tighter and tighter. Two. Your eyes are now locked so tightly together that you may try to open them, but you will find them locking tighter and tighter together. One. Test them, and you will find that they are locked tightly shut. Permit the client to try to open his or her eyes, but do not prolong this for more than a few moments. However, allow sufficient time for the client to make an effort, but don't press your luck. After you see that an effort was made to open the eyes say, *Now stop testing and let yourself go down into a deeper and deeper relaxation. Relax the muscles that control your eyelids and go deeper into relaxation.* This should be followed with the heavy arm catalepsy test.

Heavy Arm Catalepsy Test

The author owes a debt of gratitude to psychologist Charles Edward Cooke for this simple but impressive test, which he introduced back in the 1950's.

Our next test will be to make your right arm so heavy that you cannot lift it. If you wish to do this, nod your head.

Wait for acknowledgement. If the client shakes his head, indicating a refusal of any particular suggestion, say, "Very well, we will pass this one." And go on to the next test.

IMPORTANT: If at any time during the session the client awakens spontaneously, the hypnotherapist has two choices. 1) Ask him to close his eyes and again relax. Talk *deeper and deeper* for a minute or so. In most cases this is sufficient to reestablish hypnosis with a depth equal or greater than that attained before. 2) Say to the client, *Wake up! You are wide awake!* Take this precaution even though the client is obviously and apparently awake because the awakening signal becomes associated in his mind with the experience of "awakening." There is also the possibility that the client is in a much deeper trance than you suspect, and has simply opened his eyes while remaining in hypnosis.

That is fine. Now relax more and more, every muscle in your body completely relaxed, relaxed and heavy. Your right arm especially relaxed, heavy and relaxed. Every fiber of every muscle in your right hand, your right arm, and your right shoulder is completely relaxed. That makes your hand and arm feel very . . . very . . . heavy . . . very heavy.

Client's hands are resting loosely on his thighs. Gently push the relaxed arm to the outside so that it will fall and hang straight down, or in the armchair, fall to the cushion. Observe the degree of relaxation. If the client *lowers* his arm rather than permitting it to *fall*, put the arm back and talk relaxation until the arm falls loosely.

See how heavy it feels? Your hand is getting heavier and heavier. Heavier and heavier, heavier and heavier, heavier and heavier, much too heavy to lift. Your arm is getting heavier and heavier. heavier and heavier. Your hand is so heavy that you cannot lift it. You cannot lift your hand. It is much too heavy to lift, much too heavy. It feels as though it were made of solid lead, solid lead, far too heavy to lift. Try to lift it. It is much too heavy to lift.

Wait a few seconds. If the arm lifts an inch or so, and the struggle to lift it is apparent, but unsuccessful, ignore it. If the arm lifts six or eight inches and is held there say:

It is getting heavier and heavier, the weight is dragging it down . . . down . . . down. Repeat this several times. If the arm drops down, you may regard it as a successful test. If not, reassure the client that although this test was not successful, he will probably succeed on the next one.

Don't struggle to lift it any more. You see, at this time your subconscious mind is far more powerful than any conscious effort you can make. If you accept a suggestion it is completely effective. Now your arm is getting lighter and lighter. Now it is completely normal and relaxed, light and normal. You may move it easily if you wish to. Will you please put it back in your lap? It moves easily now. Go deeper and deeper into pleasant relaxation.

Observe the ease with which the client returns the hand to the lap. *This is important.* Be sure that all suggestion of heaviness is eliminated. If necessary, continue with suggestions of *completely normal*. Whenever a test suggestion is *not* to carry over into the waking state as a posthypnotic suggestion, it should be completely neutralized.

Arm Catalepsy Test

Grasp the client's wrist, lift the arm to shoulder height and firmly pull the outstretched arm toward you. And, at the same time, say:

Clench your hand tightly into a fist. Now contract the muscles in your arm . . . contract them tightly. Make your arm as stiff and rigid as a bar of steel. That's it. . . . Your arm is contracted so tightly that the muscles in your shoulder joint are beginning to fuse. The muscles adjoining your elbow are locking your elbow. And the muscles in your wrist are locking. Your arm is now as stiff and rigid as a bar of steel. You have no joint at your shoulder . . . your elbow . . . or your wrist. Your arm is as unyielding as a bar of steel. So stiff and rigid. STIFF AND RIGID. The harder you try to lower or bend it, the more rigid it becomes. Test it now and you will find that the harder you try to bend it, the stiffer and more rigid it becomes. After an effort is made to bend the arm, grasp the wrist and say, *All right, stop trying. Stop trying to bend your arm. Just let your arm relax. Relax your arm. You now have complete freedom of movement in your shoulder, your elbow and your wrist. Just let your arm relax and go limp. In a moment, I will drop your arm to your lap, and when your hand drops to your thigh, you will go into a deeper state of relaxation.* At this point release the client's arm, allowing it to fall limply into the lap, and as the hand hits the thigh say, *All the way down into deeper relaxation.*

NOTE: There is an important rule you must always observe when you are experimenting with hypnosis; remove the effects of any hypnotic phenomenon you bring about, such as eye catalepsy or limb rigidity.

Awakening The Hypnotized Subject

For more detailed information about the termination of hypnosis, review Chapter 13.

> *In a few moments, but not just yet, you'll open your eyes. You have had a good rest and will come up feeling refreshed and completely relaxed. You enjoyed being hypnotized and found this experience to be pleasant and refreshing. You look forward to being hypnotized again in the future. Indeed . . . each and every time you are hypnotized, you will achieve a deeper level of hypnosis . . . even deeper than now. . . . That's right. . . . Each and every time you are hypnotized, you will go deeper and deeper . . . more quickly and more easily. All right, ready now . . . at the count of five you will open your eyes, feeling rejuvenated, refreshed, and completely relaxed. ONE. . . . You can feel the energy flowing back into your body. . . . TWO. . . . Your mind and your body feels so wonderfully relaxed, refreshed and alert. . . . THREE. . . . You feel yourself coming up more and more. . . . FOUR. . . . Your mind is perfectly clear and alert . . . and FIVE . . . Slowly open your eyes feeling wonderfully refreshed . . . alert . . . and . . . relaxed.*

Progressive Relaxation Induction

This popular method of induction consists of suggesting relaxation to the client and shifting the focus of relaxation from one group of muscles or region of the body to the next. Some hypnotists work their way down the body; others start at the feet and work their way up. The sequence of the suggestions is not important.

> *Settle back comfortably in your chair . . . in a moment I will give you a series of suggestions that will relax each and every portion of your body. Internalize this deep relaxation.*
>
> *Just listen effortlessly and your subconscious mind will automatically record and accept the things I say, do not try to analyze them. As you relax, just let things happen as they happen, without any thought as to question or analysis.*
>
> *Focus your attention now on my voice . . . close your eyes gently so you can listen effortlessly . . . there's nothing that you need to look at so let your eyes relax as your lids close . . . . Now to begin . . . go inside . . . and just think about peace . . . and experience the quiet . . . the tranquility . . . and the calmness. Take notice of your breathing. You are breathing more slowly . . . more deeply . . . now take a deep breath and breathe relaxation in . . . hold it . . . now exhale and release the tension from your body . . . and let your eyes relax still more completely . . . that's it . . . now your body is starting to relax . . . more and more deeply . . . keep your eyes closed . . . let your body go . . . and relax deeper and deeper . . . deeply relaxed. . . .*
>
> *Your body is letting go of all tension . . . it is truly relaxing . . . now take another deep breath . . . and hold it until I tell you to exhale. . . . Now release that breath . . . slowly exhale . . . and let your body go limp and loose. . . . You are now starting to feel a little drowsy . . . your body feels so very*

comfortable . . . so relaxed. . . . Now take another deep breath . . . really deep . . . fill your lungs . . . and hold it for a moment of time . . . now exhale slowly . . . that's it . . . release all the air in your body . . . and now you are floating and drifting . . . just float. Float as if you were floating on a big, billowy cloud . . . floating and drifting into deeper relaxation. . . . You feel so dreamy, so drowsy . . . as you go deeper and deeper into pleasant relaxation. . . . You are breathing slowly and smoothly . . . and with each gentle breath, you become a little more relaxed . . . with each breath . . . floating and drifting into deeper relaxation. . . .

Your body is relaxing more and more completely . . . deeper and deeper. . . . Now take another deep breath . . . and hold it as long as you can . . . now breathe out slowly . . . feeling your body go limp and relaxed . . . you are feeling so pleasantly drowsy and so sleepy . . . notice how very comfortable your body is . . . how the tension is now leaving your body . . . just allow your body to relax completely . . . and with every gentle breath, ripples of soothing relaxation pass over your body . . . allow the muscles of your face to relax . . . to let go . . . releasing tension . . . also relax your neck muscles . . . the muscles of your shoulders . . . your arms . . . hands . . . relax your chest . . . your lungs . . . your heart . . . your stomach . . . and relax all the organs inside your abdomen . . . your pelvic muscles . . . your legs and your feet . . . let them all relax. . . . Enjoy this feeling of inner calm and peace . . . . Internalize this pleasurable feeling . . . going deeper and deeper. . . . Every muscle, every nerve, every fiber of your being is now deeply relaxed . . . and you are drifting and floating into deeper relaxation. You are relaxing still deeper . . . going deeper into pleasant relaxation . . . drifting and floating into dreamy, drowsiness . . . drifting and floating . . . and with each and every gentle breath you become just a little more relaxed. . . . Allow this pleasant feeling to flow throughout your entire body. . . . You feel so drowsy, so peaceful as you drift and float with my voice. . . . You become sleepier and dreamier with every breath you breathe out . . . and deeper and deeper relaxed with every breath you breathe in . . . deeper . . . deeper . . . dreamier . . . drowsier . . . with the gentle rise and fall of your chest . . . drifting . . . deeper and deeper . . . more and more relaxed. . . . As you internalize this deep relaxation . . . in your mind and in your body . . . going deeper and deeper . . . just let go . . . more and more . . . and now go all the way down into deep pleasant relaxation. . . . You now have a feeling of inner calmness and peace . . . how pleasant it is . . . how enjoyable . . . enjoy this wonderful feeling you have created in your mind . . . every nerve . . . every muscle . . . every fiber of your being enjoys this restful peace . . . this deep relaxation . . . and with this deep relaxation your subconscious mind is becoming exquisitely receptive to suggestion. . . .

You are now so deeply relaxed that your mind is focused on every suggestion that I give you. As you rest there all calm and quiet, your subconscious mind is awake and listening and receptive . . . it can easily absorb every suggestion that I give you. You are resting calmly and quietly. Nothing will disturb your restful peace. You need pay no attention to other sounds for they are unimportant. You can hear my voice clearly. You will find that you can easily and quickly and willingly follow every suggestion that I give you. In this relaxed condition your subconscious mind will strengthen the effect of every suggestion that I give you. All of the suggestions will make the changes we want them to make.

Ultra-Fast Induction

The author has been a student of hypnotism since 1950. Through the years I experimented with many different induction techniques and selectively evaluated them. Some of these methods were embraced and adopted for my personal use, but most were discarded for various reasons. In this Chapter, I'm going to share with you an amazingly effective method of induction, a technique that I consider to be one of the very best.

But first, I'd like to tell you how this method was serendipitously brought to my attention. Ten years ago, during a break in a workshop that I was conducting for the National Guild of Hypnotists, one of the participants demonstrated for me the technique that follows. That participant was Dwight Bale from Seattle, Washington. I was so impressed with the demonstration that I asked Dwight Bale to share his method with the rest of the class. He agreed. Since then I have successfully used a modified version of this remarkable induction technique hundreds of times, and I never cease to be amazed at the rapidity in which hypnosis is induced and the depth of trance attained.

Most rapid induction techniques are too authoritarian to be used for general hypnotherapy; this method, however, can be used in a clinical setting.

The client enters hypnosis almost before he or she is aware of the fact. The procedure involves eye-fixation, deep breathing, and direct suggestion. It also employs the element of surprise, and deepening is produced through intermittent movement of the client's head. Before starting, have the client remove eyeglasses. Hold your open hand in a horizontal position about 18 inches in front of the client's face. Make a red dot with a felt tip pen on the center of the end joint of the extended index finger; the other fingers are clenched.

> *Now watch the red dot and keep looking at the dot at all times. You are to inhale whenever I raise my finger and exhale whenever I lower my finger. Now keep your eyes on the red dot.* Start at the client's eye level and about 18 inches away. Then raise your finger about 9 inches above eye level, but within the client's range of vision, and at the same time say *inhale*. Then quite rapidly say *exhale* and, at the same time, quickly lower your hand about 9 inches below eye level, but still within the client's range of vision. Then raise your finger at a rate slightly faster than normal inhalation. (Timing is important as you wish to create a response comparable to a sigh.) Tell the client to keep looking at the dot. Look at the client's eyes to be sure that he or she is following the movement of your finger and looking at the dot. Also pay close attention to the client's breathing. If the client is not taking very deep breaths, then continue with your cycle of inhalation and exhalation. Most clients are ready for the next phase after 3 or 4 cycles, with a maximum of 6 cycles. If the client is breathing deeply, after 3 or more cycles, when you stop in the upward position, suddenly open your hand, cover the eyes and in an authoritative tone of voice say SLEEP! Now

place your index finger in the center of the forehead, cup your hand and place the thumb on the left temple area and the other fingers on the right temple. The palm of your hand supports the back of the client's head. Now, slowly turn the client's head from side to side in a slow rolling motion. Be gentle. Do not move the head continuously. Through this intermittent movement of the head the client will soon learn that he or she must let you move their head, and this will compel the client to let go. Next say, *when I remove my hand you will go 10 times deeper.* Now quickly and decisively remove your hand and say *ten times deeper.* Or, if a recliner is used, say *I am going to gently tip the recliner and you will go 10 times deeper.* Or you may tell the client *when I turn off the overhead light; you will go 10 times deeper.* As you turn off the light say *10 times deeper.*

Sidney Flower Induction

Sidney Flower, the originator of this innovative method, was the editor of the now defunct *Suggestive Therapeutics*. This technique was introduced at the turn of the twentieth century.

The procedure is a counting method and—while the hypnotherapist slowly counts—the client is told to open and close the eyes on each count. You will find, as you continue counting, that the period during which the eyes remain open becomes shorter and shorter, and finally, instead of the eyes opening there will probably only be a movement of the eyebrows.

In this method the client is seated in a comfortable chair, and told to relax as much as possible. Test the relaxation by lifting an arm and then dropping it; if properly relaxed, the arm will be entirely passive and the client will not participate either in the lifting or in the return to its original position.

The client is told to look at the opposite wall but not to fixate on any point. *In a moment I will begin counting. As I say each number close your eyes, then open them and be ready to close them again by the time I have counted to the next number. At each count you are to close your eyes and then open them before the next count. Remember, at each count close your eyes and then slowly open them before the next count.*

Now . . . begin to relax by taking a deep breath in . . . in . . . in . . . and hold it . . . now exhale and relax deeply. And as I begin counting, look at the wall in front of you. One . . . two . . . three . . . four . . . five . . . your eyes are beginning to grow heavy . . . heavy . . . six . . . seven . . . eight . . . nine . . . ten . . . so very heavy. Eleven . . . as your eyes grow heavier and heavier . . . it is becoming more and more difficult to open your eyes. . . . Twelve . . . thirteen . . . fourteen . . . eyes so heavy . . . fifteen . . . sixteen . . . seventeen . . . relax . . . deeper and deeper . . . eighteen . . . nineteen . . . twenty . . . eyelids so heavy . . . relax deeper. . . . If the eyes do not remain closed continue with the count. Stop counting as soon as the client is unable to open his or her eyes. At that point say: **Now you can let your eyelids stay closed.**

Hand-Levitation Induction

Milton Erickson developed this method of induction back in 1923. Lewis Wolberg gives a summary of the hypnotherapeutic use of this technique in his book *Medical Hypnosis*[44]. Wolberg considers this procedure the best of all methods.

The advantages of the hand-levitation technique are twofold: 1) The client participates in the induction; and 2) the client sets his own pace in entering hypnosis. The disadvantages of this method are that it is more time consuming and requires more effort and endurance on the part of the hypnotherapist.

> *Please sit comfortably in your chair and relax. Now lay your hands, palms down, on your thighs and keep watching them closely.*
>
> *We will start to relax by taking a deep breath in . . . in . . . hold it . . . now exhale, let your body relax. As you relax and observe your hands you will notice that certain things happen in the course of relaxing. As you sit there quietly relaxing you will pay close attention to your hands. As you concentrate your attention on your hands you will soon notice subtle changes taking place. You may be able to feel the texture of your clothing. You may become more and more relaxed, you may experience a pleasant tingling sensation in your hands. You will be sensitive to the tiniest sensation and movement. Your concentration is so focused you are sensitive to any change of feeling in your hands. No matter what sensations you experience, I want you to observe them.*

---

[44] Wolberg, L.R., *Medical Hypnosis*, Volume I and II, Grune and Stratton, Inc., New York, 1948.

Whatever movement appears, the hypnotherapist calls the client's attention to it, and from now on this hand is the center of the client's observation.

There, you have developed movement sensations in the middle finger of your left hand. The movement will spread, causing the spaces between the fingers to widen. The fingers will slowly move apart and the spaces will get wider and wider. As your fingers spread apart, you will notice that your left hand is beginning to feel light and buoyant. Your fingers will arch up from the thigh, as they want to lift the hand. As these movements develop, your hand becomes light and buoyant. There, your left hand is arching and you will let it float upward.

As the fingers of your left hand slowly lift, you become aware of lightness in the hand. The hand is light, buoyant, and it is beginning to rise up, up, up, up. Your left hand is so very light that it commences to rise, going up, up, up, up . . . rising higher and higher. As you continue concentrating on your hand it grows lighter and lighter, rising higher and higher. Going up, up, up. It feels as if a balloon is lifting it up into the air, lifting, up, up, up higher and higher.

After the arm has lifted about five inches above the thigh, you begin suggesting to the client that he or she will grow more relaxed and drowsy.

Keep watching your hand and arm as it rises up. As it continues to rise up, you notice that your eyelids are beginning to grow heavy and your eyes want to close. As your hand and arm rise higher and higher, going up, up, up, up . . . your eyelids are growing heavy, so very heavy. Your eyes are beginning to burn and smart. As your hand and arm goes up higher and higher you become more relaxed, more relaxed, drowsy, and sleepy. Your eyelids are growing heavy; your eyelids are so very heavy they will soon close. As your hand and arm goes up, up, up . . . higher and higher, you grow more and more relaxed. Your eyelids are growing heavy; your eyelids are so very heavy they will soon close. As your hand and arm goes up, up, up . . . higher and higher, you grow more and more relaxed. As your hand approaches your face, you feel more and more relaxed. In a moment your hand will touch your face and you will then be completely relaxed. The arm will bend and your hand will move closer and closer to your face . . . closer . . . closer. When your hand touches your face you will slowly but steadily go into a deep, deep, relaxation. There, your hand is about to touch your face. Your eyelids are heavy, you are so relaxed . . . let go and relax completely. As your hand touches your face, close your eyes and relax, relax, relax. When your hand touches your face you will be deeply and pleasantly relaxed.

Eye-Fixation With Distraction

The English physician and pioneer hypnotherapist John Hartland--a contemporary of Milton Erickson—developed this method for analytically minded patients who were unable to achieve hypnosis through standard induction techniques. To give you insight into the personality of this remarkable hypnotherapist, members of the British Society for Medical and Dental Hypnosis affectionately referred to him as Dad.

(Erickson wrote the Foreword to Hartland's book *Medical and Dental Hypnosis and Its Clinical Applications*.[45])

The author is grateful to John Hartland for this outstanding induction method. Eye-fixation with distraction is a particularly effective technique for clients who have analytical minds. Those clients, who are refractory to other induction methods, often respond positively to this procedure. It is dependable and rapid with eye-closure being secured within two to three minutes.

I have modified the procedure slightly. Instead of focusing on the tip of a pencil, I have the client fixate on a colored thumbtack in the ceiling. The position of the induction chair should be situated so the client is compelled to stair upwardly and slightly backwards. Holding the eyes in this position creates eye fatigue and helps to secure eye-closure.

An important aspect of this procedure is the preliminary instruction. Also, timing is important. After you begin the induction, carefully pay attention to the eyes. The moment you notice the client is having difficulty in keeping the eyes open, in an authoritative tone of voice say, "SLEEP!"

Position your chair beside the induction chair and lightly to the rear, so you can see the reaction of the client's eyes.

In a moment I will have you look up at a spot on the ceiling. When I tell you to begin I want you to start counting to yourself, not out loud but to yourself. Beginning with the number 300. I want you to count backwards. Counting slowly and with an even beat, slowly and rhythmically, just

---

[45] Hartland, J., *Medical and Dental Hypnosis and Its Clinical Applications*, 2nd Ed., Baillière Tindall, London, 1971

like the beat of a metronome. If you make a mistake in your count and follow say 278 with 276, don't try to correct your mistake, just continue with your count — counting slowly and rhythmically. Try not to listen to my voice. Although you will be able to hear my voice, try not to listen to it. Just mind your counting. Do you understand what you are to do?

Good. Now I want you to sit back comfortably in your chair and fix your gaze on the red dot (colored thumbtack) *in the ceiling. Do not allow your gaze to wander. Look at that spot. As you stare at the spot you may notice that the red dot will become blurred, or very sharp and clear, or even changes color as it goes in and out of focus. Now begin your count, counting slowly backwards from 300. Mentally to yourself . . . not out loud. Do not try to listen to my voice . . . you'll still hear everything that I say . . . but try not to listen . . . just stick to your counting. Keep on counting until I tell you to stop.*

Breathe slowly in . . . and out. As you exhale you are beginning to relax. You notice that you are breathing more slowly, more deeply, more rhythmically . . . and your muscles are releasing tension and relaxing. As you breathe quietly in and out you notice that your eyes are becoming very . . . very tired. They may feel like blinking . . . the spot on the ceiling may look a little blurred. Your eyelids are beginning to grow heavy . . . very heavy . . . they are beginning to blink. It is difficult to keep your eyes open. There . . . they are beginning to blink. Just let everything happen . . . exactly as it wants to happen. Don't try to make it happen . . . don't try to stop it happening. Just let everything please itself. . . . Presently your eyes will blink more and more. . . . And as they do . . . your eyes will become very . . . very tired. As soon as they feel they want to close . . . let them go . . . and let them close entirely on their own. Your eyelids are becoming heavier and heavier . . . they are starting to close . . . closing . . . closing . . . now close your eyes and go to sleep. Go to sleep! Sleep very . . . very deeply. Give yourself up completely to this pleasant, restful sleep. To this pleasant, relaxed, drowsy feeling. Stop counting now . . . and sleep . . . sleep . . . sleep.

Induction With Mechanical Aids

Many devices have been used to induce and deepen the hypnotic state. These devices are called "hypno-aids" and range from a simple object of fixation such as a pendulum, to sophisticated electronic instruments.

Mechanical devices provide a fixation point for external focus. As attention is centered on the hypno-aid, irrelevant sights and sounds become more distant. Thus, a hypnotic response may be more readily produced.

Keep in mind that while mechanical aids are effective if used properly, they are also unnecessary.

William S. Kroger, in his book *Clinical and Experimental Hypnosis*, made the following cogent remarks about hypnotic induction with the use of mechanical aids:

> All mechanical techniques depend to a degree on expectancy and rapport. The prestige factor is very important. If the subject expects to be hypnotized by a device and has confidence in the person who controls

the instrument, then hypnotic relaxation can be induced readily in a susceptible subject.

We will consider three of the more popular fixation objects: 1) The metronome used in musical instruction; 2) the flame of a candle; and 3) the hypnotic disk.

The metronome is a clockwork device with a pendulum; it is used to help a person maintain regular tempo in practicing on the piano, etc. The electronic metronome makes an intermittent sound or flashing light. Setting it at sixty beats per minute is the range found to be most satisfactory for induction.

A simple but effective object of fixation is an ordinary candle. The flickering flame and gentle movement draws the subject's attention to a very narrow point of focus. As the flame changes in shape and color, it produces a dreamy lassitude. Concentration on the flame will result in eye fatigue and will accelerate eye closure.

Perhaps the best know hypnotic aid is the spiral hypnotic disk. To use an analogy, the hypno-disk can be likened to the body of a whirlpool. The spinning vortex of the whirlpool maintains its outward form, but its components change unceasingly. The whirling hypno-disk creates the illusion of pulling the eyes toward the center of the disk as it revolves. With each revolution the spiral constantly increases (or decreases) in size. Because of its illusory effect on the subject, the revolving hypno-disk is an excellent mechanical aid.

Using Feedback to Facilitate Induction

Andrew Salter, a New York psychologist, has refined an induction procedure, which utilizes the client's subjective experiences while in hypnosis. This method is based on Salter's theory that hypnosis is a conditioned reflex.[46]

Salter believes that suggestion has greater intensity, if it has a meaningful connection to the client.

Everyone's hypnosis experience is unique. There is much variance in the reactions of individuals, and each client is asked about his or her feelings or sensations in hypnosis. In a post-induction interview Salter has the client describe precisely every nuance of his or her hypnotic experience. This data is taken down in exact detail, word for word. Sometimes a session is tape-recorded. (Greater accuracy and clarity are thus achieved.) In the next hypnosis session the recorded subjective experiences are incorporated in the induction verbalization. Feedback of the material that was brought forth in the post-induction interview, through the power of association, will deepen and enhance the client's hypnotic experience.

---

[46]Salter, A., *What Is Hypnosis?*, 4th Ed., Farrar, Straus & Giroux, 1973

CHAPTER 15
Aid To The Medical Profession

The author has been a student of hypnotism since 1950. I had the good fortune of studying hypnotism under the tutelage of Dr. Rexford L. North, who later became the founder of the National Guild of Hypnotists. Dr. North was a fascinating man and a wonderful teacher. He was by all odds the premier hypnotist of the late 1940's and early 1950's, as a showman, a teacher, and a therapist.

In appearance Dr. North was the very image of most people's idea of a hypnotist. He had a dignified professional bearing, tiny Lilliputian eyes behind glasses, and a trim Van Dyke beard. He was stone deaf and his voice had an eerie quality about it; he nevertheless managed to modulate it well enough so it did not clash with the rest of the image he projected.

Charismatic is the impression he made on others, enthusiastic in his approach to whatever he did, it is no wonder he was idolized by the students who came to his Hypnotism Center in Boston. All who are still alive and active in hypnosis today, including Dr. Dwight Damon and Maurice Kershaw, and the author of this book remember Dr. North with keen affection and credit him with inspiring them to careers in the profession. He was foremost in getting dental hypnosis accepted by the medical and dental authorities of the Boston area, through a series of practical demonstrations of its effectiveness in 1949-1950.

When I entered this fascinating field, the use of hypnosis as a therapeutic modality was virtually nonexistent. Back then only a small number of maverick doctors used hypnosis openly in their practices. Milton Erickson, William Kroger, Louis Wolberg, and a few other brave souls had the courage and fortitude to use hypnosis in their medical practices, and advocate its use by other practitioners.

At that time hypnotherapy, as we know it today, did not exist; and none of the medical or dental schools then provided postgraduate training in hypnosis.

While attending college in Davenport, Iowa I started teaching, on a small scale, what essentially was the Rexford L. North hypnotism course. In the beginning all participants were fellow students. Those students told others and my course became popular. To my astonishment even members of the faculty--my professors--enrolled in my course. This unforeseen success encouraged me to advertise, and soon I was conducting classes in the larger cities in Iowa and Illinois. I was a student by day and a teacher of hypnotism at night.

This situation provided me with a unique opportunity. Since postgraduate training in hypnotherapy was not available in the mid-1950's, my courses attracted many health professionals. (It was not until 1958 that the Council on Mental Health of the American Medical Association gave official sanction for the use of hypnosis by its members.) At the request of these doctors, I was called into their offices to hypnotize patients with various medical problems, such as obesity, smoking, insomnia, wryneck, bad habits, for the alleviation of pain in terminal cancer cases, and anesthesia for medical and dental procedures.

The following will illustrate my early involvement with hypnotherapy. The first newspaper story is about a young man who had a morbid dental phobia and was in dire need of dental care. To this patient, hypnosis was indeed a godsend. The story appeared in the Davenport Sunday Times-Democrat.

Tooth Extraction Under Hypnosis

Jim McMahon took a sideways glance at the ten teeth scattered about the dentist's table, grinned broadly, exposing his brand new upper plate and quipped: "When do we go to lunch?"

If it was a remarkable statement to make immediately after having ten teeth pulled, it was no more unusual than the extraction process with no anesthetic whatsoever.

He felt no pain, either before or after the extraction process, for McMahon breezed through the entire process with no anesthetic whatsoever.

He felt no pain, either before or after the extractions, because he was in a deep hypnotic trance, induced by his dentist, Dr. Adrian Lampe of Davenport, a trained hypnotist.

No sooner was the last tooth extracted than Dr. Lampe inserted McMahon's new dentures. Elapsed time for the entire operation--about a half hour, and

McMahon strolled out looking as if he'd always worn an upper plate. A few hours later, he went to work.

Along with several other professional men, Dr. Lampe recently completed a course in hypnotism under John C. Hughes, Davenport instructor. Since then, the dentist has successfully used hypnotism while filling teeth and making extractions.

Turns Over Control

Hughes was present in the dentist's office as McMahon climbed into the chair. He explained he would begin the hypnotic induction and then turn control over to Dr. Lampe.

"Close your eyes," Hughes intoned. "Just relax. You're beginning to feel very, very tired and sleepy. Your legs are beginning to grow heavy. Your entire body is growing heavy."

The voice droned on, McMahon's breathing became heavier. "All feeling of sensation in your upper jaw and the tissue surrounding your teeth will soon be completely gone," Hughes suggested. He continued the suggestions in a soft voice. McMahon's arms were now completely limp.

Still cameras clicked and movie cameras whirred (the film is to be used for lectures by the dentist) and the five people in the room occasionally conversed, but McMahon didn't move. He was now in a complete state of trance and Hughes told him he would now obey commands from the dentist as well as himself.

Probing in the patient's mouth, Dr. Lampe continued the induction, repeating over and over, "Your teeth and gums are becoming very, very numb. You can no longer feel any sensation in your upper jaw. You are very, very relaxed."

He tapped the patient's mouth. Dr. Lampe continued the induction, repeating over and over. "Your teeth and gums are becoming very, very numb. All sensation is leaving your upper jaw. You are very, very relaxed."

He tapped the gums with a sharp instrument. McMahon didn't stir. Dr. Lampe gave him the suggestion that time would pass very rapidly, that the time in the chair would only seem a moment.

Felt No Pain

One by one, the teeth came out. McMahon's relaxed hands never left his lap. As the dentist exerted pressure on the teeth, McMahon moaned ever so slightly. Later, he explained that he felt no pain whatsoever, only the pressure, the same as one feels with novocain.

When Dr. Lampe left the room briefly, he transferred control of the patient back to Hughes, and resumed it on his return. Again, there was the constant repetition of relaxation and numbness of the upper jaw.

Soon, the extraction was completed and the denture firmly inserted. McMahon was told how fine he would feel upon awakening, that the dentures would cause him no discomfort and that he would feel no post-dental pain.

McMahon was awakened. He looked like he'd just had a pleasant nap. "When do we go to lunch?' he grinned. Then his hand flew to his mouth and he fingered the unfamiliar dentures.

Dr. Lampe handed him a mirror, and McMahon stared in amazement. "This sure seems funny," he admitted. He had a little difficulty speaking.

He had been given a posthypnotic suggestion by the dentist that any time he was told to go back to sleep, he would do so immediately. The doctor gave the command, and McMahon's head snapped back. He was again in a deep trance.

When you awaken, you will find you have no difficulty speaking," he told McMahon. Then he awakened him, and the Davenport student spoke in a near normal voice.

"I feel good," McMahon said afterwards. "I didn't feel any pain at all, only the pressure. I was aware of what was going on, I could hear the sounds in the room, but I didn't feel anything. I know the denture is there because I'm not used to it, but it doesn't feel uncomfortable."

"You know," he confided. "I had a terrifying fear of the dentist. Now, I actually enjoy it. My wife is going to be up here soon, too, and have work done the same way."

Dr. Lampe said he recently hypnotized a patient for a sectional removal of three badly impacted molars. The operation took two hours.

He said patients who undergo hypnosis in dentistry (called hypnodontics) feel no sensation of pain; even several hours after the work has been performed.

They are completely relaxed, a state not induced by novacaine where the patient is awake and sees the work being done. Through hypnosis, hemorrhaging and the amount of saliva can be controlled.

Heals Faster

"The healing process is also, much faster than it is by conventional methods. Healing is usually nearly completed within two or three days, compared to as much as two weeks by other means," he said.

"Hypnosis is a blessing to patients who may be allergic to novocaine or cannot have it administered for health reasons," the dentist pointed out.

"Through hypnosis, dentistry can be completed in a much shorter time. Ordinarily, it would have taken three different sittings to extract McMahon's ten teeth," the Davenport dentist continued.

"I'm convinced all dentists should have a working understanding and make use of hypnotism in their work, Dr. Lampe declared."

Painless Childbirth

With the publication of a newspaper feature story about my use of hypnosis in a childbirth case, to my surprise, I became embroiled in controversy. This article appeared under a headline emblazoned in red, and generated criticism from some members of the medical profession.

The mother, Mrs. Buller of Moline, Illinois, had difficult and painful labor in the birth of two other children, and decided with this pregnancy that she would try hypnosis.

With the consent of her medical doctor, Mrs. Buller engaged my services for the latter part of her pregnancy and for the labor and delivery. She was easily hypnotized and achieved a deep level of hypnosis in all of her conditioning sessions.

An hour before she left for the hospital, I hypnotized Mrs. Buller over the telephone and gave her a posthypnotic suggestion which transferred hypnotic control to the attending obstetrician. Though the doctor had no previous experience with hypnosis, the transfer worked flawlessly.

The delivery was a complete success. Mrs. Buller suffered no pain, and--although she carried out all of my posthypnotic suggestions--she was 100 percent conscious throughout the delivery. She was so thrilled with the ease of her delivery that a few weeks later she enrolled as a student in my hypnotism course.

The Davenport morning newspaper, The Democrat, featured the painless childbirth story on its front page under the byline of its best-known staff writer, Jim Arpy. It caused quite a stir in newspaper, medical and hospital circles of the Quad-Cities, and hypnosis remained a topic in the local news for several weeks. (This publicity greatly increased enrollment in my hypnotism classes.)

Some elements of the medical profession were openly critical because at that point in time the American Medical

Association had issued an edict to the effect that hypnosis was dangerous, unless administered by a medical doctor. My response to the press, to that question, was: "Anyone with adequate training in the basic sciences, such as a chiropractor, M.D., osteopath, or dentist, is qualified to use hypnosis as a therapy. The A.M.A. should certainly not be allowed to monopolize hypnotherapy."

The article that follows appeared in the International Chiropractic Journal under the byline of Graham Kinney.

PSC Hypnotist Recommended by Mayo Clinic

A student at the Palmer School of Chiropractic has been recommended by an orthopedic surgeon at the famous Mayo Clinic, of Rochester, Minnesota, as "the best man for the job" of helping a crippled youth take a new lease on life, through hypnosis.

The student, John C. Hughes, is a nationally known hypnotist and is in his senior year at the PSC.

He confines his chiropractic adjusting to the school's Student Clinic, but outside of school hours he has helped many patients regain health and vitality through hypnotherapy. He also has succeeded in referring several of his patients to chiropractors, with gratifying results to all parties.

Hughes is uncertain how the Mayo Clinic happened to hear of his ability, but he believes that one of the physicians or dentists to whom he taught hypnotism might have been responsible.

The mother of the crippled Davenport youth read a report in a Davenport newspaper how Hughes had helped patients overcome physical and mental disabilities, fears and depressions. Her son had undergone extensive surgery at the Mayo Clinic for a congenital condition but had suffered mental and physical after-effects.

She and the youth sought Hughes' opinion. He suggested they obtain the advice of the Mayo Clinic orthopedic specialist who performed the operation.

The surgeon, Dr. Henderson said in reply: "There is no reason from our standpoint why hypnotism would be at all injurious to you, and you might try it. I don't believe there is anybody here (at the Mayo Clinic) better qualified to do the hypnotism than John Hughes in Davenport. I certainly would have no objection to your giving it a try."

From the first treatment, the youth made dramatic and rapid progress. Within two weeks his confidence and gait improved so much that he was able to walk without the support of a cane or crutch. Within two months he was able to negotiate stairs by himself—a feat that was impossible before hypnotic treatment.

CHAPTER 16
Painless Childbirth Guideline

1.) In conditioning a client for childbirth you should strive for as deep a level of hypnosis as possible. You will not always succeed in achieving deep hypnosis in the early stages of preparation. Some clients require more time than others, but with sufficient time a deep level of hypnosis can be induced in most clients.

2.) Your first efforts after hypnosis is induced, and maybe even while inducing it, are directed toward complete relaxation and removal of all fear and dread that may exist. Much of the pain and discomfort of childbirth is due to tension and fear, both of which can be removed by hypnotic suggestion. Impress upon the client's subconscious mind the idea that childbirth can and should be a perfectly natural, wonderful and pleasant experience, every moment of which she will thoroughly enjoy. This thought will replace the thoughts of fear and dread.

3.) Make sure the client will feel the muscular contractions and other evidences of the beginning of labor, but with a total absence of pain or physical discomfort. While she is in deep hypnosis, assure the client that she will have sufficient warning in advance to advise her doctor of approaching birth and that she will have ample time to get to the hospital for delivery. However, also give her assurance that labor will not be unduly long. That the baby will be born quickly and easily after the normal period of labor.

4.) Warn the client that bringing a baby into the world is hard work and entails weariness. Insist that she must do everything to cooperate, such as "bearing down" in order to facilitate and speed the delivery, and tell her that she will be tired when it is over. Suggest that following the doctor's orders, she will fall asleep and sleep soundly until she is rested or the doctor tells her to awaken.

5.) Suggest to her that the delivery will be entirely normal, the presentation correct and the period of labor short.

6.) Positively state that she will be able to "hold off" delivery until she is in the delivery room.

7.) While the client is in deep hypnosis, decisively state that there will be little loss of blood during or after delivery, and that there is no possibility of weakness due to loss of blood or shock. Stress that all she will feel is tiredness from the hard work of brining the baby into the world. Also, tell her that she will bring her own baby into the world, and that it will not have to be delivered for her. (It is a well-established fact that in all cases of delivery employing hypnotic suggestion there is a remarkable lessening of hemorrhage either before, during or after delivery.)

8.) When possible, transfer rapport to the physician in charge so the patient will respond to his or her suggestions as she does to yours. In this way you make certain that she follows all of the doctor's orders. She will instantly go to sleep or wake up at the doctor's command. She may be fully conscious of everything (even pain) or the state can be changed from analgesia to complete anesthesia if the doctor so desires.

9.) Always give suggestions to ensure strict compliance with the doctor's orders concerning diet or any other conduct. You may find it necessary to remove from the client's mind the effects of old wives tales, such as the newborn being "marked" by prenatal impressions from the mother. And sometimes it is necessary to straighten out the client's ideas about sex, marital relations and even childbirth itself in order to remove tension and restore peace of mind. This is more effective, of course, if done while the client is in deep hypnosis.

10.) Many physicians mistake unconscious reflex action for evidence of conscious pain. For instance, one doctor was certain that his patient felt pain because she winced, writhed and groaned during delivery. This rarely happens, and when it does, subsequent questioning always reveals that even if they did feel pain at the time, which is highly doubtful, patients have no recollection of it when it is all over.

11.) You should welcome the opportunity to talk over cases with the physician in charge. Always take advantage of the opportunity to show how easily the doctor can control the client--how readily she responds and reacts to the doctor's suggestions. This is, of course, for the doctor's own self-assurance in what is often a new experience.

12.) The question of fees for this service is an individual matter. You should establish a set fee per visit for a maximum number of visits, beyond which you allow the charge to go regardless of the number of visits necessary.

CHAPTER 17
The Art Of Self-Hypnosis

Back in chapter four of this book, it was stated that since it is possible to suggest actions to our own subconscious minds as well as having them suggested by others, it should be possible to hypnotize one's self. In later chapters, this was followed up by accounts of self-stimulation of the body's immune system to overcome illness, and other instances of self-hypnosis. You should thus be fully prepared to accept the idea that self-hypnosis is possible, and is in fact in the great majority of cases quite easy to induce, and its beneficial results are fully as effective as those of hypnosis induced by another person. It may be sometimes even more effective, for one may know even better than the most skilled therapist exactly what result will be of greatest help to one's own particular problem.

Many therapists recommend self-hypnosis, either as an adjunct to their own treatment of the client, or to replace it altogether once the problem has been identified. Dr. Roger Bernhardt, a noted psychoanalyst and hypnotherapist, advocates people learning simple self-hypnosis to handle their everyday crises and thus gain ability to overcome larger ones, or keep them from ever developing.

Almost everyone has, without realizing it, been in a self-hypnotic state. As has been pointed out, anyone totally absorbed in a book or movie or a musical or stage performance is in at least a hypnoidal or even light trance, induced by their cortex filtering out all distraction. The same can happen in an absorbing work task, in romantic love or in religious meditation or prayer. To purposely self-hypnotize is simply to allow this natural tendency of the mind for abstraction to have full play, but consciously directed by you toward some particular mastery of yourself that you want to achieve, whether it be to quit smoking or some other detrimental habit, or be rid of a phobia or shyness or hostility toward others, or to build physical or mental skills. For that is what all hypnotherapy aims at, to gain mastery of one's self, to enable one's mind and body to function properly at their fullest capability. Whether it is the therapist who attains this for you, or you do it yourself through self-hypnosis, the same tool is employed, the same goal sought and the same victory achieved.

The degree to which this mastery over our lives can be gained is of course not absolutely limitless—though Dr. Bernhardt says he finds himself sorely tempted to use that term—but it is far beyond that which most people are able to exert over themselves without hypnosis. How vast an alteration of human society might occur if hypnotic self-mastery should come to be attained by a majority, or even a substantial minority, of all people, was pointed to by the great English scientist J.B.S. Haldane almost a generation ago: "Anyone who has seen even one example of the power of suggestion through hypnosis must realize that the possibilities of human existence will be totally altered when we can standardize its application and remove it from the magical."

The standardization of hypnotherapy as a normal part of medical and dental practice is now in a rapid process of acceptance. Even so, the transformation of the face of society that Haldane foresaw will require that individuals begin to practice self-hypnosis as a matter of frequent or even daily routine, for the purpose of drawing on the power of their minds to cope with the stresses of modern living and to avoid or overcome the damage that stress engenders.

In this chapter we will review and highlight what self-hypnosis can do and how it can be made an essential part of one's life strategy. In the next chapter we will discuss specific, easily learned methods for inducing self-hypnosis.

Many people have more or less without knowing it, grown into the practice of inadvertent self-induction, and are practicing self-hypnosis even if they have never heard of it or do not think they want to do it. Thoughtful meditation, quiet self-consideration of one's problems and the means of handling them; all these and similar things can induce a focused state of mind in which the power of self-suggestion becomes operative.

Whatever the method, and whether self-hypnosis is sought on purpose or entered into unawares, that power can become an enormously effective tool for taking control of one's life. There has to be, of course, a positive attitude toward it—and where that is weak or lacking altogether, hypnotherapy can instill and strengthen it.

Dr. Bernhardt groups the specific applications of self-hypnosis under four main classifications, and these appear to fit most of the needs that it can meet. These groupings are:

1. Habits: — smoking, drinking, overeating, drug use, poor work and study performance, nervous mannerisms (nail-biting, etc.)
2. Emotions: — fear, timidity, anger, depression.
3. Health problems — colds, tiredness, chronic pain, asthma, etc.
4. Sexual: — impotence, low urge, frigidity, etc.

It will be noted that these are all within the range of the mind — both the conscious and subconscious — to control. Hypnosis is not meant to be a treatment for serious physical conditions and dangerous acute infections. Even when it brings relief from pain, the underlying condition must be identified and treated by standard medical means. Hypnotherapy can however help in locating and relieving a psychological trauma that may be at the root of the physical problem.

Self-hypnosis helps the above four categories of problems by generating, through correct suggestions, feelings of greater openness and affection toward others, cheerfulness, tact and poise, purposefulness, ambition and courage. It can also speed the acquirement of physical and mental skills, as well as organizational abilities, creativity and application to work, often all well beyond what the person had believed his or her limits of attainment to be.

In addition, hypnosis can alter the mind's perception of time, and make it seem either much shorter or longer than the passage of it measured by a clock. This can be of great usefulness in many ways. For instance, it is possible to instill an effective suggestion that an anticipated uncomfortable half-hour in the dentist's chair will last only two or three minutes and not be uncomfortable. By clock time, you will have spent thirty minutes in the chair, but your perception of time will have been only two or three minutes, and you leave with no unpleasant recollections. This can work the other way, to expand the usefulness of an available brief span to that of a considerably longer one. You may, for instance, find yourself needing an hour's preparation time for a business presentation or a school exam, and you have only 15 minutes to do it. Self-hypnosis can enable you to cram an hour's work into that quarter-hour--and do it well, with no sense of hurrying or being flustered.

Dr. Theodore X. Barber of the Cushing Hospital in Framingham, Massachusetts, and Dr. Roger A. Straus, both among the most prominent practitioners and teachers of hypnotism—we have already cited from Dr. Barber earlier in this book—lay primary stress on the central fact that hypnosis is something you do, not anything that is done to you. Human beings are not intricate pieces of machinery like cars or computers, to which something can be done by a mechanic or technician to fix it so it runs smoothly. All healing work, be it spiritual or mental or physical, is really done by ourselves—the treatment is only a means of getting us started on doing it.

When a person does what the hypnotherapist suggests, it is the client that is doing it. If the client did not act on the suggestion, it would only be so many wasted words. The action occurs because for the moment, the client's mind is accepting what is being suggested as reality, and is therefore following it out to consequences, which in that context are real.

This key principle was first stated about 70 years ago by the pioneering clinical sociologist, W. I. Thomas, as follows:

"Whatever a person believes is real, or takes for granted as being real, is real in its consequences."

Changing one's life thus becomes a function of defining what is reality. It is our sense of what the total picture is, of what in it affects us and how we respond to it. We ourselves can determine all this, and act to alter it in ways that are beneficial to us. Self-hypnosis enables us to do this, by freeing our imaging capabilities from the limits that our usual lives with all their stresses and constraints have imposed on them, until we have become conditioned to thinking that our lives are set in rigid patterns from which there is no escape.

That is the fallacy of determinism, which is the basis of such current philosophies as behaviorism--that our lives are determined for us by where and to whom we are born, and by our environment. Actually, we are free. Our biological parents and the social world, in which we find ourselves, merely provide the raw material out of which we build our lives and our selves. We do the building; we decide the shape, through our inner imaging and feeling. Self-hypnosis provides the most effective tool for doing this.

The current interpretation of how our brains function is that their left and right halves work in differing and contrasting ways. In chapter seven we learned that the left-brain is the thinking, calculating, planning half, which is constantly carrying on this work even when we are not aware of it. The right-brain is the imaging, feeling, and creative half, in which thoughts and mental pictures flow freely without associating as they do in the left-brain.

Useful though this concept of the left and right brains is; it should not be carried too far, or the two halves portrayed as hostile opposites. The subconscious mind operates through both, simultaneously and without distinction. When, through self-hypnosis, you create the images you want to act on—such, for instance, as seeing yourself freed of the disabling smoking habit—it is the left brain that starts to plan the steps by which to realize this, while the right brain elaborates the image and gives it life and attractiveness.

As hypnosis educator, Daniel L. Araoz, has pointed out, both the right and left-brain activities are essential to properly functioning, healthy mental life. Neither is sufficient by itself. Your left brain can come up with effective ways to reduce weight, stop smoking, manage time better, and so on, but unless the right brain chimes in with the feeling, the motivation and the conviction that you can and will do it, nothing will change. Similarly, your right brain can strongly motivate you to do all sorts of desirable things, and convince you that you can and will do them—but unless the left brain is called on to devise the practical ways and means, again nothing will come of it.

Through hypnosis, and most especially self-hypnosis, the activity of both brain halves can be coordinated and balanced, making possible a rich and rewarding life.

The creation of a new and better life pattern takes place in your subconscious. It is you who are doing the creating. As your thinking and your feeling become aligned with what you want yourself to be, it is natural and no longer an effort for you to act like you want to. This takes time to bring about; but we are beginning to understand that it can be achieved more quickly if we do not challenge ourselves to resist, by insisting on no-failures-allowed formulas.

William James, perhaps the greatest of pioneer psychologists, laid it down as a principle that until the new and better habit is securely rooted, no exceptions must be allowed. You cannot even once revert to the old bad habit.

But that is going about it the hard way. It conflicts with what has been called "the law of reversed effect"—i.e., the harder you try, the more difficult it becomes. It is exercising will power and not imagination, and we have already seen in this book that the imagination will always master the will. By imaging, constantly and repeatedly, at every opportunity, and particularly in self-hypnosis, how you will act and conduct yourself under your new and better habit, it will bit by bit become your spontaneous tendency to actually behave in that way. If along the way, you stumble now and then, you don't allow that to break the continuity of the pattern you are creating through imagery. You just pick yourself up and keep on going, in the way you really want to.

To be effective, imagery cannot be random, jumping from one mental scenario to another. Not many people can guide and maintain a particular imagining more than very briefly. Guided imagery has thus become a critically important hypnotherapy technique. If a therapist is treating you, he will provide and sustain the guidance for your imagining, until you develop the ability to do it on your own. If you are doing self-hypnosis, there are a number of road maps that have been worked out to help you do purposeful imaging. The author will suggest some of these in the next chapter. They will enable you to call on and develop your own powers of imaging and of directing your subconscious mind what you want it to do and what sort of person you want to become.

CHAPTER 18
Self-Hypnosis And You

In this chapter you will learn a simple and effective way to induce hypnosis in yourself. Since at least a light hypnotic state is a prerequisite for purposeful and productive imaging, it is essential that you first master the technique of self-hypnosis if you are not being guided by a hypnotist. Even if you are, it is an acquirement of great and lasting value to know how to induce self-hypnosis, whenever you wish, and thus be able to capture a wider range of brain activity for conscious use.

An understanding of autosuggestion, the underlying force of self-hypnosis, and the role it plays in the lives of all, is needed as a preliminary to learning the method. Autosuggestion is a way of directing your own personality—which can be defined as the sum of the mental and emotional characteristics that together make up your individuality; that which sets you apart and distinct from any and all others.

Every moment of your life the myriad stimuli of sense perceptions infiltrating your mind are creating and shaping the unique personality that is you. The term "unique" is used in the full strictness of its dictionary definition, as having no duplicate or counterpart. Alexis Carrel, the Nobel Prize laureate psychologist, more than half a century ago expressed in his great book *Man the Unknown* this basic truth:

> Human beings [that is, as abstract conceptions, such as when we say I'm a human being, or someone else is a human being] are not found anywhere in nature. There are only individuals. The individual differs from the human being because he is a concrete event. He is the one who acts, loves, suffers, fights and dies. On the contrary, the human being is a Platonic ideal living in our minds and in our books.

Your personality and individuality thus are different from any other person who has ever lived, is living now, or is yet to be born. Even identical twins, formed from the same ovum and possessing the same genetic make-up, are different individuals. The forces outside ourselves, that through unceasing experience mold and shape our personalities, are never and cannot ever be the same for any two or more individuals.

Thus when the power of autosuggestion works on your personality, it does so in a way that fits only it and no other one. It is the realization of this, which makes it possible to transcend—to rise above and re-shape—whatever defects may exist in your personality. They are your own unique defects, different from any one else's. It is in your power to overcome them, no matter what may have happened to others.

You can, of course, take inspiration from the way that many noted men and women throughout history have attained greatness despite personal limitations and adverse circumstances. They transformed obstacles and misfortunes into success, through visualizing and constructing in their minds the positive images of the specific missions and objectives they sought to achieve. They believed in themselves; they utilized, knowingly or unknowingly, the power of autosuggestion to its fullest.

Every human act or deed is in fact brought about through our suggesting it to ourselves. "As a man thinketh in his heart, so is he," was written in the Bible (Proverbs 23:7) nearly thirty centuries ago, and it is still just as true now as it was then. *You become what you think about.* All that you do and say stems from what you think (and thus suggest to yourself). Whether your actions, words and thoughts are positive or negative in their effect and impact depends entirely on the mode of your thinking.

Within reasonable limits of practicality, you can really become the better person you want to be if you train your self-talk (autosuggestions) to constantly emphasize the positive aspects of everything. Whatever your hopes, ambitions and goals, to achieve them you must cultivate positive thinking until it becomes a constant habit.

You are endowed with the reasoning brain that sets you and all other humans apart from and above all other living creatures on this planet. The human mind, whose instrument the brain is, possesses an infinite complexity and resourcefulness that make it the greatest of all the wonders of the universe. It is your privilege, and your responsibility, to learn to employ your mind and brain to the fullest degree that you are able to.

Unless, however, you go about it in the right way, you may be trapped by the very complexities that make your mind so marvelous. Its subconscious layer, the one through which autosuggestion and hypnotic suggestion work, does not possess the critical faculty of your conscious mind. It will accept and believe anything it is told, without discrimination beyond that of any moral code already ingrained into your personality. It will just as readily accept harmful suggestions as beneficial ones.

It appears to be a very basic human characteristic to look obsessively at the darker side of life. This can easily become a destructive force in our personalities, leading to a lack of confidence in our own abilities--what psychologists call the inferiority complex. Probably no one is wholly free from it. How many times have you wanted very much to do something, but did not take that crucial first step, because you had no faith in your ability to do it? If allowed to become habitual, this self-doubt destroys and undermines any attempt to improve our condition and ourselves.

Any honest examination of your own personality will reveal that you often feel insecure and inadequate. Yet if with equal honesty you appraise your assets and your attributes of talent and capability, you will in all probability discover that they far outweigh your shortcomings. The limits they place on you are in large measure self-imposed, the result of thinking about them instead of your positive qualities. All your thoughts and feelings about yourself, become autosuggestions that direct your actions for either benefit or harm.

Negative thinking is without a doubt widespread in present-day society. The vast majority have so negatively conditioned their minds and emotions that they deny themselves enjoyment of life to its fullest. Small wonder then that this is so often called "the Age of Anxiety," when so many are consumed by anxieties that are largely needless. Never before has positive thinking and constructive autosuggestion been needed as much.

And it would take the exertion of only a small part of the mental effort that is now misdirected or not used at all, to effect a vast improvement in the lives of many. Over a century ago, William James estimated that the average adult made use of only 10 percent of his or her mental faculties. Even less, it would seem, is being utilized today. Through self-hypnosis, you can put these dormant and unused powers of your mind to work for you. You will learn to function mentally at the deeper levels of relaxation of mind and body thus expanding your range of consciousness.

"Knowledge is power," it has been said from antiquity. It might be more accurately rephrased as "Knowledge is potential power." Knowledge and information have effect and power only insofar as they are made use of. People start a great many things and never properly finish them, because they have never learned to use their knowledge, to make their initial enthusiasm and energy habitual. We are flooded with information these days, but few know how to avail themselves of it or how to sort out the really useful from the rest.

Self-hypnosis is the key that enables you to start making effective use of what you already know for personal achievement and success. Once it becomes a habitual mode with you, an integral part of your individuality and personality, you will live more richly and productively. The regular practice of constructive autosuggestion through self-hypnosis will help you to gain poise and self-confidence, and to get away from always putting things off. You will become more creative, less inhibited, and efficient in both thought and action.

Self-hypnosis cannot, of course, accomplish these things if you are unwilling to accept the mental discipline it requires. Nor should you regard it as a universal prescription for self-improvement. These cautions aside, it is nevertheless beyond question the single most effective means to that end known to modern science.

This brings us to the actual methodology of inducing self-hypnosis and using it for implanting positive autosuggestions. There are countless self-help books available these days in bookstores and supermarkets, all plugging the same theme of positive thinking (autosuggestion). A great many have the same defect--they tell you how to present positive self-affirmations to the conscious level of your mind where it is virtually impossible to prevent negative counter-suggestions from making their way in and canceling what you have been suggesting positively.

On the conscious level of the mind, one thing will inevitably suggest another, which may be totally opposite in polarity, and you cannot prevent this. In self-hypnosis you avoid this bind, for you are in control of what you are suggesting to the subconscious, which in hypnosis is not open to counter-suggestion. More correctly, the critical factor of the conscious mind is lulled into a state of suspension, so to speak, and unable to nullify your positive affirmations.

Faith, i.e. strong and unshakable belief, has always been considered--from Biblical times on--an essential component of any mental or spiritual effect. Even when asserted with some degree of doubt, its constant re-affirmation tends to fix the subconscious on a positive track. Your suggestions, to have any result, must be accompanied by your belief that they are going to work. So simplistic a formula as Emile Coué's "Day by day, in every way, I am getting better and better," which had a vogue and large following in the early part of the twentieth century, worked for many—even those who though skeptical, gave it a try—because by its repetition it came to be believed in.

Repetition brings about belief, and belief brings about results. That is the equation, which tells how self-hypnosis and autosuggestion work. The will, as was pointed out in an earlier chapter, has no part in this. Affirmations of something as true, and reinforcing that affirmation through repetition, are the essentials for the attainment of what you ardently desire within the limits of practicality. It is not possible, for instance, to set a broken bone by autosuggestion. It is however certainly possible to speed up its healing by that means, once the fracture has been properly set and placed in a cast.

Autosuggestion is more effective when done in the hypnotic state, for in that state one is deeply relaxed and there is no hindrance to transmitting suggestions to the subconscious. Self-hypnosis is simply the placing of one's self, by one's own effort, in that deeply relaxed state, instead of having it induced by a hypnotist.

You may very naturally have certain hesitations and even apprehensions about inducing hypnosis in yourself, so it is essential to first remove them. One of the most usual fears is that it may be dangerous. As we have seen in Chapter Six there is no danger whatsoever in the induction process or the hypnotic state, in themselves; but there is a potential danger in their misuse, specifically in removing pain without having first determined its physical cause.

Pain is in most cases a signal by the body that something is more of less seriously wrong and needs attention. To use hypnosis for the removal of abdominal pain that might be appendicitis would be ill advised, for it could terminate fatally, with a ruptured appendix and peritonitis. It is absolutely essential, and I cannot too strongly emphasize it, that the physical source of any pain be fully determined by competent medical examination before attempting to relieve or remove it by means of hypnosis.

On the other hand, there are numerous cases of pain for which no physical cause can be found, or which persists even after the supposed cause is removed. Such pain is usually the result of anxiety or tension neuroses, and can be greatly diminished by hypnotic relaxation, as also can conditions like arthritis and rheumatism, once they have been diagnosed and identified. Cancer can sometimes be remitted or even healed through long and patient hypnotic therapy involving imagery and autosuggestion.

Another apprehension, or more properly misapprehension, is that to self-induce hypnosis is evidence of one's having a weak and easily impressionable mind. Quite the contrary, such persons hardly ever succeed in self-hypnosis. They tend to resist the whole idea. Intelligent, highly motivated persons have consistently been shown in tests to do self-hypnosis best, and also to be the best subjects for hypnosis by a hypnotist.

Another misconception is that the hypnotic state is a form of sleep, and that by self-inducing it, one is putting one's self to sleep and thus out of touch with reality. As has already been made clear in this book, a person in hypnosis is not asleep but fully aware of what he or she is being told to do. The term "sleep" however continues to be used in the induction repertoires of many hypnotists because of its lulling and soothing quality, conducive to relaxation.

It is possible, of course, to suggest in hypnosis that one become drowsy and sleepy, but this is an effect of suggestion and not of the induction or the hypnotic state.

A related fear is that one will become unconscious and afterward unable to recall anything of the experience. In very deep hypnosis a person will sometimes have spontaneous amnesia of the whole episode; or, not remembering can be the result of a posthypnotic suggestion to that effect. Normally, there is no difficulty in recall, nor is the person in hypnosis unaware of his or her surroundings.

We will now shed light on important preliminary steps to inducing self-hypnosis:

1. You must have an expectant attitude of confidence that self-hypnosis will benefit you. Any doubt or skepticism will hinder your success.

2. Determine that whatever you suggest to yourself will be done by concentrating on that one thought, with full belief that it will have manifest effect either physically or mentally, or both.

3. Be prepared to repeat the suggestion, over and over again.

4. Write the suggestion out beforehand, in the strongest affirmative terms you can think of.

5. Set a regular time for your self-hypnosis training, and have a definite interval of time between sessions. Stick to the schedule, once you have set it up.

6. Before the end of each session, give yourself suggestions that will facilitate a deeper level of relaxation next time.

7. You should find a quiet place where you will be free from intrusions, loud noises and other distractions. Dim the lights, turn off the TV or stereo, disconnect the phone and ask everyone to leave you alone for a while. It isn't absolutely essential to be free from all distraction, but in the early stages it will be very helpful.

8. Remove shoes and loosen any tight-fitting garments, take out contact lenses. If possible, settle back on a recliner or other soft chair that supports your neck, head and back. Don't lie down; if you have only a sofa or bed available, use pillows or other supports to prop yourself up. Close your eyes, stay still and quiet. Let your mind relax passively, thinking about nothing in particular. After a while you will experience a sense of inner calm and peace, with perhaps a vague feeling of physical heaviness.

9. If for any reason you need to attend to some urgent matter, you will be able to arouse yourself instantly and then return to your training session after taking care of the interruption.

Trance induction is a combination of progressive physical and mental relaxation. The following method is designed to facilitate both of these states. You will be directed to focus attention on your breathing and on specific areas of your body.

Read the following Induction Script aloud, or have a friend do so, and record the reading on an audiotape that you can then play back. Always use a pleasant, modulated tone of voice in the reading, stressing the deeper tones, as they are more soft and soothing. All suggestions should be clearly phrased and stated, preferably in a descriptive manner as if you were painting a verbal picture. When you say that a part of your body is relaxing, say it in a way which projects that feeling--r-e-l-a-x-i-n-g. In the induction use a droning, gliding tone of voice, as if you were singing a lullaby.

INDUCTION SCRIPT FOR TAPE RECORDING:

To be read aloud into a tape-recorder, by yourself or by a friend. Be sure to follow the preceding instructions (about finding a quiet place for the exercise, settling into a comfortable relaxed position, etc.) before turning on the tape. Now proceed:

> *Are you settled comfortably? That's it. . . . Now let your mind relax passively. . . . I will be guiding you in a few moments into a deeply relaxed state . . . both physical and mental . . . so please do not listen to this tape while driving or doing anything that requires mental alertness. . . .*

Focus your attention now on my voice. . . . You do not have to concentrate intensely. Just listen effortlessly and your subconscious mind will automatically record and accept the things I say. All you need to do is to listen and experience the feelings suggested. Close your eyes gently so you can listen effortlessly . . . there's nothing that you need to look at . . . so let your eyes relax as your lids close. . . . Now to begin . . . go inside . . . and just think about peace . . . about quiet . . . tranquility . . . calmness. Take notice of your breathing. Notice the movement of your chest as you breathe in . . . and out. As you breathe in notice the air filling your lungs. The expansion of your chest. Now start to relax and take a deep breath . . . breathe in . . . and as you exhale, release the tension. As you release the air notice how your chest and lungs returns to normal rest. . . . Allow your eyes to relax still more completely . . . that's it. . . . Now your body is starting to relax . . . more and more deeply . . . keep your eyes closed . . . and let your body go . . . just floating and drifting . . . just float . . . float as if you were floating on a big, billowy cloud . . . and relax deeper and deeper . . . deeply relaxed. . . .

It may be possible to hear noises and sounds other than my voice . . . but you will ignore everything except my voice . . . listening only to my voice . . . you will not think of anything else . . . because this experience is so pleasant, so relaxing, and so restful . . . you will not want to think of anything else . . . if other thoughts come wandering into your mind . . . do not dwell on them . . . and they will leave as quickly as they came. . . . You will find any outside noises and sounds becoming ever more distant . . . more subdued . . . because it is so pleasant, so restful to listen to my voice. . . .

Your body is letting go of all tension . . . it is truly relaxing. . . . Now take another deep breath . . . breathe in . . . and hold it until I tell you to exhale. . . . Now release your breath . . . slowly exhale . . . and let your body go limp and loose. . . . You are starting to feel a little drowsy . . . pleasantly so. . . . Your body feels very comfortable . . . you are so relaxed. . . . Now take another deep breath . . . really deep . . . fill your lungs and hold it . . . now exhale slowly . . . release all the air in your body . . . and now you are drifting and floating into deeper, deeper relaxation . . . it is so pleasant. . . . You feel so pleasantly relaxed and so drowsy . . . more and more . . . deeper and deeper . . . you are breathing slowly and smoothly . . . with each and every breath, you become a little more relaxed . . . with each gentle breath . . . drifting and floating into deeper relaxation. . . .

Now visualize your body relaxing more and more completely . . . deeper and deeper. . . . Take another deep breath . . . breathe in . . . and hold it . . . now breathe out slowly . . . feeling your body go limp and relaxed. . . . You are feeling so pleasantly drowsy and so sleepy . . . notice how very comfortable your body is . . . how the tension is now leaving your body . . . just allow your body to relax completely . . . and with every gentle breath, ripples of soothing relaxation pass over your body. . . . Allow the muscles of your face to relax . . . to let go . . . relaxing and releasing tension . . . also relax your neck muscles . . . the muscles of your shoulders . . . your arms . . . your hands . . . relax your chest . . . your lungs . . . your heart . . . your stomach . . . relax all the organs inside your abdomen . . . your pelvic muscles . . . your legs and your feet . . . let them all relax . . . enjoy this feeling of inner calm and peace . . . internalize this pleasurable feeling . . . going deeper and deeper . . . every muscle, every nerve, every fiber is now deeply relaxed. . . .

You are relaxing still deeper . . . going deeper . . . drifting and floating into dreamy, drowsiness . . . drifting and floating . . . and with each and every gentle breath you become just a little more relaxed. . . . Allow this pleasant feeling to flow throughout your entire body. . . . You feel so drowsy, so peaceful as you drift and float deeper and deeper. . . . You become sleepier and dreamier with every breath you breathe out . . . and deeper and deeper relaxed with every breath you breathe in . . . deeper . . . deeper . . . dreamier . . . drowsier. . . . With the gentle rise and fall of your chest   . . . drifting and floating . . . deeper and deeper . . . more and more relaxed. . . .

As you internalize this deep relaxation . . . in your mind and in your body . . . going deeper and deeper . . . you let go . . . more and more . . . and now go all the way down into deep pleasant relaxation. . . . You now have a feeling of inner calmness and peace. . . . How pleasant it is . . . how enjoyable . . . enjoy this wonderful feeling you have created in your mind . . . for every nerve . . . every muscle . . . every fiber of your being enjoys this restful peace . . . this deep relaxation. You are now experiencing this soothing relaxation flooding through your brain . . . your mind and your body are completely relaxed . . . totally . . . deeply . . . wonderfully. . . . Enjoy the peace . . . well being . . . contentment . . . enjoy this restful inner calm and peace. . . . With this deep relaxation your subconscious mind is becoming exquisitely receptive to suggestion. . . .

You are learning how to relax completely . . . how to control both your mind and your body. . . . Every time you listen to this training tape, you will maintain and increase your ability to enter the realm of self-hypnosis. . . . Practice twice or more daily, until you are fully master of it. . . . Soon you will be able to enter self-hypnosis simply by taking a long deep breath and then slowly exhaling, while mentally counting from one to five . . . with each number you count, you will go deeper and deeper into relaxation . . . pleasant deep relaxation. . . . As you breathe in deeply, you will effortlessly focus all your awareness on this beautiful state of being you have created in your mind. . . .

One. . . . Your mind and body are deeply relaxed . . . deeply, deeply . . . you now take a long, slow deep breath and hold it . . . now slowly exhale all the air from your body . . . counting slowly from one to five. . . . Each time you practice this, you will go deeper and deeper into self-hypnosis. . . . You enjoy this wonderful state of peace and relaxation and eagerly look forward to experiencing it again. . . .

Two. . . . You are finding this deep relaxation very enjoyable. . . . You will look forward to each practice session with pleasurable anticipation . . . and you will practice twice or more daily until you fully master this state. . . . You will allow your mind to quietly relax each time. . . . Soon all you will need to do to enter self-hypnosis, will be to take a long deep breath . . . just one . . . and slowly exhale, while mentally counting from one to five . . . with each number you will go deeper and deeper into pleasant relaxation . . . just let go . . . let go   . . . and go all the way down into pleasant, restful relaxation.

Three. . . . Whenever you want to enter self-hypnosis . . . you will take a deep breath . . . breathing in deeply . . . and after holding it for a moment of time . . . slowly exhale all the breath from your body . . . counting one to five . . . effortlessly, automatically you will go down . . . down . . . down into deep self-hypnosis . . . each and every time you do it. . . .

Four. . . . When you reach your desired level of self-hypnosis . . . all the suggestions you have made to your subconscious in previous sessions will repeat themselves . . . over and over, making an indelible impression on your subconscious mind. . . . The instructions you have practiced and carried out for entering self-hypnosis will be automatically assimilated by your subconscious . . . effortlessly, naturally. . . .

Five. . . . In your self-hypnotic trance, your mind will accept totally . . . completely . . . the beneficial suggestions you have made to it . . . and that have been repeated over and over . . . suggestions that you have prepared and written before entering into self-hypnosis. . . . In this state your subconscious mind is exquisitely receptive to suggestion . . . and you begin to benefit from your own suggestions immediately. . . .

You will continue to further develop your ability to enter into still deeper and deeper levels of self-hypnosis. You will always be able to return to full waking consciousness . . . no matter how deep your self-hypnosis . . . simply by counting back from five to one. At the count of one . . . your eyes will open, your mind will be clear and alert and you will emerge with a wonderful feeling of vitality surging through your mind and body.

SUGGESTIONS TO TERMINATE SELF-HYPNOSIS:

I am now going to count back from five to one. At the count of one . . . you will open your eyes . . . and emerge from this pleasant experience feeling refreshed and completely relaxed. . . . Your mind is perfectly clear and alert. . . . You will have an incredibly euphoric feeling of well being. . . . Now you are slowly starting to come up. Five . . . you feel yourself beginning to come up from this deep level of relaxation. . . . Four . . . you feel energy flowing into your arms and legs . . . coming up more and more. . . . Three . . . your mind is focused . . . it is clear and alert. . . . Appreciate how wonderfully refreshing this experience has been. . . . Two . . . move your fingers . . . you will soon be in full waking consciousness. . . . One. . . . In a moment you will open your eyes . . . you can feel energy surging through your mind . . . through your body. . . . Enjoy this wonderful feeling of well-being. . . . You are now fully alert. . . . Wide. . . . Wide awake.

CHAPTER 19
How To Use Self-Hypnosis

If you have mastered the self-hypnosis induction technique in the previous chapter, and can now place yourself in the hypnotic state whenever you wish, you are now ready to go on to the practical beneficial applications of your acquirement. Yet it will be helpful to review first some of the essential points we have already covered, and to expand on them so as to assure that you have a fuller understanding of what you will be doing and how it will bring about the changes for the better that you want in your life.

Take a look back now at what you have learned about self-hypnosis in the pages you have read. You now have a grasp of how wide-ranging and vital a skill it is––a skill that is not difficult to master, that enables you to set clear life goals for both the short and long term, and gives you the ability to direct your subconscious mind to achieve them. You now know that it is possible through autosuggestion, to take charge of your attitudes, habits and ways of doing things, and to shape them so that you will be a better, healthier, more successful individual.

In short, hypnosis is to you no longer a thing of mystery, shrouded in superstition and occultism, but a highly practical method of getting our lives under control so that we can fulfill ourselves in accordance with whatever our particular gifts and talents are.

A few practical suggestions are in order at this point, to help you in applying what you have learned and to bring about the results you want. In addition to the induction tape already described, you should have at least two additional blank tapes on which to record the suggestions and directions you wish to implant in your subconscious mind while you are in self-hypnosis. Write these out on paper first, clearly and specifically, then read them aloud onto the tape, so that you can hear them played back while in hypnosis. That way they can be repeated over and over, repetition being—as already stated—a very effective way of implanting suggestions.

A large notebook is also a very useful tool in this work. Write down the experiences of each self-hypnotic session—how well it went (or didn't.) Keep track of your progress. Keep track of the results you are getting. Record the visualizations you have--which ones work best, or are easiest to call up in your mind. It will become a fascinating, unending project that will mark the milestones of your attainment.

Suggestion works through visualization. You have to picture in your mind the things you are implanting in it. You should strive to make the visualization as total and as real as your imagination is capable of doing. Keep practicing this in every self-hypnotic episode. Don't make hard work of it! Simply let the images flow as you call them up. Let your mental eye rest on the details, colors, shapes, faces, attire, landscape, etc. Most importantly, visualize yourself as living the way you are suggesting to your subconscious that you want to be.

Remember always the key principle of letting things happen effortlessly. The harder we try to make them happen, the more difficult they become. And don't hesitate about translating your suggestions into visual imagery of your own choice. Never worry about whether they are the images some teacher or master would define as the correct ones. If you feel they are right for you, then that's all that matters.

Negatively phrased or imagined suggestions do not work. They defeat themselves. To suggest to yourself that you will not smoke any more, or eat chocolates any more, or whatever it is you want to stop doing, simply erects a mental barrier against its fulfillment. The answer is to re-define the object—to strip it of the attribute that long habit has invested it with in your mind, of being some powerful reality that compels you to partake of it.

You can re-define by suggesting to your subconscious that it view chocolates, or cigarettes, or whatever, as simply a substance that you can look at with detachment and in isolation from any other substance. You can then further suggest that it happens to be a substance you don't need; and since you don't need it, you don't have to take any of it. You have now disarmed it, for it is no longer an enemy too powerful for you to resist, but merely a neutral entity, a substance that you dispassionately consider and decide you neither need nor want.

It is of course quite probable that you will find yourself being tempted--more than once--to return to the habit from which you have freed yourself. Here again, the answer is in visualizing the situation beforehand, and in rehearsing the handling of it with the same detachment that won your freedom in the first place.

This technique, of re-defining all the threatening and difficult and troubling problems in your life, and thus altering them to discrete units that you can examine and assess coolly, extends the reach of self-hypnosis to all phases of your existence. You will not of course find any instant solutions to your problems, or cures for whatever illnesses you may have, but you will have gained a way of handling them that more than likely will lead you to some positive resolution of them.

Listing is a helpful tool for problem handling. Write out a list of the specific things that are bothering you. Then make a second list of what you could realistically do about them. This will make you think in positive terms of solutions that are feasible in your circumstances (self-hypnosis is not a means of generating miracles). Then, during your self-hypnotic sessions, implant suggestions for your actually carrying out the solutions you have thought of. Picture yourself as really doing them.

Keep doing this, session after session. Repetition is the key to results. The daily or twice daily self-hypnosis induction and creative visualization is not only the surest way to achieve them, it is in fact the only way. As in anything else, application and discipline count. Merely wishing for a better future will not bring it about.

It is true that at times in actual problem resolution and self-management or improvement, informal techniques improvised on the spot, as the situation warrants or demands, will work best. But it is only through having trained yourself in formal self-hypnosis routine that you will know how to improvise and make it work for you.

By familiarizing yourself with and mastering a set, unvarying routine of induction and awaking, you free your mind of the burden of details. It's like learning to drive a car, which consists of innumerable details that have to be correctly done; but once you have mastered them, your mind attends to them without conscious effort and is free to turn to other matters or to devise instant strategies to handle a sudden driving emergency.

Some hypnotists recommend a rehearsal. Simply imagining yourself going through the self-induction, self-suggestion and awaking routine, at least a few times, without actually doing it, as a good way of acquiring the mental discipline for its daily or twice-daily repetition. You must become skilled at this routine and discipline so that you enter and leave it as a matter of course, as much so as your getting dressed and eating. You will have no anxiety, fear, or worry about losing yourself in some realm you can't get back from. You will use self-hypnosis because it will enable you to live better now and in the future. You know what to do in hypnosis, and how to come out of it at will, when you want to.

You are, in short, free to implant your own suggestions for self-improvement, free to follow them fully, free to choose not to do things that harm you, such as addiction of any sort.

As you visualize and mentally review what you plan and intend to do, and what through self-suggestion you program yourself to carry out, you are in a sense creating the future . . . and as you afterward recall your visualization, you are literally remembering future events. You must not, however, allow yourself to fall into the blind alley of living only in an imagined future, pushing all your rewards and happiness off into it. They will never be realized if you do that. Allow yourself all the rewards you can in the present, to sustain and encourage you to keep at it until you reach your objective.

Visualization has been defined as the mental eliciting of desired responses. If you desire, for instance, to be able to control your reactions in difficult and stressful situations, in self-hypnosis you can direct your mind to visualize such a situation and see yourself as reacting in a controlled way within it. Now you can go to the next step . . . suggesting to yourself that you will actually conduct yourself in the way you have visualized, in a situation of that kind. Through repetition, and the visualizing of a number of scenarios, you can acquire and practice a self-mastery under varied pressures and stresses.

Self-mastery can be not only of feelings and emotions, but also of physical processes in your body. Indeed, it is not easy to draw the precise line between the mental and emotional on one hand, and the physical on the other. Our knowledge of mind-body relationships has vastly expanded over the past two or three decades, though even yet it is imperfect. At least we do now understand that mind and body continually interact, and that the old concept of "mind over matter" — having as its premise that somehow we could exert "will power" over our bodies to make them do what otherwise they could not — is erroneous.

Not through forceful exertion of will, if there is such a thing, do we influence what takes place in the body, but through what we image and visualize as happening. Of course, if it is to be of practical benefit, the imaging has to be goal-directed — toward the removal or healing of some physical detriment or impediment. It must not be a mere random flitting of pleasurable thoughts; the visualized scenario however can be improvised and shaped in the light of the actual situation you are dealing with.

You may begin imaging for mastery of your physical self with simple exercises such as visualizing biting into a sour lemon, and noting how readily your salivary glands respond, as if you were actually tasting the lemon. The next step would be to image warming various parts of your body — an ability that in itself can be of considerable therapeutic value, as warming is produced by an increased blood flow which helps to heal wounds and other injuries, and relieves pain in congested muscles and joints. (Conversely, imaging a reduced blood flow to a wart or tumor can be effective in shrinking and finally getting rid of it.) The visualization at this level is still very simple, you image your hand, for instance being dipped in warm water, or baking in the hot sun. Once learned, the technique works rapidly, usually only a few seconds to warm chilly hands or feet, or even your whole body.

Mastery or control of pain is a more difficult matter. It is essential, first of all, to observe the caution we stated earlier: get the pain medically analyzed and diagnosed so that you will not risk your health or even your life by hypnotically removing a pain that could be a danger signal of a serious condition. Next, it is important to understand the difference between the way in which the physical brain responds to pain, and the way in which hypnosis handles it.

The brain's response is basically biochemical; it makes and emits certain substances called endorphins, akin to opiates, which block or reduce the pain signals traveling along the nerves. While stimulation and enhancement of endorphin release can be attained through hypnotic imagining, it is not the primary means through which pain is hypnotically controlled.

Under hypnosis we seek to alter our perceptions of pain so as to either ignore it, or notice it only slightly. Using the concept of re-defining already described, we instruct our subconscious to look at pain in a different way so that it becomes something to be considered in isolation, apart from whatever is causing it. An example might be the dentist's drill. We are free to decide to ignore it because there are a lot of other things we would rather be paying attention to.

To do this successfully you must first have mastered self-hypnosis. There is a close bond between tension and pain. If you are tense you cannot calmly look at the dentist's drill and freely decide to pay no attention to the sensations it is imparting to your nerves.

The various "natural childbirth" techniques that have been developed over the last two generations, from Dr. Grantley Dick-Reade's pioneering approach to the Lamaze and Bradley methods, all are based on a few essential points, removing tension through relaxation and an understanding of the birth process so it can be looked at calmly, and imagining a mental enhancement and easing of it. Though they are not usually considered as hypnotic therapy in the strict sense, in essence they are the same as what you learn to do in self-hypnosis.

But because birth, besides being a source of pain to the mother, is also a process she wants to be knowingly a part of and assist to its completion, she has to employ a different sort of imaging from that we can make use of in other pain-causing situations. Since there is little or nothing we can do to assist the dentist to finish his work, other than being quiet and relaxed, we can image ourselves totally away from his office. We can visualize being instead at the beach, or sailing, or skiing, or hiking, or golfing, or doing whatever we find enjoyable and where pain of any kind is the last thing we would think of.

So powerful is this imaging, once you have fully learned to initiate and continue it, that you can use it to do away with taking aspirin or other common pain relievers in most ordinary pain situations such as headaches and rheumatic or arthritic inflammation. In cases of intractable pain, as in some lower-back problems and advanced cancer, imaging can be more effective than high doses of narcotics in bringing pain down to the limits of endurance. Post-operative pain can often be dispelled, with reduced or eliminated need of Demerol or other analgesics that sometimes cause dependency.

There are other techniques that can be utilized for particular types or pain, or for special bodily areas, such as inducing through suggestion a total numbness in an affected part. As you progress in self-hypnosis, you will want to avail yourself of several detailed instruction manuals readily obtainable now. Many can be found in the resources listing at the end of this book.

Important far beyond even pain control and relaxation, however, is the value of visualization and imaging for effecting real change and improvement in your life. Here again, there are detailed manuals now available—and most who practice these techniques develop the ability to devise their own scenarios. This book aims simply to scan the whole field of hypnotism in order to discern and define its essence and usefulness, so we can only describe in a general way some of the most effective imaging scenarios for positive life changes. We must also present representative visualizing and imaging techniques for promoting healing as distinguished from simple pain relief. This is first aid, as it were, for without physical health and freedom from serious disease, it is difficult if not impossible to fully alter our lives into more productive, achieving, happier ones.

Visualization for change can be summed up under two broad and distinct headings: *receptive* and *volitional*. In the first, you allow the images to simply flow, without any effort on your part, while you are totally relaxed and receptive, seeking and having asked for guidance on a choice of life paths to take. The images are usually highly symbolic and require patient and skillful interpretation, usually with the help of a professional. Here in this book we are more concerned with the volitional, in which you purposely and purposefully set the mental stage and program the imaging you enact on it. An accurate and striking comparison of these two principal kinds of visualization, which one writer on the subject has made, is that in receptive visualization you listen to your subconscious, while in the volitional mode your subconscious listens to you telling it what to do.

As with any skill, it takes time and effort to master visualization. Your first attempts may result only in lifeless, wooden imaging. If you persist, you will find that gradually they acquire life, color and motion. Again, repetition is the key.

Keep doing it, regularly, every day. Soon you will find it possible to visualize virtually at will.

Common-sense cautions need to be observed. Visualization and imaging are not to be used as means of acting out any criminal or violent fantasies that may be hidden in your mind. If you are troubled by dominant negative images presenting themselves, get professional help without delay. Nor should you ever allow visualization to become mere daydreaming, keeping you from meeting your commitments and responsibilities in the real world. It is not a refuge in which you fulfill impossible goals and achieve feats beyond your capabilities.

Visualization is an exercise for enabling you to attain realistic, practical goals. For this purpose you allot to it a certain, limited amount of time daily. You are in control of your life; you can program it within sensible, reasonable limits—which however can extend much further than most people realize. Visualization through self-hypnosis is a method, proven in thousands of cases already, through which you become all that you can be.

Practice the use of each of your five senses, one only at a time so as to fully concentrate on it, for in hypnosis you are not deprived of your awareness of any of them. With your eyes closed, visualize various geometric shapes, such as triangles, circles, squares, etc., in differing colors and combinations of patterns; until you can actually see them. Then practice hearing sounds that you create in your mind, voices of people you know, cats mewing and dogs barking, music on various instruments, wind and rain and waterfalls, and so on; until you actually hear them. Visualize touching objects that are not physically there--such as chair slats, balls, toys, etc., developing your ability to feel them and recognize wood, leather, paper, and other materials that are only the constructs of your mind.

Taste and smell are perhaps senses more easily visualized than others; even in very light hypnosis, most people can readily image and taste many foods, and perceive a wide variety of imaged odors. In deeper hypnosis, and with constant daily practice, these two senses can be developed into very powerful aids to visualization.

As you become more proficient, image yourself as the director of a movie in which you have full power to arrange the set and command the actors. You have in fact even greater power than a real-world movie director, for you can make yourself as large or small as you wish, in your scenario. Try recalling actual movies you've seen, and yourself as actually living the emotions and situations the actors portrayed.

It is helpful to visualize a special place in which you act your imaged scenario. This can be a room done just the way you want it, a quiet beach, a peaceful valley, or any location that especially appeals to you and in which you feel comfortable and secure. Keep practicing this repeatedly, until you can enter your "special place" as easily as you walk into an actual room.

In advanced imaging, which shades into shamanistic techniques and practices, a guide, who can often be an animal, is visualized. This requires training under someone who is experienced at it, and for most ordinary purposes of visualizing for life change, is not necessary. Very effective results have been obtained even without having developed the ability to mentally create a "special place," though it is a helpful attribute for enhancing your imaging.

One of the most common motivations for self-improvement is weight loss, and it can usually be achieved more satisfactorily and lastingly through visualization, than by any diet or exercise program. Such programs tend to be mere quick-fix performances, with no lasting effects because they do not address the underlying causes of over-eating and lack of body fitness. Through purposeful imaging, in which you visualize yourself making rational decisions for proper eating and sensible exercise, you can achieve an attractive personal appearance without fad or crash diets, or dangerously strenuous exercise. You do it by deciding to do it, and instructing your subconscious to carry out your decision.

Smoking, as well as other undesirable habits, can be overcome in the same way, as has already been pointed out. However, when alcoholism or drug addiction is involved, professional guidance and support are a necessity. Insomnia often yields readily to suggestion and imaging; you instruct your subconscious that this time instead of awaking in the usual way from self-hypnosis, it will just fade into normal, restful sleep, which you visualize yourself as enjoying.

Depression, inability to control anger, and excessive anxiety are conditions that visualization is particularly effective in treating and correcting. In most cases you can do this on your own, though some professional guidance may be advisable. By visualizing yourself as happy rather than depressed, calm and self-controlled under stress instead of flying off the handle all the time, and as being in control of your life circumstances without constant worry over what might happen, you gradually achieve the attainment of these preferable conditions.

Persistence, repetition and patience are the essential prerequisites for success. They cannot be evaded, shortcut or wished away. Visualization and imaging, and self-hypnosis, which enable you to use them effectively, are not a means for producing miracles. Properly and continuously used, however, they can shape your life to be the way that you want it.

Measuring your progress also becomes important in any long-term visualization program for life improvement and skills enhancement. Even though you may be aware of how you are becoming a better person, less shy, valuing yourself and your abilities more (if shyness and low self-esteem have been barriers blocking you), learning faster and applying better what you are learning, and so on, it is both reassuring and reinforcing to keep a notebook journal of this progress.

It helps too to visualize some outline of time and specific attainments that you are programming yourself to achieve by certain dates. But be realistic in setting these goals and targets, knowing that they will not come with miraculous completeness or suddenness. On the other hand, don't set them in some far-off indefinite future—"Some day I want to do this or be that." You will not attain objectives so vaguely defined. Dr. Milton Erickson was a master of the technique of having his patients set realistic timetables and goals--he would say, for instance, "Well, you can't attain that big an objective in just six weeks, but how about three months from today? Have the secretary set your next appointment for that date, then come back and tell me how you did it." And usually they did, and were ready for the next goal. Sometimes they would even call a couple of weeks in advance, to say that they had already achieved their target and wanted to come and tell him about it.

Erickson was of course simply elaborating on what he had found to be the highly effective method of diverting attention from the immediate subject. Had he said, for instance, "You can overcome this bad habit" — whatever it was — "in six weeks and I'm telling you to do it."; the chances of success would have been much less. But by conceding in advance his patients' probable objections to too short and fixed a deadline, he turned their attention to what seemed easier; and they were able to do it.

There are many detailed guides now available on how to meet through self-hypnotically guided imaging and visualization, whatever your particular needs in life improvement may be — such as learning more effectively, enhancing memorization, developing self-confidence, etc. The list is virtually endless. You owe it to yourself, if you are serious, to examine and select those which will be especially helpful for your situation and requirements. The most important thing that you have to know before you can even start, is that through hypnosis--whether guided, or self-induced, or a combination of both--it is now possible to open wider doors of realistic personal achievement and satisfaction.

It is the purpose of this book to make you — the reader — aware of the reality and the availability of hypnosis, and the gateway it offers into the realms of imaging and visualization. Through these, as modern science is coming increasingly to recognize, the human mind can assert its supremacy over the material forms of existence. In no sphere is this more astonishingly evident than in that of our physical bodies. Many of its diseases and disorders can be effectively healed and prevented through hypnotically guided imaging and visualization. This augments the technology of traditional medicine and surgery, and sometimes obviates the necessity for their use.

CHAPTER 20
Understanding Psychology
An Overview For The Hypnotherapist

Psychotherapy is a broad classification of therapy that is aimed at dealing with psychological disturbances. It is the use of psychological techniques by a *professionally trained individual* to help a client change unwanted behavior and adjust to his or her environment. In short, it is the use of language to make positive changes in the life of another.

There are many types of psychotherapy. All, however, have three basic goals. The first goal of the therapist is to be sure that his or her techniques do not bring harm or intensify the problems of the client. The second goal is that the therapist should seek to reduce the individual's present discomfort. And finally, the therapist should attempt to aid in the development of a healthier and more adjusted individual. It is important to keep these goals in mind as we examine the many techniques that are used to relieve psychological suffering. First, let us examine the professionals who administer therapy to the six million Americans who seek professional help each year.

The Therapists

The psychiatrist is a medical doctor who has received a degree in medicine and has taken part in a residency program (usually 3 years), specializing in emotional disorders. Psychiatrists may specialize in any of the psychotherapy techniques, and they are the only professionals who can prescribe drugs or conduct psychosurgery.

The psychoanalyst is often a psychiatrist who has had a great deal of training in psychoanalytic techniques. As part of this training, psychoanalysts must themselves undergo psychoanalysis. Psychoanalytic therapy is very time consuming and involves some very specialized techniques.

The clinical psychologist has received a Ph.D. or Psy.D. in clinical psychology from a graduate school. This training generally takes from 3 to 6 years after receiving an undergraduate degree. The clinical psychologist receives extensive training in therapy techniques, methods of testing, and interpreting psychological theories.

The counseling psychologist has earned either an M.A. or Ph.D. Most counseling psychologists take a 1-year internship, during which time they work with clients under the direction of a practicing counselor. Generally, counseling psychologists are trained to deal with adjustment problems rather than psychological disturbances. The aim of counseling is to help the client adjust to the situation rather than "treat" a specific disorder.

The psychiatric social worker has a master's degree in social work and often has served an internship. Social workers have special training in interviewing techniques, and they may visit individuals in their home to collect information, interview relatives and friends, and make assessments. Social workers are often called upon by juvenile courts to make reports about the family environments of delinquents.

The psychiatric nurse is a registered nurse who has received special training in dealing with psychological disorders. Mental institutions employ psychiatric nurses, where they are responsible for a wide variety of activities, including patient care and making careful observations of patient behavior.

An Introduction To Psychotherapy

A word of caution: **Unless you have the requisite professional credentials, as listed above,[47] do not use hypnosis in the treatment of psychological disorders, except under the direction and supervision of a qualified specialist.**

An exact definition of mental illness is hard to come by. The difficulty in defining mental illness lies in a problem peculiar to psychology, as opposed to other sciences: psychology mixes science and *morality*.[48] As a human being, the psychotherapist is subject, as most of us are, to equating "abnormal" with "bad." "Bad" is a moral judgment from society; "abnormal," strictly speaking, should be a purely objective evaluation.

---

[47]Worchel, S., Shebilske, W., 1983. *Psychology: Principles and Application*, Prentice-Hall, Inc. Englewood Cliffs, NJ
[48]Scarr, S., Zanden, J.V., 1987.*Understanding Psychology*, Random House, New York, NY

Usually the normal person is one who is able to function at a satisfactory level, though not necessarily a perfect level. Thus, a person who suffers from short periods of moderate depression, who has a temper tantrum about once a month, and who has occasional fantasies about sexual conquests or becoming a great celebrity is probably as close to normal as most of us get.

A workable definition[49] of the mentally ill person has been proposed. It consists of three parts, any one of which probably signals mental illness, although frequently in a mild form.

1. The mentally ill person probably suffers discomfort more or less continuously; such discomfort is typically found in people who are anxious, worried, or depressed.

2. The mentally ill person behaves in a bizarre fashion; he or she may see things that are not there (hallucinations), or constantly misrepresent what is actually going on (have delusions), or be markedly different from most people, like the person who can't go to work because they are afraid to ride the elevator up to the office.

3. The mentally ill person is inefficient, unable to adequately perform a life role that formerly seemed quite comfortable.

For most purposes, this threefold definition—discomfort, bizarre behavior, and inefficiency—works quite well.

---

[49]McMahon, F. B., 1972. *Psychology, the Hybrid Science,* Prentice-Hall, Inc., Englewood Cliffs, NJ

We will review the most common psychological disorders. The hypnotherapist should keep in mind, however, that the symptoms for psychological disturbances are not always obvious or clear-cut.

Anxiety Disorders

Anxiety is a vague, generalized apprehension or feeling that one is in danger. For people who experience anxiety disorders the world is fraught with apprehension and fear. Until recently, mental health professionals termed them "neurotic." But since little consensus exists on the meaning of "neurosis," in 1980 the American Psychiatric Association DSM-III (*Diagnostic and Statistical Manual of Mental Disorders*) eliminated the term as a category.

Generalized Anxiety And Panic Disorders

Persons who suffer from generalized anxiety disorder experience frequent high levels of tension for months on end. However, they do not know why they are apprehensive or fearful. Since their anxiety is not limited to a particular stimulus or situation, it is termed "free-floating." At times the anxiety blossoms into a full-fledged attack, which may include choking sensations, racing heart, chest pains, dizziness, trembling, hot flashes, and numbness and tingling in the hands or feet. Moreover, sufferers frequently have a nagging worry that disaster will befall them or their loved ones.

In other cases of anxiety, people experience what is termed panic disorder. They have sudden, intense attacks of fear, apprehension, or terror. Usually, the bouts of anxiety begin in late adolescence or early adulthood. The attacks are more acute than in generalized anxiety disorder, and they differ from normal responses to danger in that there seems to be a sudden activation of the body's alarm system for no explainable reason. During an attack, sufferers complain of rubbery legs, a pounding heart, dizziness, hot flashes, nausea, or choking feelings. Others say their surroundings become strange, unreal, or foggy. The attacks may last from a few minutes to hours.

Phobias

Severe anxiety focused on a particular object or situation is called a phobia. A person with a phobia has an intense, persistent, irrational fear of something. A phobia can develop toward almost anything. Common phobias include:

- *Acrophobia*--fear of high places
- *Agoraphobia*--fear of open places
- *Claustrophobia*--fear of closed, cramped spaces
- *Nyctophobia*--fear of darkness
- *Panthophobia*--fear of disease
- *Thanatophobia*--fear of death
- *Xenophobia*--fear of strangers

Phobic individuals develop elaborate plans to avoid the situations they fear. For example, people with agoraphobia may stop riding on buses or shopping in large, busy stores.

The first attack may occur with no warning, perhaps when the person is on a bus or in a supermarket. Should the attacks become more frequent, the victim comes to associate them with these places. Very shortly a sense of "anticipatory panic" wells up every time the victim finds himself or herself in such a setting. The home is seen as a refuge, the only place the person feels safe. In time the victim may become totally "housebound."

Obsessions And Compulsions

Some people experience an uncontrollable and unwelcome pattern of thoughts, called an obsession. For instance, a young mother may periodically be flooded with thoughts of knifing her child, a business executive may feel persistent anxiety lest he lose control and run through the office shouting obscenities, or a person may be plagued with the recurrent thought, "I wonder if I locked the door before leaving home?" The images, words, or presumed desires intrude into awareness, against people's will and beyond their conscious ability to stop them.

People may also feel constrained to perform repeatedly certain irrational and ritualized actions. This behavior is called a compulsion. For example, a person may feel compelled to avoid walking on the cracks of sidewalks or to touch every third windowpane along the walkway of shopping centers. Frequently, obsessive thoughts are tied to compulsive acts. Thus persistent thoughts about being germ-ridden may cause people to wash their hands countless times during the day.

Persons with obsessive-compulsive personality disorder do not have specific obsessions or compulsions. Rather, they will display a style of behavior--inflexibility, perfectionism, stubbornness, frugality, and punctuality--that runs throughout their daily activities. They are typically dependable and reliable workers, have high standards and ethical values, and appreciate order and discipline. They live highly ritualized lives and allow themselves little expression of spontaneity.

Somatoform Disorders

In somatoform disorders ("body-form" disorders), people experience physical symptoms for which there is no apparent organic cause. Sufferers do not intentionally seek to mislead either themselves or others about their physical condition. Their difficulties are quite real. Often they complain of backache, stomach pains, or chest pains (a condition categorized as *psychogenic pain disorder*). Others report blindness, deafness, the loss of sensation in body limbs, false pregnancy, or partial paralysis, (a condition categorized as *conversion disorder*).

Conversion disorders get their name from the belief among some psychotherapists that clients experiencing the disorders "convert" anxiety into physical symptoms. From time to time most people experience mild conversion disorders; for instance, you may become so frightened or terrified that you cannot move. Later you may comment that you were "frozen stiff." But people suffering a conversion disorder do not momentarily lose functioning due to fright. Their difficulty persists.

Conversion disorders should be distinguished from hypochondriasis, in which a person who is in good health becomes preoccupied with imaginary ailments and blames his or her problems on them. They should be distinguished from psychosomatic illnesses, in which emotional problems produce real physical damage such as ulcers or high blood pressure. In conversion disorders, something real has happened to the victim, but not physically. Once the psychological problem has been solved, the person's normal functioning is restored.

Dissociative Disorders

In dissociative disorders, it is psychological rather than physical functioning that is affected. People experience a disturbance in memory or identity. The disorders get their name from the psychoanalytic view that one part of the mind or consciousness splits off, or "dissociates," from another part. These psychological phenomena fascinate many people, and so a good deal is heard about amnesia and "split personalities." Actually, dramatic cases are quite rare. On the other hand, temporary dissociative states, in which people cannot remember what happened to them, are common.

Amnesia, or loss of memory, may be an attempt to escape from problems by blotting them out completely. During wartime, for example, some hospitalized soldiers block out their names, when they were born, where they lived, and their war experiences. However, the amnesiac remembers how to speak and usually retains a fund of general knowledge. Another explanation of amnesia rests on the distinction between automatic and effortful encoding of information. Information that normal people encode automatically may require effort in amnesiacs, leading to memory impairment.

In fugue, another type of dissociative disorder, amnesia is coupled with active flight to a different environment. The person may suddenly disappear and "wake up" three days later in a restaurant two hundred miles from home. Or on discovering himself or herself in a new location, the person may establish a new identity—assume a new name, take a job, and even marry—repressing all knowledge of a previous life. A fugue state may last for days or for decades. However long it lasts, the person comes out of it with no memory of what he or she has done in the interim. Fugue, then, is a sort of traveling amnesia, and it probably serves the same psychological function as amnesia: escape from unbearable conflict or anxiety.

In multiple personality, a third type of dissociative disorder, the individual seems to have two or more distinct identities. Robert Louis Stevenson's story *Dr. Jekyll and Mr. Hyde* provides a fictional illustration of this disorder.

In cases of multiple personality, the various personalities are relatively independent and distinct, with only a small degree of personality linkage among them.

Two predisposing factors seem to be implicated in the disorder. The first is an underlying capacity to go into a spontaneous hypnotic trance. The second is an early childhood of harsh abuse. According to one view, the child uses the hypnotic state as a kind of psychological protection, a temporary defense against an unbearable situation. The temporary defense becomes stabilized when the child is repeatedly confronted with the same kinds of circumstances. Each personality allows the child to cope with certain kinds of difficult realities without other aspects of his or her personality having to know about or confront them.

Affective Disorders

Mood disturbances underlie affective disorders. (Affect is the term psychotherapists use to refer to a person's emotional state or mood.) From time to time everyone undergoes changes in mood, ranging from elation to sadness. However, moods of elation or depression can be abnormal when they persist for long periods, interfere with a person's daily functioning, and distort an individual's outlook on life. At times the disorders can be life threatening, culminating in suicide.

Depression

By depression, psychotherapists do not mean the blues — those feelings of gloom and despair that pervade everyday life at one time or another. They do not mean the short-term bout of sadness and anxiety that accompanies a stressful experience. Rather, depression is an affective disorder characterized by a mood drop that lasts for months (severe depressions average about eight months), even years. As depression deepens, people commonly experience insomnia, disinterest in work, loss of appetite, reduced sexual desire, low energy, hopeless feelings, persistent sadness, and profound emotional despair. Often even routine tasks become difficult for depressed people to perform and they have difficulty concentrating, remembering things, and getting their thoughts together. Some people also suffer deep anxiety as part of their depression.

Depression is frequently termed "the common cold of mental ailments." It is much more widespread and pervasive than is sometimes thought. The National Institute of Mental Health estimates that seven out of every one hundred Americans are affected by depression at any given time.

Mania And Bipolar Disorders

Another mood disorder is mania, in which people experience an extended "high"--they feel revved up and on top of the world. More often, they alternate between elated, excited "highs" and dejected, depressed "lows." This latter disturbance is termed bipolar disorder and also, by some mental health professionals, manic-depressive disorder.

When in the manic phase, these people vibrate with energy and have a decreased need for sleep. Their thoughts and feelings race at machine-gun speed. Frequently, the "high" spirals out of control and sufferers become confused and disorganized.

Bipolar swings between highs and lows may occur over the course of several days to several months. Some people experience interim periods of normality. Others may have only brief highs and long lows or, more rarely, brief lows and long highs. And then there are people who are normal most of the time except for relatively minor dips and elevations.

Psychoanalysis

The origins of psychoanalysis can be traced to Sigmund Freud's observation that the physical symptoms of patients suffering from hysteria tended to disappear after apparently forgotten material was made conscious. From this he developed the basic postulate of psychoanalysis: the existence of a dynamic unconscious that influences every action but operates with material that is not subject to recall by normal processes. This so-called forgetting he termed repression and he made the conscious recognition of repressed experiences the keystone of psychoanalytic therapy. After experimenting with hypnotism to probe the unconscious, Freud introduced two techniques—free association, whereby patients voice their thoughts exactly as they arise, and dream interpretation; these are still the main therapeutic tools of psychoanalysis. In addition, Freud and his followers developed a vast theory of the human psyche that stresses the role of two instincts—the sexual instinct and the death instinct. According to the theory, these two drives balance one another in the well-adjusted individual; if dammed up, they produce neurosis. Freud also developed a theory of the human personality, dividing it into three parts: the id (reservoir of unconscious instinctual drives, dominated by the pleasure principle and desirous of instant gratification); the superego (internal censor, or conscience); and the ego (mediator between the id, the superego, and the demands of society or reality).

Psychoanalysis is the longest of the therapies; it can go on for years with two or three or even five meetings a week. When hypnosis (hypnoanalysis) is used as an adjunct to psychoanalytic methods such extended treatment is unnecessary.

Client-Centered Therapy

Carl Rogers and other humanistic psychologists believe that the root of many disorders is in childhood. However, their approach is very different from that of the psychoanalysts. The humanists argue that we naturally strive to reach our potential and lead a fulfilling life. However, as children we often learn that other people have expectations about how we should behave. We also learn that the way to get rewards is to live up to others expectations. If we follow these lessons, however, we may lose touch with our own desires and feelings. When this happens we become unhappy and experience anxiety.

According to Rogers, given the proper conditions people will become more self-aware and happy, and they will strive to meet their own goals. In short, Rogers suggests that people will reduce their own anxiety and mature by their own efforts if they are given the right opportunities. Therefore, the aim of therapy is to provide the proper setting for this self-growth to occur. The "proper setting" is one in which people do not fear social rejection for expressing themselves. The goal of the therapist is to create this condition by giving clients unconditional positive regard; that is, accepting and caring for them no matter what feelings or behaviors are revealed in the sessions. Therapists need to show a genuine warmth and concern for their clients. In this way, their clients will gain enough confidence to begin the self-exploration process and strive toward personal fulfillment.

The emphasis in therapy is on the client rather than on the therapist. The client determines what will be discussed during therapy; in other words, the therapy is client-centered. The therapist does not attempt to diagnose or interpret the client's condition. According to the humanists, a diagnosis serves no purpose and only places the client in a dehumanized category. Instead, the therapist responds to the person as a unique individual and attempts to experience the world from the client's position, as the client sees it. In doing this, therapists mirror and rephrase what they hear the client saying.

Rational-Emotive Therapy

Rational-emotive therapy (RET) is a form of therapy developed by Albert Ellis in the late 1950's. Ellis believes that people behave in deliberate and rational ways, given their assumptions about life. Emotional problems arise when a person's assumptions are unrealistic. A RET therapist would not look for incidents in the past, as a psychoanalyst would. RET therapists do not probe; they reason.

The goal of rational-emotive therapy is to correct false and self-defeating beliefs. There are a number of irrational and destructive attitudes that can lead to depression. Among the most common are:

1. It is necessary that I be loved by every significant person in my environment.

2. It is absolutely necessary that I be completely competent, adequate, and achieve in all areas or I am worthless.

3. If something is dangerous, I must be constantly concerned about it.

4. It is a terrible disaster if things do not turn out the way I want them to turn out.

Since it is these attitudes that are the root of anxiety, Ellis argues that therapy should be aimed at restructuring the way people think. In order to do this, therapists must take an active and direct teaching role.

To teach the client to think in realistic terms, the RET therapist may use a number of techniques: role-playing; modeling (to demonstrate other ways of thinking and acting); humor (to underline the absurdity of his or her beliefs); and simple persuasion.

Ellis believes that people must take three steps to cure or correct themselves. First, they must realize that some of their assumptions are false. Second, they must see that they are making *themselves* disturbed by acting on false beliefs. Finally, they must work to break old habits of thought and behavior. They have to practice, to learn self-discipline, to take risks. When self-defeating thoughts and feelings are changed, the client will learn to both feel and behave in more adaptive ways.

Gestalt Therapy

Developed by Fritz Perls, a psychoanalyst, in the 1950's and 1960's, Gestalt therapy aims to make the person "whole" or "complete" by developing self-awareness, overcoming incapacitating defenses, releasing pent-up feelings, and giving full range to the potential for growth. Although taking its name "Gestalt" (meaning "pattern" or "configuration" in German) from a distinct school of psychological thought, the approach does not strictly follow traditional Gestalt theory. However, it resembles other humanistic approaches in its emphasis on the expressive and dynamic aspects of people, rather than on the unhealthy and distorted features stressed by psychoanalytic theorists.

Clients of Gestalt therapy are encouraged to immerse themselves in the here and now. More particularly, they are asked to experience things rather than imagine them and to feel rather than think. Therapeutic techniques teach people to pick up cues associated with bodily sensations, perceptions, and feelings. More particularly, therapeutic work is directed toward the identification of a person's needs and of legitimate ways by which these needs can be met. People are helped to come to terms with themselves--to accept themselves for what they *are* and to give expression to their true feelings and desires in a responsible manner. In brief, each person is encouraged to do his or her own thing.

The relationship between the client and the therapist reflects the "living in the now" emphasis. It attempts to drive home the need to get in touch with one's feelings and to express them without fear or embarrassment. Suppose that toward the middle of a session a client runs out of material to discuss and sits mute, staring blankly out the window. Instead of waiting for the client to speak up, a Gestalt therapist would say what he or she feels: "I can't stand the way you just sit there and say nothing. Sometimes I regret ever becoming a therapist. You are impossible . . . There, now I feel better." The therapist is not blowing off steam in an unprofessional way. The therapist does this to encourage (by example) the client to express feelings, even if it means risking a relationship.

Behavior Therapies

Psychoanalysis and the human potential movement have sometimes been criticized for being "all talk and no action." In behavior therapy there is much more emphasis on action. Rather than spending large amounts of time going into the client's past history or the details of his or her dreams, the behavior therapist concentrates on finding out what is specifically wrong with the client's current life and takes steps to change it. Thus the aim of behavior therapies is not to alter a person's personality (which is the aim of psychoanalysis) but to change only certain problem behaviors. The approach has proven of particular value in the treatment of anxiety disorders.

The idea behind behavior therapy is that a disturbed person is one who has learned to behave in the wrong way. The therapist's job, therefore, is to "reeducate" the client. The reasons for the client's undesirable behavior are not important. What is important is to change the behavior. To bring about such changes, the therapist uses techniques based on the principles of learning. The strategy rests on the assumption that learning depends on the connections or links that people make between two events.

Systematic Desensitization

One technique used by behavior therapists is systematic desensitization. Therapists use this method to help clients overcome various fears. These anxieties may be associated with closed spaces, heights, death, sexual encounters, public speaking, flying in airplanes, or social contacts. Systematic desensitization involves gradually confronting clients with various levels of a fear-rousing stimulus after they have first been trained to relax.

In systematic desensitization, the therapist takes the client through the feared situation step by step. In contrast, in "implosive" or "flooding" therapy, the therapist guides the client through the entire feared situation all at once, either by imagining it (*implosion*) or actually experiencing it (*flooding*). For instance, a client may fear her father's anger should she assert herself. In implosion, the therapist would have the client imagine telling her father something of which he would certainly disapprove, and then hold the scene in mind until her anxiety peaks and decreases. As an example of flooding, if a client fears heights, the therapist may accompany him to a high building and have him look out a window. The client remains in the anxiety-provoking situation until it no longer elicits anxiety. Flooding resembles the end stages of desensitization but without the gradual build-up to the feared situation.

Aversive Conditioning

Another form of behavior therapy is aversive conditioning. People learn to associate a strong negative response with an undesirable behavior such as drinking, using drugs, gambling, or smoking. The aversive stimulus may be an electric shock, a loud noise, or nausea.

Cognitive-Behavioral Therapies

Psychologists Martin Seligman and Aaron T. Beck stress the part that negative thinking plays in depressive disorders. Depressed people look at life through dark-colored glasses. They dwell on bad experiences, minimize their accomplishments, and forget happy times. These elements constitute the *cognitive* components of depression. Depression is also characterized by *behavioral* components, including withdrawal, lack of energy, insomnia, and loss of appetite.

Cognitive-behavioral therapists attack their clients' problems on both the cognitive and the behavioral levels. They insist that depressed clients confront their negative view of themselves and the world and question the evidence that they use. And they assist their clients in tackling the behavioral aspects of their problems by scheduling positive self-reinforcements.

Cognitive Therapy

In recent years, cognitive therapy has gained considerable popularity and acceptance. Beck assigns primary importance to the fact that people *think*. In turn, how they think and the conclusions they reach determine what they feel and do. Thus Beck reasons that if depressed people come to see themselves as winners instead of losers, they will feel better. His approach is designed to correct these major distortions characteristic of depressed people: seeing themselves as deficient and unworthy; seeing the world as frustrating and unfulfilling; and seeing the future as hopeless.

In early sessions, Beck has his clients record their daily activities in a notebook, plan productive activities, and schedule enjoyable events. He also assigns tasks at which the client is likely to succeed (it can be as simple as getting out of bed, preparing a snack, or writing a letter). These measures "break into" the self-defeating and circular components of depressive thought. They focus the client's attention on his or her behavior and away from melancholy preoccupation. Simultaneously, they provide the client with a sense of accomplishment.

Later, the client and the therapist work together to pinpoint the client's distorted, negative, and unrealistic thoughts. Clients are made to confront their pessimistic ideas and see that they do not make sense. For example, they come to recognize the danger of such either-or premises as "Either I'm popular with everybody or I'm a total flop." They learn to realize that such unreasonable and inflexible expectations lock them within cycles of inevitable failure, that their pursuit of unattainable goals feeds their feelings of guilt and worthlessness.

Finally, the client and therapist set about to modify the maladaptive beliefs. They seek to increase the client's problem-solving repertoire through the acquisition of effective verbal and behavioral strategies. Research suggests that cognitive therapy is a particularly effective type of directive therapy in combating depressed feelings associated with hopelessness and in strengthening a person's sense of worth and self-esteem.

CHAPTER 21
Smoking Cessation Guidelines

Medical authorities contend that cigarette smoking is the single most important source of preventable death. The annual death toll from diseases attributed to smoking, 435,000, is sixteen times the fatality rate of motor vehicle crashes and more than the total number of Americans killed in World War I, Korea, and Vietnam combined. The Environmental Protection Agency lists tobacco smoke as the country's most dangerous airborne carcinogen.

As a result of the aggressive anti-smoking campaign launched by Everett Koop, when he was the United States Surgeon General, many people have quit smoking. While the percentage of smokers has been dropping for some years, there are still 50 MILLION Americans over the age of 17 who smoke cigarettes. And nine out of ten smokers report that they want to quit, so there is still a large market out there.

This procedure is a two-session stop smoking program for office use. (It is based on the very successful group system that we developed.)

When the appointment is made tell the prospective client that it is a two-visit program. Collect the total fee on the first visit.

The objective of the first visit is to bolster the client's resolve to quit smoking. Although specific suggestions to quit smoking are not given during the first office visit, the client is hypnotized to facilitate re-induction on the second visit and to generate a confident expectation of success.

Follow This Sequence

Stress the importance of commitment, and that it is never too late to quit smoking. Fact: *No matter how long a person has smoked, when they stop the body starts regenerating.* Emphasize all the health benefits of quitting. Point out the stabilizing force of the subconscious mind, and how, through hypnosis, it will empower the client to stop smoking quickly and permanently. Preparation is an important part of the quitting process. Schedule the next appointment within one week. Designate the appointment date as the client's *quit-day*. This is an important event! (Quitting day is not important for what day it is, but rather because it adds momentum and a focal point to the client's commitment to quit.) The client is told to mark their quit-day on a calendar, counting down each day. Tell the client to get rid of all smoking paraphernalia on quit-day: cigarettes, matches, lighters, ashtrays, etc.

Motivation is an important aspect of this program. Success depends on the depth of the client's commitment to quit. Wanting to stop because of the liabilities is not enough. The client has to go the next step beyond wanting to quit to making a commitment to quit. The client has to say: "I will quit smoking, and under no conditions will I ever go back to smoking."

On the second visit, following hypnotic induction, the client is given a reinforcement CD.[50] To assure long-term success, it is necessary to use the CD on a daily basis for the full time recommended.

Exercise will provide a way to manage weight gain, and reduce stress as well. The client will not gain weight if he or she drinks several glasses of water every day and begins a realistic exercise program, such as walking. Walking is one of the best all-round physical activities. The massaging action the leg muscles exert on the veins as one walks improves the flow of blood back to the heart. Walking not only improves the leg muscles but also the pumping action they provide. Walking costs nothing, there are many possible daily opportunities for it, and it can be enjoyable thus reducing stress and the urge to smoke. A sensible exercise regimen can help reduce stress, control weight and protect the client from heart and blood vessel disease

Smoking Cessation Guidelines For The Client

On the second visit, following hypnotic induction, give the client a reinforcement CD and a copy of the following guidelines. These guidelines emphasize the importance of listening to the reinforcement CD on a daily basis. It also lists the more common symptoms of recovery; strategies to avoid weight gain, breathing exercises and other strategies to manage urges.

---

[50] A prerecorded reinforcement CD is included with the National Guild of Hypnotists Ultimate Smoking Cessation packet and is available through the NGH Bookstore.

You've Kicked The Smoking Habit For Good!

You've done something many millions of people wish they could do. You've quit smoking. Smoking is something in your past and you're glad to have it ended. The suggestions that you stop smoking, implanted in your subconscious mind while you were in hypnosis, have empowered you with the strength and determination to live up to your commitment as a non-smoker.

As with any great change in one's life, quitting smoking means you will be going through a transition period adjusting to being an ex-smoker. Most people don't have any unsettling physical or mental changes as a result of giving up cigarettes. During the transition period, however, your body is in the process of repairing itself, slowly returning to a healthy state as the poisonous effects of nicotine leave it. Don't be surprised if you experience some symptoms of recovery. Most symptoms, if any do occur, will disappear within two to three weeks. Remember you are breaking your dependence on an addictive substance--nicotine--as well as changing an established habit pattern and it is natural to have some inconvenience. Accept any symptoms as part of your body changing and purging itself of a poison.

How To Use Your Reinforcement CD

To stay free of smoking forever, you must sustain your commitment. Maintaining your commitment as a nonsmoker will involve your persistent use of the reinforcement CD, which you received with these guidelines. Daily use of this CD will bolster your resolve to remain a non-smoker. Thus assuring your immediate and long-term success. The CD must be used as follows: daily for the first forty-five days, and then every other day for the next month. By that time your transition period will be over, or winding down rapidly, and you will have been fully and effectively confirmed in your having quit smoking forever.

It doesn't matter what time of day you play the CD, or even if it's a different time each day. But you must keep to the schedule of listening to it daily for six weeks, and then every other day for another month. You are not to make excuses for skipping or for concluding that you don't need it any more. Long experience has shown that for complete success in quitting smoking forever, it is absolutely vital to listen to the reinforcement CD according to this schedule.

Also, you must not play the CD while driving or engaged in any activity demanding mental alertness, for it can make you drowsy. If possible, don't play the CD in a noisy or action-filled environment. You should find a quiet place where you will be free from intrusions, loud noises and other distractions. Dim the lights, turn off TV and radio and stereo, disconnect the phone and ask everyone to leave you alone for a while. It isn't absolutely essential to be free from all distractions, but it will be very helpful.

Remove shoes, loosen any tight-fitting garments, and take out contact lenses. If available, settle back on a recliner or other soft chair that supports your neck, head and back. Don't lie down; if you have only a sofa or bed available, use pillows or other supports to prop yourself up.

If for any reason you need to attend to some urgent matter, you can arouse yourself instantly and then return to your reinforcement session after taking care of the interruption. IMPORTANT: *Do not commence where you left off and start listening to the CD from the beginning.*

Some Common Symptoms Of Recovery

What are some of the symptoms of recovery that listening to the CD will help you to deal with and take in stride, as mere temporary inconveniences?

For a few days, perhaps longer if you have been a very heavy smoker, you might find that you cough more; raising up a lot of mucus, often stained brown because of the tobacco tars trapped in your breathing system. Nicotine has an anesthetic effect on the tiny hairlike "cilia" that line your nasal, tracheal, and lung passages. In a healthy person the cilia continually "sweep out" all intrusive material such as germs, mucus, and dirt from your lungs.

In a smoker, the cilia stops functioning and all this material piles up in the breathing system. That is why smokers develop shortness of breath, a hacking cough, wheezing and so on. But very soon after you stop smoking, the cilia resume activity and relentlessly "sweep out" all this accumulated respiratory garbage inside you. Don't be alarmed or worried; it's part of the repair process and it'll soon be over. Then you'll be able to breathe clearly and cleanly again, smell and taste things distinctly, and wake up in the morning with a clear throat and nose.

A slightly sore or dry throat sometimes follows on quitting smoking. This too is part of the repair job. It won't last long. Drink fluids to ease it. But go very easy on alcohol for a long time after quitting; it tends to counteract all the positive instructions to your subconscious. Relapse is frequently associated with alcohol. In the beginning, you should try to avoid drinking alcohol. The first few times you drink after quitting, you must be extremely cautious. Just have one or two drinks. Try to be with a non-smoker. It is important to explain to the person that you may need support. Make up your mind now that you will not smoke if you've had a few drinks, even though it seems like a good idea at the time. *It is definitely not a good idea.* When you're drinking it's easy to rationalize yourself back into smoking.

Don't talk yourself into smoking again. Many people reach a point in their nonsmoking lives when they feel they have the situation "under control" and that having a cigarette "just once" won't hurt. This could easily be the beginning of a short road back to smoking, just as before.

You may feel a bit light headed for a while. That's just your lung cells starting to take in again the amount of oxygen you normally need, and that smoking has deprived you of by hindering the oxygenation of the cells. Your body will soon readjust to this new, normal oxygen ratio.

If you feel a little listless, tired or lethargic for a few days, that's simply your pulse rate and blood pressure coming back to normal, from their abnormal stimulation by nicotine. Again, your body will soon readjust.

The Reality Of Weight Gain

Weight gain is a fear that has needlessly deterred thousands from quitting smoking. Some people gain weight after giving up smoking, since they start to burn calories a little more slowly. Also, food tastes better and some people use food instead of cigarettes when they want something to do with their hands. But there is no rule that says you will gain weight. Don't forget that a few extra pounds are not nearly as bad for you as smoking. Although there is no inevitability about putting on weight when one quits, it is understandable that after having been habituated to putting a cigarette in and out of your mouth about 400 times a day, if you were an average smoker, you will almost without realizing it, be putting something else in your mouth all the time. Only now, it'll be food--and pretty soon you'll be adding pounds, If that is food heavy in carbohydrates (flour and sugar). But it doesn't have to be. The most important foods to avoid are sweets—donuts, cakes, cookies and candies. Sweets may increase your urge for cigarettes. Eating sweets will cause most people to gain weight when they stop smoking. Instead, drink lots of water—it helps to flush the nicotine poisons out of your body; eat salads and carrot sticks; chew on swizzle sticks. In a few weeks at most, you will have got rid of the urge to have something in your mouth, and by following these common-sense suggestions you will have gained no more than two or three pounds, if even that much.

Also, now that you start to breathe better and don't get "winded" as easily, you'll find yourself wanting to be more physically active. What kind of exercise is best? Walking is perfect. Start taking longer walks, and brisker ones. Work up to two miles in 45 minutes. Increase your participation in swimming, biking, jogging, aerobics—anything brisk and steady that you like and can do for at least 10 minutes at a time, then 20 minutes, and then 30. Do it at least three times a week. This activity will more than offset any slight weight gain you may have.

Breathing Exercises To Manage Urges

There will be the occasional moments when your hands will fidget and reach for a cigarette. Your subconscious mind has been instructed, in hypnosis, that these urges will soon pass. Hypnosis has given you the power to eliminate the craving for a cigarette.

If you are in a situation in which you used to smoke, it is only natural that you will think about a cigarette. Instead of thinking self-defeating thoughts like, "I'd love to have a cigarette right now," remind yourself how far you've come and how much you've accomplished. Tell yourself that you do not smoke nor do you want to. And if you go right on with what you are doing and take a long, slow, relaxing breath that thought will readily pass by. Even if you do nothing about the urge, it will pass in a few seconds. Distracting just puts you in control.

There is an effective quick inhalation exercise that will help you cope with a stressful situation. First, form your mouth into a small circle, as if you were inhaling on a cigarette or going to whistle. Then take a breath, inhaling through the circle you formed with your mouth. Throw your head back gently. Now exhale through your mouth in the same manner, and relax. Repeat as necessary. Breathing exercises will help you to reduce tension.

The Rubber Band Method

A tip from a successful ex-smoker: An American Cancer Society contest to come up with new ideas on how to break the smoking habit was won by Mrs. Janet MacAinsh of Howell, Michigan, who said that she had broken her twenty-six year pack-a-day habit with the help of a rubber band. She kept the rubber band on her wrist and snapped it against her skin whenever she felt the urge to light up. Be sure the rubber band is loose enough that it doesn't block blood flow or leave a mark on the skin when it is removed. According to Edward Lichtenstein of the University of Oregon, preliminary research suggests that this approach really does help people curb their urge to smoke.

Review Your Reasons For Quitting

You can further strengthen your commitment and its instruction to your subconscious mind, by often thinking—really thinking, putting your thoughts in the forefront of your conscious mind--about the many positive things you're gaining by having quit smoking. Freedom from worry about cancer, emphysema, strokes, and heart attacks. More resistance to colds and infections. Set a good example for your children.

Smoking makes your clothes and hair smell. Smoking is a waste of money. You'll sleep better, work better, and play better. Greatly increased self-respect--go ahead, boast of your victory over smoking to family and friends. There's nothing wrong with bragging about having done something that was right for you and those around you. Your friends and relatives can congratulate you as you check off another week—or month—as a nonsmoker. You'll have new freedom to take up new activities, new interests, and new friendships.

Repeat over to yourself the wonderful fact that your body is constantly replacing and renewing the millions of cells of which it is composed. In the course of somewhere around five to seven years, depending on your body size, every cell will have been replaced and your body totally changed into a wholly new one. All of the old nicotine-permeated cells will have been discarded and you'll be as clean of tobacco components as if you had never smoked. For that cleansing and renewal, the minor discomforts of the transition period after quitting, aren't even worth mentioning.

Reward Yourself For Not Smoking

Congratulate yourself each time you get through the day without smoking. After one week, give yourself a reward. It can be something you buy, like a record, or something you like to do, like seeing a movie. After three months give yourself that silk blouse, pair of shoes, tennis racket, or whatever else you have had your eye on. After a year you might take an extra vacation-- a weekend in the Caribbean, for example. The money you will save in just the first year of not smoking will more than pay for your rewards. No matter how you do it, make sure you reward yourself in some way. It reminds you of the fact that what you're doing is important.

Stay Smoke-Free For A Lifetime

Remember always when thinking on your victory over smoking and that you will never go back to it, to avoid such terms as "giving up smoking". You are not giving up anything in getting rid of something as destructive to you as smoking, any more than a freed prisoner gives up his chains and shackles. You are gaining--gaining freedom, health and longer life, a whole new and better life in fact. And you have done it through the proven methodology of hypnosis, which enabled you to contact and draw on the vast powers of your subconscious mind.

Congratulations and good luck!

Smoking Cessation Induction Script

Hypnotize your client as deeply as possible. Then begin:

Congratulations on your commitment to yourself. Hypnosis will increase your determination . . . your willpower . . . and your self-control . . . so that you will . . . from this time forward . . . never . . . ever again smoke another cigarette. Before you leave I will give you some smoking cessation guidelines that I have prepared for you and a CD . . . it is important that you read the material and listen to the CD daily as instructed. Keep in mind that you do this exercise for your own benefit . . . consider it a gift to yourself.

Now relax deeper . . . going deeper into pleasant relaxation . . . drifting and floating into dreamy, drowsiness . . . and with this deep relaxation your subconscious mind is becoming exquisitely receptive to suggestion . . . you are now so deeply relaxed that your mind is focused on every suggestion that I give you. As you rest there all calm and quiet . . . your subconscious mind is awake and listening and receptive . . . it can easily absorb every suggestion that I give you . . . you are resting calmly and quietly . . . nothing will disturb your restful peace . . . you need pay no attention to other sounds for they are unimportant . . . you can hear my voice clearly . . . you will find that you can easily and quickly and willingly follow every suggestion that I give you. In this relaxed condition your subconscious mind will strengthen the effect of every suggestion that I give you . . . all of the suggestions will make the changes we want them to make . . . and because of the suggestions . . . you will have no need or desire to smoke . . . you will have no cravings for cigarettes . . . you will no longer have the impulsive habit of smoking . . . the pattern of habit you had to smoke is being erased now . . . you will not need to reach for a cigarette because you are tense or bored or nervous . . . anytime in the future you ever think of smoking . . . the very thought will be a signal to take a long . . . deep breath   . . . and as you slowly exhale that breath . . . all the reasons not to smoke will immediately come back into your mind . . . because the suggestions you have received . . . you are no longer a compulsive smoker . . . because you made an absolute commitment to stop smoking . . . you made a value judgment to stop smoking . . . you made a choice between a healthy life . . . and cigarettes . . . realizing that you cannot have both . . . you have chosen to quit smoking . . . and you no longer feel threatened by the thought of stopping smoking. You are determined and committed to succeed . . . and proud of the absolute commitment that you have made to yourself . . . because you have stopped smoking . . . there is no further reason to think of yourself as a smoker . . . no further reason for trying to smoke . . . visualize yourself through the day feeling good . . . healthy . . . and relaxed. Without the odor of cigarettes . . . without the expense of cigarettes . . . without the coughing . . . without having to constantly light cigarettes . . . being totally and completely free of the addiction . . . without the poisons of cigarettes in your body . . . you will become calmer . . . much more relaxed . . . any time at all in the future that you ever find yourself becoming upset anxious or worried. . . . If thoughts of smoking comes to your mind . . . you need only to take a long . . . deep breath . . . and release the breath slowly . . . and you will immediately relax . . . completely and totally . . . mentally and physically . . . a single deep breath will automatically relax you . . . for your commitment not to smoke is permanent . . . but you will deal with it on a minute-to-minute basis. You will not be tempted by others who are smoking . . . you now recognize that smoking was a poison to your body . . . the taste of smoking was poisonous . . . and there was no pleasure . . . no enjoyment from tasting poisonous gases entering your mouth . . . going down into your lungs and poisoning your body . . . no longer are you . . . or will you ever be again . . . a slave to that disabling habit . . . you will now see other people's smoking as a weakness . . . and your not smoking as a strength . . . you no longer have any desire to inhale the poisonous tars . . . the poisonous nicotine . . . down into your lungs . . . turning them black and filling them with mucus. The thought of inhaling a cigarette now will be like inhaling dirt or mucus to your mind. . . . This thought will be so revolting to you . . . so disgusting to you . . . that your desire to stay away from cigarettes permanently . . . completely overwhelms the old desire to smoke . . . the fear of emphysema . . . of heart disease . . . of cancer . . . of shortness of breath . . . of poor circulation . . . reinforce your need to stay away from that terribly disabling habit. . .

Now relax deeper . . . sinking down deeper and deeper . . . you need not pursue any other thoughts . . . just the feeling that you are relaxing deeper . . . and as you rest . . . once again you think of your purpose of stopping smoking . . . the image of yourself now with a cigarette is a very ugly one . . . you will never again choose a cigarette over your own health . . . you will now choose your health over the cigarette . . . you will not replace the smoking habit with any other negative habit . . . such as overeating . . . in fact . . . your appetite will in no way increase   . . . you will have absolutely no craving . . . no desire for additional food . . . and now you will fully understand that by having stopped smoking . . . you will completely reverse the cycle of illness and disease . . . begin instead the process of cleaning all of the filth . . . all the damage out of your lungs . . . out of your body . . . the process of restoring your health . . . of repairing the damage . . . and restoring your strength and vitality. . . .

All the suggestions you have received . . . and all the suggestions you will receive . . . will be totally effective . . . and the strength of the suggestions will never waver . . . will never lessen . . . they become a permanent state of mind . . .

continuing every minute of every day . . . and every day now . . . without your cigarettes . . . without smoking . . . you will become physically and mentally stronger . . . without cigarettes robbing your energy and dulling your senses . . . you will become more alert . . . more energetic. And every day without the cigarettes constricting your blood vessels . . . forcing your heart to pump harder . . . you will find that your nerves grow stronger and steadier . . . and for the next few days . . . you will become so deeply interested in your new feelings of health . . . that your mind will not be preoccupied with smoking . . . you will only regard cigarettes with disgust . . . so even if the thought of a cigarette momentarily occurs to you . . . take a long . . . deep breath . . . and as you slowly exhale you will automatically relax . . . then go right on with whatever you are doing . . . and the thought will easily pass by . . . no longer having any effect upon you . . . the thought will dissipate and disappear . . . from now on you will see cigarettes in their true perspective . . . as a filthy . . . disgusting habit . . . you will never again associate the thought of a cigarette with pleasure . . . and as you remain more relaxed . . . less tensed . . . you will develop much more confidence in yourself . . . much more confidence in your ability to do whatever you have to do . . . without the need of a cigarette . . . you will have confidence in your ability to stay away from cigarettes . . . and because of this . . . every day you will feel more and more independent . . . independent of the smoking habit . . . and you will know that no matter how difficult or trying things may be . . . you will be able to cope with them easily and efficiently . . . without any need for a cigarette at all . . . and because all of these things will happen exactly as I tell you they will happen . . . you will feel much happier . . . much more content . . . much more cheerful . . . much more optimistic . . . remember . . . there are absolutely no circumstances under which you will ever again choose to smoke. . . .

Just relax . . . deeper and deeper . . . deep pleasant restful relaxation . . . with repeated use of the re-enforcement CD you will receive today . . . you will steadily increase your ability to relax . . . you enjoy this peaceful relaxation and will look forward to listening to the CD.

Use appropriate suggestions to re-alert the client.

CHAPTER 22
Pain Management

IMPORTANT: *In the alleviation of pain, hypnotherapy should be used only in those cases that have been screened by a thorough physical examination to establish the diagnosis. Pain is often a warning signal, a symptom of an underlying disorder that needs to be treated. Therefore in all cases involving the management of pain – chronic as well as acute – get a medical referral. Therefore, hypnosis should be used only when there is certainty that there is no underlying organic disorder, or under the supervision of a qualified specialist.*

It has long been known that hypnosis can control to a very substantial degree, if not totally, even the severest pain, as in extensive burns and in advanced cancer. To relieve the stress and anxiety that exacerbate chronic pain we should first have an understanding of the pain mechanism, and how the mind can distance itself from the perception of pain. Hypnotherapy for pain relief ranges from moderate to very effective. Its long-term success is related to the client's hypnotizability, and his or her commitment to reinforce the suggestions with self-hypnosis. However, the client's susceptibility to hypnosis is not the only criterion for the production of analgesia. This fact is illustrated in the following story as told by British medical hypnosis expert John Hartland, whom we cited In Chapter 16 in this book:

"Some years ago I was undertaking the hypnotic training of a young married woman in preparation for her confinement. She was a good subject, and I had already taught her self-hypnosis as a result of which she was able to produce a state of complete relaxation whenever she wished to do so. She had previously achieved so deep a state of hypnosis that I had no doubt that I should easily succeed in inducing a complete analgesia to pin-prick. Unfortunately I was mistaken and this did not occur, and the most I was able to achieve was a slight blunting of sensation to painful stimuli — all attempts to secure a complete analgesia failed completely. Despite this, I continued to impress upon her mind the fact that during her confinement she would be able to relax and free herself from tension so completely that she would still be able to abolish pain and merely experience the discomfort of her uterine contractions. Several weeks later she appeared with her right arm in a sling. It seemed that she and her husband had been involved in a car accident, as a result of which she had developed acute pain in her right arm and shoulder. Worried at her distress, he left her sitting by the roadside and hurried to the nearest farmhouse to seek assistance. When he returned, he was amazed to find that during his absence she had put herself into the hypnotic state and had completely abolished all pain and discomfort."

Dr. Harland summarizes, "It must, therefore be possible for hypnosis to secure complete relief from pain arising from pathological or physiological processes in cases in which it was impossible to produce any marked degree of insensitivity to pain caused by an artificial, external stimulus." (Clients with organic pain problems do better because they are more highly motivated to obtain pain relief.) Experiments at Harvard University led to the conclusion that pain of the pathological variety is much more susceptible to suggestion than artificially induced pain.

Present-day medical science conceives pain to be essentially of two kinds: *nociceptive pain*, in which the body perceives damage to tissue which is reported as pain by the pain receptors in the brain; and *chronic pain* in which tissue damage may or may not occur. Nociceptive pain is of short duration and usually can be alleviated by standard painkillers. Low-back trouble, following a herniated disc or other injury, is the most common cause of chronic pain. But amputations, arthritis, trigeminal neuralgia, headaches, and cancer also produce the kind of pain that may fluctuate in intensity, but seldom disappears completely.

Until recently, nobody really understood how the mind relieved pain. We know now that chronic pain feeds on itself, creating a self-reinforcing cycle that must first be broken and then reversed to bring relief. Pain is so highly subjective, a combination of physical sensations and emotional response that the longer it persists, the more dominate the emotional components become. The client's emotional reaction to pain must be resolved before pain can be relieved.

Some pain victims unwittingly intensify their pain. When they insist on their disability, resorting to crutches, corsets, or even total bed rest, their muscles degenerate and become a source of constant pain themselves. This sets in motion a vicious cycle of pain malingering and muscle degeneration.

One of the most plausible explanations for pain perception and relief is the gate-control theory advanced in 1965 by Ronald Melzack, a psychophysiologist at McGill University, and Patrick Wall, a neuroanatomist at University College, London. They suggested that different nerve fibers conduct different messages. The larger fibers conduct the sense of touch, heat, and cold. The smaller fibers conduct pain. When the large fibers are stimulated by rubbing, hot packs, acupuncture, etc., they overload the circuits and close a "gate" in the spinal cord that prevents the small fibers from transmitting pain signals to the brain. When the large fibers are not stimulated, the gate remains open and the small fibers have a chance to get their pain messages through.

Melzack and Wall attempted to explain pain's emotional components in the same way, suggesting that positive emotions, such as joy, excitement, or pleasure, close the gate, while negative emotions, such as fear, anxiety, and depression, open it. Despite an enormous amount of research, no "gate" mechanism has ever been positively identified and it has remained a theory.

Now, pertinent evidence is starting to accumulate in two areas: not only are emotions related to the flow of neurotransmitters (the chemical messengers) in the brain, thus directly affecting the transmission of pain signals, but the brain itself is capable of producing a powerful analgesic substance. This substance, endorphin (endogenous morphine), is five to 10 times more powerful than morphine and has recently been shown to inhibit the transmission of pain signals through the spinal cord. Although evidence is still scanty, it seems likely that many pain-killing methods have this common denominator, the ability to stimulate endorphin.

There are two pain sectors, already noted above as those connected with severe burns and advanced cancer, which combine both nociceptive and chronic pain, that is either partially or wholly uncontrollable by even massive amounts of pain-killing drugs. In these two sectors, tissue damage continues to occur. Burn patients suffer it in skin grafting of burned areas and excision of the grafts from unburned areas, as well as in bandage changing and sloughing off (debridement) of dead or dying tissue. In advanced cancer, the tumor is still attacking and damaging fresh tissues all the time, with resulting ever mounting intensity of pain.

Hypnosis, as stated above, has proven capable of relieving and controlling these two highly refractory pain sectors. The hypnotherapist must with great skill enable the clients in each to overcome the fears that are making the pain worse and locking them into a state of hopelessness. This is achieved through deep relaxation and dissociation from the pain, in which the burn victim ceases to fear the treatment procedures since he or she will be in control; and the client with cancer no longer fears that there is nothing ahead but continual severe pain. Through self-hypnosis they will not need the presence of the hypnotherapist to initiate these self-protective dissociative states; though the therapist will continue to come to counsel, encourage and direct them. Though pain-killing drugs are usually still needed, the dosages often can be greatly reduced, and in any case become much more effective.

Intensive and extended hypnotherapy treatment is sometimes required in chronic pain cases where the underlying causes are involved and complex. Migraine, arthritis and rheumatism are typical of such diagnoses. For relief to be more than temporary, long and patient work with the client is necessary. Self-hypnosis with directed visualization for deep relaxation and letting go of deep-seated, long-held resentments, will usually bring positive results. Mobilizing the immune system to resist infections and to check it from attacking the body's own cells, as in arthritis, is important. Efficacy of pain medications and a reduction of their dosages can be brought about through suggestion, once proper relaxation has been achieved.

Phantom limb pain, a common complaint among amputees, has been overcome through hypnosis. Suggestions are implanted that the stump is healing completely and no longer causing pain. The cause of phantom limb pain would appear to be a subconscious conviction that the amputation wound is unhealed and hurting. Removing the erroneous belief results in the disappearance of the pain and discomfort.

Hypnoanalgesia

Before the discovery of chemical anesthesia, hypnosis was the only effective way to mitigate pain. As we saw in Chapter 1 James Esdaile, a surgeon practicing in India in 1845 performed several thousand minor operations and over three hundred major surgeries (including amputations of limbs and breasts and the removal of huge scrotal tumors) painlessly on patients who were in "mesmeric coma." Understandably, in the pre-anesthesia era, many surgical patients died of neurogenic shock. Dupuytren, writing about this period, stated: "Pain kills like hemorrhage." In those days, to undergo surgery was tantamount to signing one's death warrant. Using mesmerism to mitigate pain, Esdaile reduced the mortality rate from 50% to only 5%.

Despite its documented effectiveness hypnosis will never be a substitute for chemoanesthesia, as not everyone can be hypnotized deeply enough for the production of complete anesthesia.

Except in the fields of obstetrics and dentistry, and in some surgical cases where chemical anesthesia in contraindicated (for example, geriatric patients who are at risk for heart surgery) hypnoanesthesia is rarely used today. This is unfortunate since the use of hypnosis allays fear and tension, reduces anoxemia (deficiency in the oxygen content of the blood), facilitates the induction of inhalation anesthesia, and reduces the amount of analgesia and anesthesia needed. Also, chemically induced anesthesia impedes postoperative healing, as it retards the body's ability to regenerate and repair damaged tissues.

Hypnotically induced analgesia can diminish the excruciating pain of second and third degree burns, and in terminal cancer cases. Eventually the body builds up a natural immunity to barbiturates and narcotics, and the dosage must be increased. Unlike these palliatives, hypnosis is free from harmful side effects.

Glove anesthesia is often used as a technique to mitigate pain. It is a partial or total loss of physical sensation in the area of the hand that would be covered by a glove. It can be used to control pain by transferring the glove anesthesia to another part of the body. In the case where glove anesthesia is to be transferred to the jaw or abdomen, for example, the client is told to place the anesthetized hand on that area. "As you touch your jaw (abdomen) the numbness you have in your hand will be transferred to that part of your body. You will have the same freedom from pain there. You may feel pressure, but no pain. At the same time, feeling will return to your hand." (One or both hands can transfer the glove anesthesia.) Through self-hypnosis it can be used in childbirth cases, and in severe pain problems.

Induction Script for Glove Anesthesia

Hypnotize the client as deeply as possible, then say ...

> *And now you are deeply relaxed. . . . And with each and every gentle breath you will go deeper . . . and deeper . . . into pleasant deep relaxation. . . . Nothing will disturb this pleasant restful hypnotic experience . . . as you go deeper . . . and deeper. . . .*
>
> *You will be aware of this hand (lightly touch back of the right hand) becoming numb . . . and insensitive to feeling. . . . Your right hand is growing numb and insensitive to feeling. . . . Soon your right hand will become so numb, heavy, and woodenlike that it will be devoid of feeling. . . . Your right hand is growing numb and insensitive to feeling. . . . It now has the feeling of a thick leather glove around it . . . as you are aware of this glovelike feeling, nod your head. . . . Good. . . . Your right hand is numb, heavy, and woodenlike . . . and insensitive to feeling. . . . Now transfer this numbness to your face. . . . With every movement of your hand toward your face, it will get more numb and woodenlike. . . .*

That's it. . . . Now, when your hand touches your face, press the palm of your hand close to your face. (The hand lifts and is pressed to the face.) . . . When you are certain that this numbness is transferred from your hand to your face, drop your hand and your arm. . . . Good. . . . Now go deeper and deeper . . . into pleasant deep relaxation. . . .

Crasilneck and Hall[51] test the glove anesthesia with a blunt nail file. After the client acknowledges an awareness of the hand being numb and insensitive, say . . .

Now open your eyes and notice that I am sticking your finger quite severely with a nail file, but no pain . . . and with a little more force I would break the skin . . . no pain. . . . I stop. . . . I now suggest that normal feeling return to the finger. . . . Now, I am going to stimulate the same finger. . . . Now you are withdrawing your finger. . . . You withdrew it . . . yes . . . with only slight pressure . . . demonstrating to you the power of your inner mind over your body in the control and feeling of severe pain. . . . The anesthetized finger felt nothing with severe stimulation . . . but when the finger that was not anesthetized was touched ever so lightly you experienced feeling.

Example of Induction for Pain Relief

Hypnotize the client as deeply as possible, then say ...

Now that you are deeply relaxed . . . take in slow, deep breaths . . . and as you exhale, mentally say to yourself, "Re-

---

[51] Crasilneck, H.B., Hall, J.A., *Clinical Hypnosis Principles and Applications*, 2nd Edition, Grune & Stratton, Inc., N.Y., © 1985

lax." . . . Pay attention to your breathing and continue to repeat, "Relax" as you exhale. . . .

As you continue to breathe deeply, slowly, and comfortably, begin to notice any tension in your head and your scalp and, as you breathe out, let your head and scalp relax. Notice any tension in your jaw, and let your jaw relax. . . .

Breathe deeply, slowly, and comfortably, and continue to let your body relax. Let your neck and your shoulders relax . . . and your arms and your hands. . . .

And now let your back relax . . . and then your chest . . . and then your abdomen . . . and then your pelvis. This release of tension allows your heart and your lungs and your stomach . . . all your organs . . . to relax. Breathe deeply . . . slowly . . . and comfortably . . . and relax. . . .

Continue downward and let your hips relax . . . and your legs . . . and . . . your feet. . . .

And now with your body more relaxed, begin to imagine yourself in a place where you are feel safe, comfortable, and protected. . . . Take a moment to imagine this place of great safety and comfort as you continue to breathe slowly . . . deeply . . . and comfortably. . . .

When you feel ready . . . begin to focus on the area of pain and relax this area. . . . Breathe in . . . breathe out . . . and relax the area of pain. . . . Picture the area as a tight rubber band and hold this image for a couple of seconds. . . . Now let the rubber band go limp; let the area of pain relax. . . .

Do this again. . . . Consciously tighten the area of pain for a couple of seconds and then relax . . . relax the area of pain. . . .

As the area relaxes, send healing light into it . . . imagine healing light going into the area of pain. . . .

And as the area relaxes, feel blood flowing to it . . . feel energy flowing to it. . . . Relax the area and make room for the blood and energy to flow into it. . . .

Breathing slowly . . . deeply . . . and comfortably . . . begin to imagine the color of your pain. . . . What color is your pain? . . . Change the color to whatever color you like. . . . Picture the color more intense . . . and then less intense. . . .

Continue to breathe slowly . . . deeply . . . and comfortably . . . now begin to imagine the texture of your pain. . . . It is rough? . . . Is it smooth? . . . Is the pain hard . . . or soft? . . . Change the texture to whatever you would like. . . .

Make your image of the pain larger . . . and smaller. . . .

And now as you continue to breathe slowly . . . deeply . . . and comfortably . . . send your breath into the area of pain. . . . Imagine that your breath brings healing light into the area. . . . Imagine a warm healing light flowing into the area of pain. . . .

Calling on your inner wisdom for strength and support, recall the difficult life circumstances or unhealthy beliefs this pain is protecting you from. . . .

Now imagine yourself doing whatever is important for you to do to take care of a difficult challenge in your life. . . . What is the first step toward meeting that challenge? . . . When will you initiate this action? How? ...

And now imagine what your life will be like after this difficulty has gone away. . . . Imagine how your life will improve, how your relationship with yourself and with others will improve. . . .

And now imagine that the painful area is becoming normal again. . . . Imagine you are pain-free. . . . You feel good . . . you feel strong. . . .

And when you are ready . . . become aware of your breathing again and aware of the sounds in the room. . . .

Arouse the client from hypnosis.

CHAPTER 23
A Marketing Tool For Referrals

Running a private hypnotherapy practice is the same as running a small business. The key to creating, building, and maintaining a thriving practice is to become a successful marketer. To build a solid referral base, marketing must become an integral part of what you do.

Some hypnotherapists have the wrong attitude about marketing and perceive it as "selling," or an aggressive imposition on other people. There is a difference between marketing and selling. We must understand what marketing is: *Marketing is educating people about your services.*

One way to "educate people about your services," is through public speaking. In addition to generating new referrals, speaking in public will provide you with community visibility and enhance your professional image.

If you are like most people, you would prefer to face a firing squad than get up before an audience. If the very thought of giving a speech causes you to experience a wave of panic, take comfort in knowing you are not alone. In the *Book of Lists*,[52] fear of public speaking is listed as the number one

---

[52]Wallace, A., Wallechinsky, D. and Wallace, I. The book of lists, NY: Morrow Books, 1983.

phobia in America. Fear of dying is number six. When you feel vulnerable, you experience "stage fright." Everyone wants to look good before an audience. If you believe the audience will evaluate your performance negatively, you will become nervous and develop the classic symptoms of stage fright.

You may ask, "How can I overcome my fear of speaking in front of a group of people?" If you understand the cause of stage fright, the solution is simple. *Stage fright is self-generated. Its cause is negative self-talk.* In this book we have learned that every human act or deed is in fact brought about through our suggesting it to ourselves. As previously stated: "As a man thinketh in his heart, so is he," written in the Bible nearly thirty centuries ago, is as true now as it was then. Thus, you become what you think about. All that you do and say stems from what you think (and suggest to yourself). Whether your actions, words, and thoughts are positive or negative in their effect and impact depends entirely on the mode of your thinking.

The major cause of nervousness, about an impending talk, is the imagined fear of bungling and looking incompetent to others. Speech consultant, Dorothy Sarnoff, expresses this concept in her book *Speech Can Change Your Life*.[53]

> Knowing he does not speak well, he is almost destroyed by panic from the moment he agrees to speak right through the speech itself. Suddenly, he realizes he is putting up for public judgment his personality, his thinking, and his worth as a person. To speak in public is to unveil a picture of yourself and you wonder, "will

---

[53]Sarnoff, D. Speech can change your life. NY: Dell Publishing Co., 1970.

I have their respect for what I have to say and the way I handle myself?"

Anxiety, through negative self-programming, is profoundly influenced by the emotions. The resultant physical symptoms of fear—pounding heart, shortness of breath, trembling hands, dry mouth and throat—establish a vicious circle. If, in your imagination, you picture yourself faltering and doing badly, the end result is fear. This fear, then, becomes a self-fulfilling prophecy. The foreboding fear of looking ridiculous is now confirmed by intense anxiety and discomfort.

Since suggestion works through visualization; you have to vividly picture, in your mind's eye, the suggestions you are implanting in it. You should make the visualization as total and as real as your imagination is capable of doing. "I see myself walking to the lectern, I feel relaxed and confident. I look at my audience and smile. I am happy to be here. I know my material and I enjoy sharing it with them. I begin talking in a loud, strong voice. I speak slowly, clearly, pleasantly. As I establish eye contact with individual members of my audience, I notice they are paying close attention and smiling. I feel relaxed and at ease. I feel happy and confident. My confidence comes from knowing that I have something worth saying, and that I will say it in a way worth listening to. When I finish talking they applaud for a long time." Keep practicing this in every self-hypnotic episode. Don't make hard work of it! Simply let the images flow as you call them up. Most importantly, see yourself delivering your talk the way you are suggesting to your subconscious that you want it to be.

As you visualize and mentally act out what you plan and intend to do, and what (through self-suggestion) you program yourself to carry out, you are, in a sense, creating the future... and as you afterward recall your visualization, you are literally remembering future events.

You will recall that visualization was defined as the mental eliciting of desired responses. You can banish the paralyzing fear of stage fright, by mentally "seeing" yourself being calm and reacting in a controlled way. As the motivational speaker Wayne Dyer so wisely said, "You'll see it when you believe it." The secret lies in understanding that nothing happens accidentally. You must begin to accept full responsibility for your thoughts. Once you do so, you can bring about whatever you want from life.

The elimination of stage fright involves three specific steps: 1.) a positive mental attitude (self-hypnosis is the acme of scientifically applied positive thinking), 2.) preparing your material thoroughly, and 3.) from knowing that you have something worth saying, and that you can say it in a way worth listening to.

WHERE TO SPEAK

Many civic and charitable organizations are constantly looking for speakers to address their regular meetings. Among these are the Lions, Kiwanis, Rotary, churches, synagogues, parent-teacher associations, etc. Also, special events, such as taking charge of a booth at a health fair. All can serve as an arena in which you can inform the audience about you and your hypnotherapy services.

LEARNING TO SPEAK

An organization dedicated to the training of the art of public speaking is *Toastmasters International*.[54] Most Toastmasters Clubs meet weekly and there are breakfast, lunch, dinner, and evening meetings to accommodate a variety of job situations. Regardless of where you live, it is probable that you will find at least one Toastmaster club in your community. There are 250,000 members in over 12,000 clubs worldwide.

Toastmasters is a worthwhile organization for the novice speaker, the veteran, or anyone in between. It is an excellent way to perfect the art of public speaking in a positive and relaxed atmosphere.

Speaking engagements will keep your name, face, and reputation before the public, thus building up the base of potential referrals from people who know of you and your hypnotherapy practice.

Public speaking is, and should be for you, a gratifying, even exhilarating, activity. For a few special minutes, you are in the spotlight with a grand opportunity to make a vital contribution to your career.

Good luck!

---

[54] Anthony, R. How to make a fortune from public speaking. NY: Berkley books, 1985.

Glossary

ABREACTION: The act of reviving the memory of a repressed disagreeable experience and giving expression in speech and action to the emotions related to it, thereby relieving the individual of its influence.

AFFECT BRIDGE: A technique by which significant memories are recovered by inducing an intense emotional state in a client and asking him or her to remember a past instance when he or she felt the same way.

AGE PROGRESSION: Simulated time orientation. The hypnotic subject hallucinates living in the future while retaining his or her chronological age.

AGE REGRESSION: In age regression the subject plays a role acting out past events in the framework of the present. A re-experiencing of earlier events in life, usually limited to a specific time or time period.

AMNESIA: Loss of memory; inability to recall. It may result from organic or functional causes and may be generalized or for a circumscribed period of time. In *retrograde amnesia* there is a loss of memory for events over a period of time prior to a trauma, as in the case of cerebral concussion. Hypnotic amnesia is always a reversible forgetting. It may occur spontaneously or be suggested, and may be partial or total.

ANALGESIA: The loss or reduction of pain sensation without the loss of consciousness. When analgesia is produced in hypnosis it is called *hypnoanalgesia*. If used to decrease pain, hypnoanalgesia can be retained by posthypnotic suggestions.

ANESTHESIA: The loss of all sensory modalities. An agent, that causes insensitivity to pain. In chemically induced anesthesia there are two types: *general,* which produces unconsciousness; and *local,* which causes a specific area of the body to be insensitive to pain. In the context of hypnosis this is called *hypnoanesthesia,* and is used in major surgical and dental procedures.

ANOREXIA NERVOSA: A life-threatening psychoneurotic symptom in which the client, usually a young woman, diets to the point of emaciation. As a rule, the anorexic has a loss of appetite with a loathing for food.

APPROACH: System of operation or way of working, characteristic *modus operandi.*

AUTHORITARIAN: The approach of hypnotic suggestion that is commanding and forceful in nature. The hypnotist's imposing suggestions communicate it.

AUTOHYPNOSIS: This term is synonymous with *self-hypnosis.*

AUTOSUGGESTION: Self-suggestions; refers to suggestions made by the subject to oneself.

BULIMIA: The bulimic has an insatiable appetite for food. Bulimia is a psychoneurotic disturbance resulting in a morbid increase of appetite whereby the individual wishes to eat constantly.

CATALEPSY: A condition characterized by a rigidity of the skeletal muscles. May be accompanied by *waxy flexibility* in which the limbs of a cataleptic individual remain in almost any position they are placed, as though made of molded wax. The medical term for this phenomenon is *cerea flexibilitas*.

CLINICAL HYPNOSIS: The therapeutic uses of hypnosis.

CONSCIOUS: Awareness; alertness; referring to the state of being subjectively aware. That which is known and experienced. The left hemispheric function, which maintains an interpretative contact of the individual with the environment.

DELUSION: An irrational belief tenaciously held in spite of all evidence to the contrary.

DISSOCIATION: The inherent ability of the hypnotized subject to become detached from the immediate environment. The subject can step out of himself, as it were, just as if he were viewing his body from another part of the room. Also, the dividing up of the psyche into two or more parts functioning independently at the same time (e.g., automatic writing).

ENDORPHINS: Any of several peptides secreted in the brain, that have a pain-relieving effect like that of morphine. The body naturally produces these analgesic chemicals.

FORENSIC HYPNOSIS: Legal application of hypnosis.

FRACTIONATION: A procedure for deepening hypnosis by repeatedly hypnotizing and dehypnotizing a subject.

GLOVE ANESTHESIA: A hypnotically suggested anesthesia in the area of a hand normally covered by a glove. The hand is made insensitive to stimuli in a circumscribed area from the fingertips to the wrist. A condition that is neuroanatomically impossible.

HETEROHYPNOSIS: Hypnosis induced by a hypnotist.

HYPERMNESIA: Memory recall with retrieval of forgotten information. The brain stores everything, forgets nothing, and most memories can be recovered when the proper association pathways are stimulated.

HYPERESTHESIA: Heightened sensibility to touch.

HYPERSUGGESTIBILITY: The capacity to respond to suggestions above a norm. The subject who is readily influenced and achieves a profound level of hypnosis is said to be *hypersuggestible*.

HYPNAGOGIC: The state intermediate between wakefulness and sleep.

HYPNOANALYSIS: The use of hypnosis in combination with psychoanalytic techniques.

HYPNOIDAL: Resembling hypnosis. When the term *hypnoidal* is used in the context of hypnotic susceptibility, it designates the lightest degree of hypnosis.

HYPNOSIS: An altered state of consciousness characterized by hypersuggestibility. It is a trance-like state psychically induced, usually by another person, in which the subject responds to the suggestions of the hypnotist.

HYPNOTHERAPY: Any therapy in which the use of hypnosis constitutes the core of the treatment.

HYPNOTIC: Pertaining to or associated with hypnotism.

HYPNOTISM: The study and use of suggestion. The science of hypnosis.

HYPNOTIZABILITY: Refers to suggestibility or individual susceptibility to hypnosis.

HYPNOTIC SUSCEPTIBILITY: A personality characteristic that determines a subject's ability to be hypnotized and to attain a given depth of hypnosis.

IDEOMOTOR ACTION: The involuntary capacity of muscles to respond instantaneously to thoughts, feelings, and ideas.

IDEOSENSORY ACTION: The involuntary capacity of the brain to evoke sensory images; these may be kinesthetic, auditory, visual, olfactory, gustatory or tactile.

ILLUSION: A common misperception of some sensory stimulus. All sensory modalities are subject to illusions.

IMAGERY: The ability to perceive or mentally recreate ideas, pictures, or feelings.

INDUCTION: The production of hypnosis by the use of specific procedures.

INDIRECT HYPNOSIS: The production of hypnosis without the subject's awareness.

MATCHING: An approach developed by the late Milton Erickson, and used by John Grinder and Richard Bandler in their system of neurolinguistic programming (NLP). The technique consists of adopting parts of another person's behavior, such as particular gestures, facial expressions, forms of speech, tone of voice, and so on. Done skillfully, it helps create rapport.

NEGATIVE HALLUCINATION: A hallucination in which the subject fails to perceive something that is present.

OPERATOR: Synonymous with hypnotist or hypnotherapist.

PERMISSIVE: This approach to hypnotic induction is the opposite of authoritarian. A *permissive suggestion* is made in such a manner as to give the subject the option of responding. The subject, not the hypnotist, is made the perceived source of the response. Permissive suggestions never have an intimation of authority or command.

POSITIVE HALLUCINATION: A perception of a stimulus that does not exist in objective reality.

POSTHYPNOTIC RESPONSE: Acts carried out after the termination of hypnosis in response to specific suggestions are called posthypnotic. A suggestion given during hypnosis serves as the stimulus and the act becomes the response.

GLOSSARY

POSTHYPNOTIC SUGGESTION: A suggestion given during hypnosis that occurs in the subsequent waking state.

REVIVIFICATION: A reliving of a prior period of life. In revivification the hypnotized person returns to a physiological state believed to have existed at the time to which the subject has returned. All memories following the age to which the subject has been regressed are removed.

SELF-HYPNOSIS: Hypnosis induced in oneself. The ability to influence positive self-improvement through the inner processes of focused awareness.

SOMNAMBULISM: In everyday usage the term somnambulism is used for sleepwalking; in the lexicon of hypnotism somnambulism is used to designate the deepest stage of hypnosis.

SUBCONSCIOUS MIND: The psychic processes of which an individual is not conscious. They are often associated with the part of the mind involving imagination, memory, and creativity. The subconscious mind is particularly accessible through hypnotic suggestion.

SUBJECT: This term denotes an individual submitting to an induction of hypnosis. If hypnosis is being used for hypnotherapy the term *client* should be used.

SUBJECTIVE TIME: Time as perceived by a subject (as opposed to real time).

SUGGESTIBILITY: The capacity to respond to suggestion. The propensity of a subject to accept and act on suggestions.

SUGGESTION: Hypnotic communication.

TIME DISTORTION: The ability of hypnotic suggestion to make subjective time seem to pass more rapidly or more slowly than real time.

TRANCE: A term widely used by Milton Erickson and his followers. The term trance is often used synonymously for hypnosis.

TRANCE LOGIC: The suspension of critical judgment on the part of a hypnotized subject and his or her ability to tolerate the coexistence of logically incompatible phenomena.

UNCONSCIOUS MIND: A term used in psychiatry to denote a postulated region of the psyche, the repository of repressed urges and wishes. The term *subconscious* is often used as a synonym for the term unconscious.

A Word About the Resources of The National Guild of Hypnotists

The author of this book strongly urges hypnotists to join the world's premier hypnosis organization, the National Guild of Hypnotists, which provides its members with the finest resources in the field of hypnotism. The Guild is a not-for-profit, educational corporation in the State of New Hampshire. Founded in Boston, Massachusetts in 1951, it is a professional organization comprised of more than 12,000 dedicated hypnotists (from 65 countries) committed to advancing the field of hypnotism. The Guild is a resource for members and a vehicle for legal and legislative action.

Dr. Rexford L. North, Director of the Hypnotism Center of Boston, founded the Guild in 1951. Within a short time, local chapters were formed and operating in many major cities throughout the US and Canada. Important resources through the years have been two publications devoted exclusively to the field of hypnotism: *The Journal of Hypnotism* and *The HypnoGram*.

This unique organization encourages an eclectic exchange of ideas, fellowship, mutual trust and cooperation among members—while promoting and protecting the science, art, and philosophy of hypnotism. Dr. Dwight F. Damon, the President of the National Guild of Hypnotists, has made a personal commitment to have hypnotherapy recognized as a separate and distinct profession. The National Guild of Hypnotists is fair-minded and has always assisted wherever needed, helping other groups and individuals regardless of their affiliations.

Each year in August the National Guild of Hypnotists holds the world's largest annual hypnosis educational conference and convention. Hypnotists from all over the world attend this event.

For more information contact:

The National Guild of Hypnotists

P.O. Box 308
Merrimack, NH 03054-0308
(603) 429-9438 (FAX) 424-8066
NGH e-mail address: ngh@ngh.net
NGH Web Page: http://www.ngh.net

Index

A

alpha brainwaves, 129, 180-181
amnesia, 114, 116, 124, 279, 313-314, 363
animal magnetism, 4-5, 9, 14-26, 29-31, 34-35
Araoz, Daniel L., 267
arms rising and falling test, 197
artificial somnambulism, 30, 32
automatic motion test, 224
autosuggestion, 44-48, 107-108, 177, 211-212, 278, 289, 364
  understanding, 271
awakening the hypnotized subject, 231

B

Barber, Theodore X., 83-84, 98, 154, 165, 265
Barth, Karl, 12-13
Berger, Hans, 180
Bernhardt, Roger, 261-262
Bernheim, Hippolyte, 37-38, 44, 88, 103, 112, 118
beta brainwaves, 129, 180
biofeedback, 155, 179-181
Bloch, Bruno, 152
Bolloch, Karen, 162
Bordeaux, Jean, 123, 125
Braid, James, 34-36, 111, 113, 118
Bramwell, J. M., 37
burns and scalds, 153

C

Carrel, Alexis, 271
Chevalier d'Eslon, 22, 26, 30
Chevreul pendulum, 195-196
chronic pain, 264, 345, 347, 349
clinical value in psychotherapy, 91
common objective signs of hypnosis, 215
conscious mind, 48, 87, 113, 119-120, 170, 226, 274, 276, 336
Cooke, Charles Edward, 224, 227
Coué, Emile, 44-50, 118, 277
counting method, 220, 237
Créteil clinic, 21

D

Damon, Dwight, 5, 78-80, 247, 271
de Jussieu, Laurent, 24

delta brainwaves, 130, 180
Dick-Reade, Grantley, 296
Digby, Sir Kenelm, 147-148
divided brain theory, 116

E

Elliotson, John, 36
endorphins, 131, 133, 296, 365
Erickson, Milton, 40-41, 43, 55-75, 83, 158, 241-242, 248, 303, 368, 370
Esdaile, James, 36, 350-351
Estabrooks, George, 53, 107
eye catalepsy test, 226
eye-fixation with distraction, 241-242
eye-locking test, 189

F

factors influencing hypnotic induction, 218
fear of getting stuck in hypnosis, 96
fear of not being hypnotized, 170
first interview, 168
Flint, Herbert, 40
Flower, Sidney, 237
four types of suggestion, 89, 211
Freud, Sigmund, 38-39, 48, 67, 73, 317

G

Gassner, Fr. J. J., 10-11
gate-control theory of pain, 348
Gerrish, F. H., 40

glove anesthesia, 351-353, 366
Gluck, Christoph Wilibald, 7
Gould, Stephen Jay, 25
Greatrakes, Valentine, 148-151
Green, Elmer E., 181
Groosbart, Ted, 152
guideline for painless childbirth, 257-259

H

Hall, Howard, 155
hallucinations, 107, 124
hand clasp test, 202
hand-levitation induction, 239
Hartland, John, 241-242, 346
heavy arm catalepsy test, 226-227
Hell, Fr. Maximillian, 8, 9, 15
heterosuggestion, 211
Hilgard, Ernest, 40-4, 82-83
Hilgard, Josephine, 114, 127
Hull, Clark, 40-41, 54-55
hypersuggestibility, 194, 367
hypnagogic, 41, 130
hypnoanalgesia, 350, 364
hypnos, 35, 113
hypnosis
  a conviction phenomenon, 167, 190
Hypnosis As A State Of Sleep, 113
hypnotic rapport, 165, 167, 214-215
hypnotizability, 83, 96, 125, 127-128, 183, 345

I

ideomotor action, 118, 191-192, 194-195
imaginative involvement as a factor of hypnotizability, 127
immune system, 86, 90, 120, 131, 133, 137-138, 141-146, 148-152, 155-156, 159-162, 261, 350
induction for pain relief, 353
induction with mechanical aids, 244
Information Theory of hypnotic suggestion, 130

J

James, William, 40, 191, 193, 268, 275

K

Kershaw, Maurice, 79, 247
Kroger, William S., 89, 104, 120, 166, 194, 211, 244, 248

L

Lafontaine, Charles, 35
LeCron and Bordeaux susceptibility scoring system, 123, 196
Leeds, Dorothy, 168
loss of consciousness, 364
lymphocytes, 144

M

M. De Maillebois, 20
macrophages, 162
Maharishi Mahesh Yogi, 177
Maltz, Maxell, 140
mantra, 44, 46, 49, 178
Marquis de Puységur, 30-34
McDougall, William, 41, 43, 53
McGill, Ormond, 192
Mead, Richard, 6
meditation
  the relaxation response, 177
Mehrabian, Albert, 168
Meichenbaum, Donald, 158-160
Mesmer, Franz Anton, 1, 3-30, 91
misconceptions, 5, 93, 101, 169-170, 206
Mozart, Wolfgang Amadeus, 7, 12
myths and misconceptions, 93

N

Nancy School, 37-38, 45, 69, 84, 112
natural childbirth, 296
neuropeptides, 131-134, 162-163
neutrophil, 143
nociceptive pain, 347
North, Rexford L., 43, 77-81, 247-248, 371

O

Oesterlein, Francisca, 8

P

pain management, 345
painless childbirth, 253-254, 257
Paradis, Maria Theresa, 11-14
Pathologic Theory, 112
Pavlov, 103, 114
Pearsall, Paul, 144
permissive versus authoritarian approach, 210
Pert, Candace, 161
physical causes of stress, 173
plenary trance, 125
posthypnotic suggestions, 66, 73, 105, 124, 138, 205, 254, 364
postural sway test, 199
progressive relaxation induction, 231
psychological causes of stress, 174
psychological theory, 54, 118
psychologically disturbed subject, 106
psychoneuroimmunology, 161

Q

Quackenbos, John D., 40
qualities of the hypnotic voice, 212

R

Race, Victor, 32-33
rapport and self-confidence, 214
re-alerting the subject, 205
receptive visualization, 298
receptor keyholes on cells, 162
rehypnotization, 205
Relaxation Test, 184, 186-187
Rhodes, Raphael, 119
Rossi, Ernest Lawrence, 131
Rousseau, Jean Jacques, 5
Royal Commission of Inquiry, 23-24
Ruff, Michael, 161
Rumpelstilskin Principle, 160

S

Sage, X. LaMotte, 184
Salpêtrière School, 38, 112
Salter, Andrew, 246
Samuels, Michael, 155
Sargent, Joseph, 181
Sarnoff, Dorothy, 358
Schultz, Johannes, 151
self-hypnosis, 44-45, 47, 56-57, 70, 72, 87, 95, 118, 140, 151-152, 178-181, 212, 261-269, 271, 275-280, 285-286, 289-290, 292-294, 296-297, 299, 301-302, 345, 349, 350, 352, 360, 364
self-hypnosis, how to induce, 271
Selye, Hans, 158
sexual fantasies, 109
shaman therapy, 156
Sidis, Boris, 40-41

Sidney Flower induction, 237
signs of hypnosis, 210, 215, 217
smoking cessation, 327, 329, 338
social causes of stress, 174
somnambulism, 30, 32, 34, 107, 112, 126, 217, 369
somnambulism artificial, 32
Straus, Roger A., 265
stress, the cardinal signs of, 174
subconscious mind, 4, 12, 86-90, 113, 119-120, 125, 137, 224-225, 229, 232, 234, 257, 261, 267, 269, 282, 284, 286, 289-290, 328, 330, 335-336, 338-339, 369
subjective experiences that may accompany hypnotic induction, 217
suggestibility, 54, 81- 82, 89, 104, 118, 120, 166-167, 169, 183-184, 191, 194, 197, 211-212, 367
suggestibility tests, 167, 183, 191
suggestion, definition of, 88

T

Temples of Asklepeia, 2

testing during hypnosis, 170, 226
theta brainwaves, 129-130, 133-134, 180
Thomas, W. I., 266
Toastmasters International, 361
tooth extraction under hypnosis, 249
Transcendental Meditation, 177
transduction, 131, 134, 160
Type 1 Herpes, 152
types of suggestions, 211

U

Udolf, Roy, 88, 167
ultra-fast induction, 235
unqualified therapy, 104
using feedback to facilitate induction, 246

V

van Swieten, Gerard, 6
volitional visualization, 298
von Bosch, Maria Anna, 7

W

weight loss, 90, 301
Wells, W. R., 116
Wolberg, Lewis, 118, 239, 248

www.ingramcontent.com/pod-product-compliance
Lightning Source LLC
Chambersburg PA
CBHW052048230426
43671CB00011B/1831